LAKE PARK HIGH SCHOOL
RESOURCE CENTER

Harlem
Renaissance

William S. McConnell, *Book Editor*

Daniel Leone, *President*

Bonnie Szumski, *Publisher*

Scott Barbour, *Managing Editor*

David M. Haugen, *Series Editor*

GREENHAVEN
PRESS ®

THOMSON

———————★———————™

GALE

San Diego • Detroit • New York • San Francisco • Cleveland
New Haven, Conn. • Waterville, Maine • London • Munich

THOMSON
———————✳—————— ™
GALE

LIBRARY OF CONGRESS CATALOGING-IN-PUBLICATION DATA

Harlem Renaissance / William S. McConnell, book editor.
 p. cm. — (The Greenhaven Press companion to literary movements and genres)
Includes bibliographical references and index.
ISBN 0-7377-1087-X (pbk. : alk. paper) — ISBN 0-7377-1088-8 (lib. : alk. paper)
 1. African Americans—Intellectual life—20th century. 2. Harlem Renaissance.
3. African American arts—History—20th century. 4. Harlem (New York, N.Y.)—
Intellectual life—20th century. 5. African Americans—New York (State)—New
York—Intellectual life—20th century. 6. African American arts—New York
(State)—New York—History—20th century. 7. New York (N.Y.)—Intellectual life—
20th century. I. McConnell, William S. II. Series.
E185.6 .H26 2003
810.9'89607307471'09041—dc21
                                                          2002032211

Printed in the United States of America

white, an effort that was ultimately a failure. In his novel *Cane*, Toomer's characters face the problems of biracial heritage, including a lack of acceptance by both black and white culture.

Countee Cullen was a poet who initially drew on religious themes to address his thoughts on love and salvation. Later, he reworked some of his motifs to contend with racial prejudice and the black experience.

Carl Van Vechten was a white patron who befriended many of the black artists of the Harlem Renaissance. Black intellectuals, however, were disappointed when Van Vechten's 1926 novel *Nigger Heaven* exploited the primitive black stereotypes that were in vogue with white audiences of the period.

The city of Harlem was a frequent theme in Hughes's poetry. Beginning as an exotic destination for whites during the Jazz Age, the community became more somber as the hardships of the Great Depression drove away the white tourists and thrill seekers. Langston Hughes follows this evolution of Harlem, using his poetry as a form of social commentary that documents the changes within the community.

Chapter 4: Challenging Racism Through Literature

During the 1920s, the dependence of black writers on the support of white patrons was critical to the success of the Harlem Renaissance. This support did have drawbacks. It encouraged the development of negative black stereotypes. It also encouraged many blacks to emulate white society in order to remain financially successful, causing many to reject the significance of their collective cultural experiences.

During the first half of the twentieth century, Charles S. Johnson's use of literary contests in magazines created a platform with which to promote black achievements. This scheme also helped destroy the racial stereotypes prevalent in American art that had fostered a sense of inferiority within the black community.

Chapter 5: The Legacy of the Movement

FOREWORD

The study of literature most often involves focusing on an individual work and uncovering its themes, stylistic conventions, and historical relevance. It is also enlightening to examine multiple works by a single author, identifying similarities and differences among texts and tracing the author's development as an artist.

While the study of individual works and authors is instructive, however, examining groups of authors who shared certain cultural or historical experiences adds a further richness to the study of literature. By focusing on literary movements and genres, readers gain a greater appreciation of influence of historical events and social circumstances on the development of particular literary forms and themes. For example, in the early twentieth century, rapid technological and industrial advances, mass urban migration, World War I, and other events contributed to the emergence of a movement known as American modernism. The dramatic social changes, and the uncertainty they created, were reflected in an increased use of free verse in poetry, the stream-of-consciousness technique in fiction, and a general sense of historical discontinuity and crisis of faith in most of the literature of the era. By focusing on these commonalities, readers attain a more comprehensive picture of the complex interplay of social, economic, political, aesthetic, and philosophical forces and ideas that create the tenor of any era. In the nineteenth-century American romanticism movement, for example, authors shared many ideas concerning the preeminence of the self-reliant individual, the infusion of nature with spiritual significance, and the potential of persons to achieve transcendence via communion with nature. However, despite their commonalities, American romantics often differed significantly in their thematic and stylistic approaches. Walt Whitman celebrated the communal nature of America's open democratic society, while Ralph Waldo

Emerson expressed the need for individuals to pursue their own fulfillment regardless of their fellow citizens. Herman Melville wrote novels in a largely naturalistic style whereas Nathaniel Hawthorne's novels were gothic and allegorical.

Another valuable reason to investigate literary movements and genres lies in their potential to clarify the process of literary evolution. By examining groups of authors, literary trends across time become evident. The reader learns, for instance, how English romanticism was transformed as it crossed the Atlantic to America. The poetry of Lord Byron, William Wordsworth, and John Keats celebrated the restorative potential of rural scenes. The American romantics, writing later in the century, shared their English counterparts' faith in nature; but American authors were more likely to present an ambiguous view of nature as a source of liberation as well as the dwelling place of personal demons. The whale in Melville's *Moby-Dick* and the forests in Hawthorne's novels and stories bear little resemblance to the benign pastoral scenes in Wordsworth's lyric poems.

Each volume in Greenhaven Press's Companions to Literary Movements and Genres series begins with an introductory essay that places the topic in a historical and literary context. The essays that follow are carefully chosen and edited for ease of comprehension. These essays are arranged into clearly defined chapters that are outlined in a concise annotated table of contents. Finally, a thorough chronology maps out crucial literary milestones of the movement or genre as well as significant social and historical events. Readers will benefit from the structure and coherence that these features lend to material that is often challenging. With Greenhaven's Literary Movements and Genres in hand, readers will be better able to comprehend and appreciate the major literary works and their impact on society.

INTRODUCTION

The United States was thriving during the years following World War I. The war in Europe had boosted the American economy. The bulk of these profits went to white Americans, who then speculated in the stock market and created more wealth. Certainly not all of white America shared in this wealth, but enough did that they earned the title nouveau riche, or "newly rich." White artisans and writers ironically found financial success by commenting on the excessive wealth and lifestyle that characterized the nouveau riche of the 1920s. F. Scott Fitzgerald's novel *The Great Gatsby* exemplifies the carefree lifestyle and lavish indulgences of people—white people—who seem to have more money than they could ever possibly spend.

For black America, the 1920s were not so carefree. African Americans living in the impoverished conditions of the South had yet to fulfill for themselves any of the cultural and financial success of white America. Even before war's end, many southern blacks drifted north in search of a better life, filling the industrial jobs left open by the soldiers in Europe. In 1919, with the war in Europe finally over, white soldiers returned home to New York to discover a shift in city demographics. The large cities in the North—New York, Detroit, Philadelphia, Chicago—underwent a large growth in their black population. Better work, better wages, and better opportunities drew a steady stream of blacks to the industrial cities of the North during the 1920s. There, they carved out communities and witnessed a level of prosperity that was as yet unheard-of in the South.

THE CULTURE OF HARLEM

Those black migrants who moved to New York settled in Harlem. The urban community offered a sense of belonging to the uprooted families. It also offered good jobs and steady wages, which created opportunities to purchase real estate, open businesses, and found churches and schools. These successes also attracted African Americans from the West Indies, who brought with them their distinctive folk culture and heritage. As author and West Indian immigrant Claude McKay writes in his book *Harlem: Negro Metropolis,* "The black masses were attracted from everywhere by the greater living space of Harlem."[1] Once in Harlem, blacks from all walks of life felt they were bound by similar cultural values. Although some of these shared values were a direct result of being set apart from white America, the black communal values that developed in Harlem also stemmed from the realization that the neighborhood was a unique achievement, something that was created and defined by black Americans for themselves. Harlem became the preeminent hub of black culture and served as a blueprint for the creation of black communities in other cities.

Accompanying the financial and communal successes of Harlem was an artistic dimension of creative achievement, which helped validate a new outgrowth of black culture. Referring back to the European Renaissance—when new wealth and lavish lifestyles helped foster unprecedented artistic growth—the Harlem Renaissance was a title retroactively applied to the burgeoning growth of black literature, theater, and other art forms that began during the 1920s. Of course, there had been notable black artistic achievements before the intense period of creative growth in 1920s Harlem. Charles W. Chesnutt and Paul Laurence Dunbar are but two examples of authors who attained some level of recognition for their work, but it was not until the 1920s that black artisans created a unique black voice that expressed the modern African American experience. Two factors converged during the Harlem Renaissance that drew serious attention from both black and white audiences and propelled the movement forward.

White Interest in the Black Community

The first of these factors was the interest the white nouveau riche had in the Harlem community. Langston Hughes said in his autobiography, *The Big Sea* (1940), the 1920s was a time when "the Negro was in vogue," because Harlem attracted many white thrill seekers wanting to experience the exciting nightlife of the cabaret and flirt with the taboo culture they could not embrace because of America's racial barriers. Whites came to hear jazz music, take in the black theater productions, and visit cabaret-style clubs and bars owned and managed by blacks. For many whites, Harlem was an exotic locale that was safe to visit, knowing they could retreat back to their own neighborhoods after having invested nothing more than spare cash in the black community. Other whites, however, took a more significant interest in Harlem. Art critics and patrons recognized the talent of black artists, playwrights, and authors. Some of these white patrons exerted financial control over black writers, obliging them to cater to white interests. Others took a more personal interest in the lives of the Harlem elite, helping them find their own voice.

One event that attracted white audiences and patrons to Harlem was the musical *Shuffle Along*, which debuted in 1921. The show, written by black writers Eubie Blake and Noble Sissle, played in several cities, including Harlem, before making its Broadway appearance. The show was significant because it was written, produced, directed, and performed by an all-black entourage. The show capitalized on minstrel themes, which were popular with white audiences. Minstrel shows required actors to apply blackface makeup and perform as simplistic caricatures of slaves and poor blacks. Although *Shuffle Along* had an all-black cast, its actors were still required to wear the blackface makeup as part of the minstrel routine that white audiences had come to expect. Even though minstrelsy was viewed as entertainment, the main attraction for white audiences was that it was a declaration of white superiority.

THE FOCUS ON PRIMITIVISM

As minstrelsy capitalized on stereotypes, so, too, did the interest in primitivism. Primitivism was the focus in art and literature on African tribal culture or on the simplistic peasant life of the Caribbean islands. Many whites believed blacks had an instinctual connection to primitive life. African Americans were thought to possess savage qualities that included beastlike cunning and sexual prowess. Of course, such attributes reflected the displaced desires of white audiences who felt their own "civilization" had made such feelings extinct. To foist these primitive ideals on to blacks was a way that white America could safely revel in the dark side of human nature.

Because it was what paying white audiences wanted, primitive themes appeared in theater productions, in literature, and even in the interior design of certain clubs. Black artists and entrepreneurs in Harlem were encouraged to propagate the stereotype to achieve success. In literature, white patrons such as Charlotte Mason, Langston Hughes's legendary benefactor, influenced writers to create art that specifically delved into these popular themes. Black writers like Zora Neale Hurston received financial support for such writing, but many of these writers eventually rebelled against their benefactors because they could not identify with the stereotypes that they created.

Primitivism was also pervasive in the field of drama, in which a black writing presence was notably absent. White writers were very interested in primitivistic themes because of their lucrative draw with white audiences. Many dramas of this period, written by white authors such as Eugene O'Neill, made use of black themes and created quality roles for black actors, but their focus on primitive themes left the impression that black life was nothing more than savage, and that blacks were indeed very different than whites. In O'Neill's play *The Emperor Jones* (1920), the lead role of Brutus Jones even embodies an image of savagery, as the "brute" in his name suggests.

Carl Van Vechten, another white writer and patron of the Negro movement, perhaps best exemplifies the positive and negative effects white patrons and the lucrative interest in primitivism had on black artists at the time. Van Vechten opened doors for many Negro writers, including Jessie Fauset and Nella Larsen. He used his vast connections to bring many young black writers to the attention of white publishers, enabling the authors to make money and establish reputations outside the Harlem community. But Van Vechten also used his involvement within the Harlem community as the basis for his novel *Nigger Heaven*, a book focusing on the primitive aspects of the cabaret lifestyle of Harlem's nightlife. Although he was considered a friend to black writers, many within the Harlem intellectual community accused him of placing too heavy an emphasis on sexual undertones and primitivistic imagery in his novel, thus promoting negative stereotypes of blacks.

With such a heavy importance placed on primitivism, the challenge facing the African American writer during this period was how to appeal to major publishers and yet maintain a strong sense of cultural identity that was not defined by white America. A contemporary critic and scholar, Arthur P. Davis, comments on this need to maintain a sense of black identity:

> We do not have actual integration anywhere [in America]. We have surface integration and token integration in many areas, but the everyday pattern of life for the overwhelming majority of Negroes is unchanged. . . . The Negro artist recognizes and acknowledges that climate [of racism]; he accepts it on good faith; he is resolved to work within that climate at all costs. In the meantime, he will have to live between worlds, and that for any artists is a disturbing experience.[2]

Like Davis, black scholar W.E.B. Du Bois recognized that there was little room in 1920 for anything but stereotypical depictions of blacks. As he states, "We can go to the stage . . . [and] we can play all the sordid parts that America likes to assign to Negroes; but for anything else there is small place for us."[3] But for many black writers and scholars, Davis's "disturbing experience" was unbearable. It became clear that a struggle would have to take place in order for black writers to change their current artistic identity. African Americans would either remain a stereotype, or they would have to rebel against white patronage in order to express a truer sense of black identity.

THE FOSTERING OF BLACK CONSCIOUSNESS

The second factor that converged during the Harlem Renaissance and worked to draw serious attention from both black and white audiences was the fostering of a new black consciousness. This new consciousness stemmed from two sources: a growing black intellectual community, and a need to write about the black experience in a forum that was in direct tension with the white world. The black intellectual community envisioned the black identity as one that moved beyond the boundary of race to create a more equitable view of blacks by white America. Du Bois envisioned one avenue of change happening through what he termed the *talented tenth*. This term implied that within a society, 10 percent of the population is gifted with above-average intelligence, creativity, and the means for obtaining success. But according to Du Bois, the responsibility of this 10 percent also involves educating and encouraging the other 90 percent to rise up to the higher level. As Du Bois states, "The Talented Tenth rises and pulls all that are worth the saving up to their vantage ground. This is the history of human progress."[4] It was his desire to foster creative achievement through an educated class of men and women who could work to elevate the rest of black society. Du Bois saw literature and art as one means of changing the view of an entire society.

W.E.B. Du Bois

Du Bois exerted much influence over the creative efforts of many of Harlem's young literary elite. One such individual was Langston Hughes. Du Bois was responsible for publishing Hughes's first poem, "The Negro Speaks of Rivers" (1921), which appeared in the *Crisis*, a journal of the National Association for the Advancement of Colored People (NAACP), for which Du Bois was then the editor. Hughes's poem draws on past cultural achievements in Africa to give a foundation for new possibilities in defining a black culture in America. Early in the poem, Hughes writes,

> I bathed in the Euphrates when dawns were young,
> I built my hut near the Congo and it lulled me to sleep.
> I looked upon the Nile and raised pyramids above it.
> I heard the singing of the Mississippi when Abe Lincoln
>   Went down to New Orleans, and I've seen its muddy
>   Bosom turn all golden in the sunset.[5]

These images represented for blacks the possibilities that exist for men and women who are part of a progressive society, not subservient to it. By focusing on what was once great in Africa, Hughes expresses a desire to achieve similar greatness in America, in an environment that is both free and equal. Writers such as Hughes were part of Du Bois's talented tenth that worked to change the American black identity.

MIXING THE CREATIVE AND INTELLECTUAL COMMUNITIES

Another member of the talented tenth was the entrepreneur Charles S. Johnson. During the years 1920 through 1924, many young authors published their works in the few forums available to black writers—mostly small black-run journals that did not reach national audiences. Johnson saw a definite need to bridge the gap between the white publishing world and the talented writers of Harlem. In 1924 Johnson attempted to unite the young literati of Harlem with the black intellectual community and representatives from the white publishing houses. This gathering happened in March 1924 and became known as the Civic Club Dinner. Arna Bontemps recounts some of the details of the event, gleaned from a letter written by Charles S. Johnson and published in his memoir, *The Awakening:*

> It was a most unusual affair—a dinner meeting at the Civic Club at which all of the younger Negro writers . . . met and chatted with the passing generation . . . and with the literary personages of the city—about 100 guests and tremendously impressive speaking. . . . It would have given you a first hand introduction to the "last worders" in literature. But principally it served to stimulate a market for the new stuff these young writers are turning out. The first definite reaction came in the form of one magazine to devote an entire issue to the similar subjects as treated by representatives of this group.[6]

The publication to which Johnson referred was the March 1925 edition of *Survey Graphic.* This edition was entitled *Harlem: Mecca of the New Negro,* and it contained poetry, fiction, and social essays regarding the direction of black culture. This edition was edited by black scholar Alain Locke and was later expanded for his book *The New Negro* (1925).

As more and more young black writers found forums in which to publish their works, it became important for the established black intellectual community to promote these new voices. Thus, the creation of new magazines and promotions by the black intellectual community worked to solicit literature by African Americans about the black experience. The magazine *Opportunity,* edited by Johnson, played an instrumental role in the discovery of African American writers. *Opportunity* held monthly contests that drew new talent with the promise of financial reward. Zora Neale Hurston, a prominent anthropologist and chronicler of black folklore in America, was one such talent discovered through the *Opportunity* contests. She recounts in her autobiography, *Dust Tracks on a Road* (1942), the substantial role these contests played in her direction as a scholar:

> Being out of school for lack of funds, and wanting to be in New York, I decided to go there and try and get back in school in that city. So the first week of January 1925, found me in

New York with $1.50, no job, no friends, and a lot of hope. . . .
[After submitting a story] I came to New York through *Opportunity*, and through *Opportunity* to Barnard. I won a prize
for a short story at the first Award dinner, May 1, 1925, and
[short story writer] Fannie Hurst offered me a job as her sec-
retary, and Annie Nathan Meyer [one of the founders of
Barnard College] offered to get me a scholarship to Barnard.
My record was good enough, and I entered Barnard in the
fall, graduating in 1928.[7]

It was also in the pages of *Opportunity* that Carl Van Doren,
a white critic and editor of the *Century*, praised the works of
the new Negro writers as engaging issues that were more interesting than the bland optimism that epitomized the majority of white magazine writing.

In essence, the renaissance had evolved into a synthesis
between two established communities: the youthful writers
of the 1920s and the older intellectual community that established groups like the NAACP and the Urban League, and
who published their works within the black social science
and university journals. Literary scholar Cary D. Wintz explains in his book *Black Culture and the Harlem Renaissance*
that "these older men and women, while sometimes partici-
pating directly in the creative aspects of the renaissance,
served chiefly as critics, advisers, and liaisons between the
younger black writers and the white literary establishment."[8] Thus, it was through the efforts of intellectuals like
W.E.B. Du Bois, Alain Locke, and Charles S. Johnson that
doors opened for black writers.

BREAKING INTO THE PUBLISHING WORLD

By the mid-1920s many black novelists began to find success. Up until 1922 poetry and short fiction were given pri-
ority by most publications. But due to an increased interest
in black themes by white audiences and publishers, novels
about the black experience began to emerge. The most significant publication of the early 1920s was Jean Toomer's
Cane (1923). Many critics heralded its publication as the
first major work of the renaissance. Claude McKay's *Harlem
Shadows* (1922) was also regarded highly by critics and was
seen as the first influential piece of black writing by an immigrant from the West Indies. In 1926 Carl Van Vechten published *Nigger Heaven*, and both Jessie Fauset and Nella
Larsen were making an impact with their novels about the
female black experience.

The end of the 1920s finally saw advancements in the publication of plays by black dramatists. By 1927, through contests sponsored by *Opportunity, Crisis, Nation,* and several other journals committed to publishing black authors, many one-act plays were published by individuals who went on to have prominent careers as dramatists. The anthology *Plays of Negro Life* (1927) was published by Harper and edited by Alain Locke. This volume contains many one-act plays by black and white writers, but the thematic expression is overwhelmingly about black life without the emphasis on primitivism. There was also an emergence of several small playhouses in Harlem that were solely owned and operated by the black community. Although the theater movement did not gain serious attention until the middle 1930s, these advancements showed a developing interest in the publication and performance of drama by blacks.

By the end of the 1920s, more socially conscious blacks believed there was a need to break away from the editorial control of white publishers, but this break would never fully happen. A rift began to appear between the younger artists and the older critics. The artists accused the intellectuals of using white standards to judge the artistic merits of a work and therefore dismissing viable black writings. The critics rejected the claim, but indeed the search for new talent flagged. In 1927 *Opportunity* suspended its fiction and poetry contests due to what it considered a lack of strong material. To counter this rejection, several established writers and artists joined together financially in an effort to create an all-black publication called *Fire!* This journal of black writing would feature the contemporaries of the renaissance movement, but it went bankrupt after just one issue due to a lack of publishing knowledge and an inability to predict the operating costs involved.

By the late 1920s, there were fewer black markets for publication, a sign that the rift between the intellectual and creative communities was still widening, and the increasing influx of white patrons and their money overshadowed the efforts of intellectuals like Du Bois and his contemporaries to foster a propagandistic effort through art. In 1928 sociologist Edward Franklin Frazier commented, "[The black creative community] looks askance at the new rising class of black capitalism while it basks in the sun of white capitalism. It enjoys the congenial company of white radicals while shunning association with black radicals."[9] Claude McKay states in his book *A Long Way from Home* (1937) "[that] among the Negro artists there was much of that Uncle Tom attitude which works like Satan against the idea of a coherent and purposeful Negro group."[10] But any financial reliance on white patrons ended on October 24, 1929; the stock market crashed and Harlem found itself in the midst of the Great Depression. The economic patronage of white audiences disappeared, and interest in the Harlem community dried up.

THE EXPATRIATES AND THE DEPRESSION

Besides shrinking financial investment, another factor helped bring the Harlem Renaissance to an end. As many white writers of the late 1920s became expatriates in Paris, their black colleagues followed. Whereas many of the white artists went to France seeking a supposedly more liberal atmosphere, African American artists became expatriates to work outside of the racial barriers that kept their work from reaching larger audiences. Ironically, it was while in Europe that many of the great black American novelists, poets, musicians, and actors achieved fame and recognition. Langston Hughes, Countee Cullen, Jean Toomer, and Claude McKay spent time in Paris and other European cities, enjoying the success that was impossible to achieve back home. Actress and singer Josephine Baker took advantage of France's fascination with primitivism to carve out her own hugely successful career. Most of these artists spent the depression years in Europe, only returning to the United States when their achievements became internationally acclaimed.

Countee Cullen

Meanwhile, the Great Depression created a new image of Harlem, one that was submerged in poverty and unemployment. The jobs that once drew blacks and immigrants alike to New York were gone. In the introduction to his anthology of the period, *Voices from the Harlem Renaissance*, black scholar and critic Nathan Huggins states, "The black man, at the height of his popularity, became the first to be sacrificed to unemployment and starvation."[11] The white audiences, with their excess of cash, also had fallen away. Harlem became a symbol of racial poverty as it transformed from a culture capital into an urban ghetto. This tarnished image of Harlem shifted the focus of African American writing toward themes of social injustice. The community remained as a major theme in many works by prominent black writers, though now it was not viewed as a neighborhood of nightlife and primitive taboos but rather as a reflection of the racism, poverty, and hopelessness that was left when the party ended.

THE RENAISSANCE DRAWS TO A CLOSE

Although the heyday of the Harlem Renaissance was during the 1920s, many literary scholars extend the period to 1940. Regardless, the common thread that united the works of the Harlem Renaissance was the creation of a new black voice in art that struggled to free itself from older stereotypes and even the white conventions of the day. The poetry, fiction, and essays of the elite writers of this time used Harlem as a hub in which to centralize the focus for their writings. Harlem symbolized, early on, the urbanization of black America. It was a major cultural center for blacks migrating from the South, and it represented the desire of all African Americans to rise above the economic depravity that characterized black America in the decades after the Civil War and emancipation.

The Harlem Renaissance is not only a history of literary and artistic achievement, but it is also a direct reflection of the social patterns stemming from the urbanization of northern cities by African Americans. Because the literature of the renaissance traces the quest for validation in a white literary world, it focuses on several issues that black writers faced as a direct result of racial bias. Even though many of the writers received economic support and even friendship from individuals within the white community, readers of Harlem Renaissance literature cannot overlook the influence exerted by white society through its control of publishing houses and through its deep pockets.

After the Great Depression sealed the economic vitality of Harlem and the 1930s found many of its writers working in

Europe, there was a brief resurgence of interest in the literature of the renaissance. But both the audience and the participants seemed unwilling to maintain that interest. In 1934 English heiress Nancy Cunard compiled *Negro*, an anthology of new black writings by many of the Harlem Renaissance writers as well as works by new African American talent. The work borrowed heavily from Alain Locke's *The New Negro* and was criticized for being no more than a reiteration of Locke's previous work. When Cunard courted the support of the principal writers of the movement, many such as Claude McKay and Jean Toomer, who were living as expatriates, refused to contribute. Some were not interested in working over the same material and issues in their previous works; they wanted to move on as writers. Others simply felt the renaissance had not delivered on its promises. They were still harboring resentment with the black intellectual community that had encouraged them to use their art as a way of erasing the distinction between black and white instead of celebrating the African American experience. Many critics have implied that the reliance of renaissance writers on themes of the primitive instead of on social conscience is what resulted in the disparity between the creative and intellectual communities. As Harold Cruse, a critic of the 1960s black arts movement, wrote in 1967, "No social movement of a protest nature in Harlem can be successful or have any positive meaning unless it is at one and the same time a political, economic movement."[12] This supports the contention of Du Bois that all art should be created for the purpose of propaganda, an idea against which the creative community rebelled.

The legacy of the Harlem Renaissance included over thirty-five writers who collectively produced twenty-six novels, ten volumes of poetry, several Broadway plays, numerous essays and short stories, and several advancements in art and music. Ultimately, the movement helped to define black culture in America and reveal its significance to the culture of the nation as a whole. It also granted recognition and respect to the achievements of this previously overlooked segment of the population, ensuring that the artistic voices of African Americans would not be silenced in future generations.

NOTES

1. Claude McKay, *Harlem: Negro Metropolis*. New York: E.P. Dutton, 1940.
2. Arthur P. Davis, "Integration and Race Literature," in *Analysis and Assessment: 1940–1979*, ed. Cary D. Wintz. New York: Garland, 1996.
3. W.E.B. Du Bois, "The Criteria of Negro Art," *Crisis*, October 1926.
4. W.E.B. Du Bois, "The Talented Tenth," in *Negro Problem: A Series of Articles by Representative American Negroes of Today*. New York: J. Pott, 1903.
5. Langston Hughes, *The Collected Poems of Langston Hughes*, ed. Arnold Rampersad. New York: Knopf, 2001.
6. Arna Bontemps, "The Awakening: A Memoir," in *The Harlem Renaissance Remembered*, ed. Arna Bontemps. New York: Dodd, 1972.
7. Zora Neale Hurston, *Dust Tracks on a Road*. New York: Arno, 1969.
8. Cary D. Wintz, *Black Culture and the Harlem Renaissance*. College Station: Texas A&M University Press, 1996.
9. Edward Franklin Frazier, "La Bourgeoisie Noire," *Modern Quarterly*, Fall 1928.
10. Claude McKay, *A Long Way from Home*. New York: Furman, 1937.
11. Nathan Huggins, ed., *Voices from the Harlem Renaissance*. New York: Oxford University Press, 1976.
12. Harold Cruse, *The Essential Harold Cruse: A Reader*, ed. William Jelani. New York: Palgrave, 2002.

CHAPTER 1

Harlem and the New Negro

Harlem
Renaissance

The Capital of Negro Culture

James Weldon Johnson

James Weldon Johnson was an American author, lawyer, and diplomat, whose writings and activities focused chiefly on black life in the United States. Johnson's best-known book is the novel *The Autobiography of an Ex-Colored Man* (1912). The book examines race relations in the United States by wrestling with the question of racial identity. Johnson's *The Culture Capital* is one of the best-known essays regarding the northern migration of southern blacks to Harlem. Writing in the mid-1920s, Johnson focuses on the importance of Harlem as a place where African Americans accumulated property and built a community that fostered intellectual as well as economic prosperity. He also cites that Harlem shall never become a point of racial tension, as the community possesses a solid economic infrastructure and a sophisticated metropolitan atmosphere attractive to various ethnic backgrounds, which makes it an asset to the rest of New York City.

In the history of New York, the significance of the name Harlem has changed from Dutch to Irish to Jewish to Negro. Of these changes, the last has come most swiftly. Throughout colored America, from Massachusetts to Mississippi, and across the continent to Los Angeles and Seattle, its name, which as late as fifteen years ago had scarcely been heard, now stands for the Negro metropolis. Harlem is indeed the great Mecca for the sight-seer, the pleasure-seeker, the curious, the adventurous, the enterprising, the ambitious and the talented of the whole Negro world; for the lure of it has reached down to every island of the Carib Sea and has penetrated even into Africa.

Excerpted from "Harlem: The Culture Capital," by James Weldon Johnson, *The New Negro: An Interpretation*, edited by Alain Locke (New York: Albert and Charles Boni, 1925).

In the make-up of New York, Harlem is not merely a Negro colony or community, it is a city within a city, the greatest Negro city in the world. It is not a slum or a fringe, it is located in the heart of Manhattan and occupies one of the most beautiful and healthful sections of the city. It is not a "quarter" of dilapidated tenements, but is made up of new-law apartments and handsome dwellings, with well-paved and well-lighted streets. It has its own churches, social and civic centers, shops, theaters and other places of amusement. And it contains more Negroes to the square mile than any other spot on earth. A stranger who rides up magnificent Seventh Avenue on a bus or in an automobile must be struck with surprise at the transformation which takes place after he crosses One Hundred and Twenty-fifth Street. Beginning there, the population suddenly darkens and he rides through twenty-five solid blocks where the passers-by, the shoppers, those sitting in restaurants, coming out of theaters, standing in doorways and looking out of windows are practically all Negroes; and then he emerges where the population as suddenly becomes white again. There is nothing just like it in any other city in the country, for there is no preparation for it; no change in the character of the houses and streets; no change, indeed, in the appearance of the people, except their color.

A COMMUNITY FOR BLACKS

Negro Harlem is practically a development of the past decade, but the story behind it goes back a long way. There have always been colored people in New York. In the middle of the last century they lived in the vicinity of Lispenard, Broome and Spring Streets. When Washington Square and lower Fifth Avenue was the center of aristocratic life, the colored people, whose chief occupation was domestic service in the homes of the rich, lived in a fringe and were scattered in nests to the south, east and west of the square. As late as the '80's the major part of the colored population lived in Sullivan, Thompson, Bleecker, Grove, Minetta Lane and adjacent streets. It is curious to note that some of these nests still persist. In a number of the blocks of Greenwich Village and Little Italy may be found small groups of Negroes who have never lived in any other section of the city. By about 1890 the center of colored population had shifted to the upper Twenties and lower Thirties west of Sixth Avenue. Ten years later another considerable shift northward had been made to West Fifty-third Street.

The West Fifty-third Street settlement deserves some special mention because it ushered in a new phase of life among colored New Yorkers. Three rather well-appointed hotels were opened in the street and they quickly became the centers of a sort of fashionable life that hitherto had not existed. On Sunday evenings these hotels served dinner to music and attracted crowds of well-dressed diners. One of these hotels, The Marshall, became famous as the headquarters of Negro talent. There gathered the actors, the musicians, the composers, the writers, the singers, dancers and vaudevillians. There one went to get a close-up of Williams and Walker, Cole and Johnson, Ernest Hogan, Will Marion Cook, Jim Europe, Aida Overton, and of others equally and less known. Paul Laurence Dunbar was frequently there whenever he was in New York. Numbers of those who love to shine by the light reflected from celebrities were always to be found. The first modern jazz band ever heard in New York, or, perhaps anywhere, was organized at The Marshall. It was a playing-singing-dancing orchestra, making the first dominant use of banjos, saxophones, clarinets and trap drums in combination, and was called The Memphis Students. Jim Europe was a member of that band, and out of it grew the famous Clef Club, of which he was the noted leader, and which for a long time monopolized the business of "entertaining" private parties and furnishing music for the new dance craze. Also in the Clef Club was "Buddy" Gilmore who originated trap drumming as it is now practised, and set hundreds of white men to juggling their sticks and doing acrobatic stunts while they manipulated a dozen other noise-making devices aside from their drums. A good many well-known white performers frequented The Marshall and for seven or eight years the place was one of the sights of New York.

THE BATTLE OVER PROPERTY

The move to Fifty-third Street was the result of the opportunity to get into newer and better houses. About 1900 the move to Harlem began, and for the same reason. Harlem had been overbuilt with large, new-law apartment houses, but rapid transportation to that section was very inadequate—the Lenox Avenue Subway had not yet been built—

and landlords were finding difficulty in keeping houses on the east side of the section filled. Residents along and near Seventh Avenue were fairly well served by the Eighth Avenue Elevated. A colored man, in the real estate business at this time, Philip A. Payton, approached several of these landlords with the proposition that he would fill their empty or partially empty houses with steady colored tenants. The suggestion was accepted, and one or two houses on One Hundred and Thirty-fourth Street east of Lenox Avenue were taken over. Gradually other houses were filled. The whites paid little attention to the movement until it began to spread west of Lenox Avenue; they then took steps to check it. They proposed through a financial organization, the Hudson Realty Company, to buy in all properties occupied by colored people and evict the tenants. The Negroes countered by similar methods. Payton formed the Afro-American Realty Company, a Negro corporation organized for the purpose of buying and leasing houses for occupancy by colored people. Under this counter stroke the opposition subsided for several years.

But the continually increasing pressure of colored people to the west over the Lenox Avenue dead line caused the opposition to break out again, but in a new and more menacing form. Several white men undertook to organize all the white people of the community for the purpose of inducing financial institutions not to lend money or renew mortgages on properties occupied by colored people. In this effort they had considerable success, and created a situation which has not yet been completely overcome, a situation which is one of the hardest and most unjustifiable the Negro property owner in Harlem has to contend with. The Afro-American Realty Company was now defunct, but two or three colored men of means stepped into the breach. Philip A. Payton and J.C. Thomas bought two five-story apartments, dispossessed the white tenants and put in colored. J.B. Nail bought a row of five apartments and did the same thing. St. Philip's Church bought a row of thirteen apartment houses on One Hundred and Thirty-fifth Street, running from Seventh Avenue almost to Lenox.

THE NEGRO INVASION AND WHITE FLIGHT

The situation now resolved itself into an actual contest. Negroes not only continued to occupy available apartment houses, but began to purchase private dwellings between Lenox and Seventh Avenues. Then the whole movement, in the eyes of the whites, took on the aspect of an "invasion"; they became panic-stricken and began fleeing as from a plague. The presence of one colored family in a block, no matter how well bred and orderly, was sufficient to precipitate a flight. House after house and block after block was actually deserted. It was a great demonstration of human beings running amuck. None of them stopped to reason why they were doing it or what would happen if they didn't. The banks and lending companies holding mortgages on these deserted houses were compelled to take them over. For some time they held these houses vacant, preferring to do that and carry the charges than to rent or sell them to colored people. But values dropped and continued to drop until at the outbreak of the war in Europe property in the northern part of Harlem had reached the nadir.

THE RECRUITMENT OF SOUTHERN BLACKS

In the meantime the Negro colony was becoming more stable; the churches were being moved from the lower part of the city; social and civic centers were being formed; and gradually a community was being evolved. Following the outbreak of the war in Europe Negro Harlem received a new and tremendous impetus. Because of the war thousands of aliens in the United States rushed back to their native lands to join the colors and immigration practically ceased. The result was a critical shortage in labor. This shortage was rapidly increased as the United States went more and more largely into the business of furnishing munitions and supplies to the warring countries. To help meet this shortage of common labor Negroes were brought up from the South. The government itself took the first steps, following the practice in vogue in Germany of shifting labor according to the supply and demand in various parts of the country. The example of the government was promptly taken up by the big industrial concerns, which sent hundreds, perhaps thousands, of labor agents into the South who recruited Negroes by wholesale. I was in Jacksonville, Fla., for a while at that time, and I sat one day and watched the stream of migrants passing to take the train. For hours they passed steadily, carrying flimsy suit cases, new and shiny, rusty old ones, bursting at the seams, boxes and bundles and impedimenta of all sorts, including banjos, guitars, birds in cages and what not. Similar scenes were being enacted in cities and towns all over that region. The first wave of the great exodus of Negroes from the South was on. Great numbers of these migrants headed for New York or eventually got there, and naturally the majority went up into Harlem. . . .

ECONOMIC PROSPERITY

These new-comers did not have to look for work; work looked for them, and at wages of which they had never even dreamed. And here is where the unlooked for, the unprecedented, the miraculous happened. According to all preconceived notions, these Negroes suddenly earning large sums of money for the first time in their lives should have had their heads turned; they should have squandered it in the most silly and absurd manners imaginable. Later, after the United States had entered the war and even Negroes in the South were making money fast, many stories in accord with the tradition came out of that section. There was the one about the colored man who went into a general store and on hearing a phonograph for the first time promptly ordered six of them, one for each child in the house. I shall not stop to discuss whether Negroes in the South did that sort of thing or not, but I do know that those who got to New York didn't. The Negroes of Harlem, for the greater part, worked and saved their money. Nobody knew how much they had saved until congestion made expansion necessary for tenants and ownership profitable for landlords, and they began to buy property. Persons who would never be suspected of having money bought property. The Rev. W.W. Brown, pastor of the Metropolitan Baptist Church, repeatedly made "Buy Property" the text of his sermons. A large part of his congregation carried out the injunction. The church itself set an example by purchasing a magnificent brownstone church building on Seventh Avenue from a white congregation. Buying property became a fever. At the height of this activity, that is, 1920–21, it was not an uncommon thing for a colored washerwoman or cook to go into a real estate office and lay down from one thousand to five thousand dollars on a house. . . .

When the buying activity began to make itself felt, the lending companies that had been holding vacant the handsome dwellings on and abutting Seventh Avenue decided to put them on the market. The values on these houses had dropped to the lowest mark possible and they were put up at astonishingly low prices. Houses that had been bought at from $15,000 to $20,000 were sold at one-third those figures. They were quickly gobbled up. The Equitable Life Assurance Company held 106 model private houses that were designed by Stanford White. They are built with courts running straight through the block and closed off by wrought-iron gates. Every one of these houses was sold within eleven months at an aggregate price of about two million dollars. To-day they are probably worth about 100 per cent more. . . .

CAN HARLEM REMAIN A BLACK COMMUNITY?

The question naturally arises, "Are the Negroes going to be able to hold Harlem?" If they have been steadily driven northward for the past hundred years and out of less desirable sections, can they hold this choice bit of Manhattan Island? It is hardly probable that Negroes will hold Harlem indefinitely, but when they are forced out it will not be for the same reasons that forced them out of former quarters in New York City. The situation is entirely different and without precedent. When colored people do leave Harlem, their homes, their churches, their investments and their businesses, it will be because the land has bcome so valuable they can no longer afford to live on it. But the date of another move northward is very far in the future. What will Harlem be and become in the meantime? Is there danger that the Negro may lose his economic status in New York and be unable to hold his property? Will Harlem become merely a famous ghetto, or will it be a center of intellectual, cultural and economic forces exerting an influence throughout the world, especially upon Negro peoples? Will it become a point of friction between the races in New York?

I think there is less danger to the Negroes of New York of losing out economically and industrially than to the Negroes of any large city in the North. In most of the big industrial centers Negroes are engaged in gang labor. They are employed by thousands in the stockyards in Chicago, by thousands in the automobile plants in Detroit; and in those cities they are likely to be the first to be let go, and in thousands, with every business depression. In New York there is hardly such a thing as gang labor among Negroes, except among the longshoremen, and it is in the longshoremen's unions, above all others, that Negroes stand on an equal footing. Employment among Negroes in New York is highly diversified; in the main they are employed more as individuals than as non-integral parts of a gang. Furthermore, Harlem is gradually becoming more and more a self-supporting community. Negroes there are steadily branching out into new businesses and enterprises in which Negroes are employed. So the danger of great numbers of Negroes being thrown out of work at once, with a resulting economic crisis among them, is less in New York than in most of the large cities of the North to which Southern migrants have come.

THE FUTURE OF HARLEM

These facts have an effect which goes beyond the economic and industrial situation. They have a direct bearing on the future character of Harlem and on the question as to whether Harlem will be a point of friction between the races in New York. It is true that Harlem is a Negro community, well defined and stable; anchored to its fixed homes, churches, institutions, business and amusement places; having its own working, business and professional classes. It is experiencing a constant growth of group consciousness and community feeling. Harlem is, therefore, in many respects, typically Negro. It has many unique characteristics. It has movement, color, gayety, singing, dancing, boisterous laughter and loud talk. One of its outstanding features is brass band parades. Hardly a Sunday passes but that there are several of these parades of which many are gorgeous with regalia and insignia. Almost any excuse will do—the death of an humble member of the Elks, the laying of a cornerstone, the "turning out" of the order of this or that. In many of these characteristics it is similar to the Italian colony. But withal, Harlem grows more metropolitan and more a part of New York all the while. Why is it then that its tendency is not to become a mere "quarter"?

I shall give three reasons that seem to me to be important in their order. First, the language of Harlem is not alien; it is not Italian or Yiddish; it is English. Harlem talks American, reads American, thinks American. Second, Harlem is not physically a "quarter." It is not a section cut off. It is merely a zone through which four main arteries of the city run. Third, the fact that there is little or no gang labor gives Harlem Negroes the opportunity for individual expansion and individual contacts with the life and spirit of New York. A thousand

Negroes from Mississippi put to work as a gang in a Pitts-
burgh steel mill will for a long time remain a thousand Ne-
groes from Mississippi. Under the conditions that prevail in
New York they would all within six months become New
Yorkers. The rapidity with which Negroes become good New
Yorkers is one of the marvels to observers. . . .

To my mind, Harlem is more than a Negro community; it
is a large scale laboratory experiment in the race problem.
The statement has often been made that if Negroes were
transported to the North in large numbers the race problem
with all of its acuteness and with new aspects would be
transferred with them. Well, 175,000 Negroes live closely together in Harlem, in the heart of New York—75,000 more
than live in any Southern city—and do so without any race
friction. Nor is there any unusual record of crime. I once
heard a captain of the 38th Police Precinct (the Harlem
precinct) say that on the whole it was the most law-abiding
precinct in the city. New York guarantees its Negro citizens
the fundamental rights of American citizenship and protects
them in the exercise of those rights. In return the Negro
loves New York and is proud of it, and contributes in his way
to its greatness. He still meets with discriminations, but possessing the basic rights, he knows that these discriminations
will be abolished.

I believe that the Negro's advantages and opportunities
are greater in Harlem than in any other place in the country,
and that Harlem will become the intellectual, the cultural
and the financial center for Negroes of the United States, and
will exert a vital influence upon all Negro peoples.

The New Negro Identity

Alain Locke

Alain Locke was a philosopher and literary critic.
His ambitions included providing a forum in which
the talents and works of African American writers
and artists could be displayed legitimately without
being curtailed by the pressures of white publishers.
His best-known collection of work by black writers,
which culled much of its material from the March
1925 edition of *Survey Graphic,* was called *The New
Negro: An Interpretation,* and was devoted entirely to
the talents of essayists, writers, and authors from the
Harlem Renaissance movement. This selection,
taken from *The New Negro: An Interpretation,* examines the ideas behind outdated stereotypes surrounding African Americans and urges the African American community to empower itself through an
increased involvement in white society. Locke sees
social integration as an end to both cultural and political discrimination, the two greatest factors working against the recognition of African American talent and ability. To Locke, such progress is being
forged in the community of Harlem.

In the last decade something beyond the watch and guard of
statistics has happened in the life of the American Negro and
the three norns who have traditionally presided over the Negro problem have a changeling in their laps. The Sociologist,
the Philanthropist, the Race-leader are not unaware of the New
Negro, but they are at a loss to account for him. He simply cannot be swathed in their formulæ. For the younger generation
is vibrant with a new psychology; the new spirit is awake in
the masses, and under the very eyes of the professional observers is transforming what has been a perennial problem

Excerpted from "The New Negro," by Alain Locke, *The New Negro: An Interpretation,*
edited by Alain Locke (New York: Albert and Charles Boni, 1925).

into the progressive phases of contemporary Negro life.

Could such a metamorphosis have taken place as suddenly as it has appeared to? The answer is no; not because the New Negro is not here, but because the Old Negro had long become more of a myth than a man. The Old Negro, we must remember, was a creature of moral debate and historical controversy. His has been a stock figure perpetuated as an historical fiction partly in innocent sentimentalism, partly in deliberate reactionism. The Negro himself has contributed his share to this through a sort of protective social mimicry forced upon him by the adverse circumstances of dependence. So for generations in the mind of America, the Negro has been more of a formula than a human being—a something to be argued about, condemned or defended, to be "kept down," or "in his place," or "helped up," to be worried with or worried over, harassed or patronized, a social bogey or a social burden. . . .

By shedding the old chrysalis of the Negro problem we are achieving something like a spiritual emancipation. Until recently, lacking self-understanding, we have been almost as much of a problem to ourselves as we still are to others. But the decade that found us with a problem has left us with only a task. The multitude perhaps feels as yet only a strange relief and a new vague urge, but the thinking few know that in the reaction the vital inner grip of prejudice has been broken.

POSITIVE CHANGES

With this renewed self-respect and self-dependence, the life of the Negro community is bound to enter a new dynamic phase, the buoyancy from within compensating for whatever pressure there may be of conditions from without. The migrant masses, shifting from countryside to city, hurdle several generations of experience at a leap, but more important, the same thing happens spiritually in the life-attitudes and self-expression of the Young Negro, in his poetry, his art, his education and his new outlook, with the additional advantage, of course, of the poise and greater certainty of knowing what it is all about. From this comes the promise and warrant of a new leadership. As one of them has discerningly put it:

We have tomorrow
Bright before us
Like a flame.

Yesterday, a night-gone thing
A sun-down name.

And dawn today
Broad arch above the road we came.
We march!

This is what, even more than any "most creditable record
of fifty years of freedom," requires that the Negro of to-day
be seen through other than the dusty spectacles of past controversy. The day of "aunties," "uncles" and "mammies" is
equally gone. . . .

First we must observe some of the changes which since
the traditional lines of opinion were drawn have rendered
these quite obsolete. A main change has been, of course, that
shifting of the Negro population which has made the Negro
problem no longer exclusively or even predominantly Southern. Why should our minds remain sectionalized, when the
problem itself no longer is? Then the trend of migration has
not only been toward the North and the Central Midwest, but
city-ward and to the great centers of industry—the problems
of adjustment are new, practical, local and not peculiarly
racial. Rather they are an integral part of the large industrial
and social problems of our present-day democracy. . . .

The tide of Negro migration, northward and city-ward, is
not to be fully explained as a blind flood started by the demands of war industry coupled with the shutting off of foreign migration, or by the pressure of poor crops coupled
with increased social terrorism in certain sections of the
South and Southwest. Neither labor demand, the boll-weevil
nor the Ku Klux Klan is a basic factor, however contributory
any or all of them may have been. The wash and rush of this
human tide on the beach line of the northern city centers is
to be explained primarily in terms of a new vision of opportunity, of social and economic freedom, of a spirit to seize,
even in the face of an extortionate and heavy toll, a chance
for the improvement of conditions. . . .

WHAT HARLEM SYMBOLIZES

Take Harlem as an instance of this. Here in Manhattan is not
merely the largest Negro community in the world, but the
first concentration in history of so many diverse elements of
Negro life. It has attracted the African, the West Indian, the
Negro American; has brought together the Negro of the North

and the Negro of the South; the man from the city and the man from the town and village; the peasant, the student, the business man, the professional man, artist, poet, musician, adventurer and worker, preacher and criminal, exploiter and social outcast. Each group has come with its own separate motives and for its own special ends, but their greatest experience has been the finding of one another. Proscription and prejudice have thrown these dissimilar elements into a common area of contact and interaction. Within this area, race sympathy and unity have determined a further fusing of sentiment and experience. So what began in terms of segregation becomes more and more, as its elements mix and react, the laboratory of a great race-welding. . . .

Harlem, I grant you, isn't typical—but it is significant, it is prophetic. No sane observer, however sympathetic to the new trend, would contend that the great masses are articulate as yet, but they stir, they move, they are more than physically restless. The challenge of the new intellectuals among them is clear enough—the "race radicals" and realists who have broken with the old epoch of philanthropic guidance, sentimental appeal and protest. But are we after all only reading into the stirrings of a sleeping giant the dreams of an agitator? The answer is in the migrating peasant. It is the "man farthest down" who is most active in getting up. . . .

RACIAL SOLIDARITY AND EQUALITY

When the racial leaders of twenty years ago spoke of developing race-pride and stimulating race-consciousness, and of the desirability of race solidarity, they could not in any accurate degree have anticipated the abrupt feeling that has surged up and now pervades the awakened centers. Some of the recognized Negro leaders and a powerful section of white opinion identified with "race work" of the older order have indeed attempted to discount this feeling as a "passing phase," an attack of "race nerves" so to speak, an "aftermath of the war," and the like. It has not abated, however, if we are to gauge by the present tone and temper of the Negro press, or by the shift in popular support from the officially recognized and orthodox spokesmen to those of the independent, popular, and often radical type who are unmistakable symptoms of a new order. It is a social disservice to blunt the fact that the Negro of the Northern centers has reached a stage where tutelage, even of the most interested

and well-intentioned sort, must give place to new relationships, where positive self-direction must be reckoned with
in ever increasing measure. The American mind must
reckon with a fundamentally changed Negro. . . .

The fiction is that the life of the races is separate, and increasingly so. The fact is that they have touched too closely
at the unfavorable and too lightly at the favorable levels.

While inter-racial councils have sprung up in the South,
drawing on forward elements of both races, in the Northern
cities manual laborers may brush elbows in their everyday
work, but the community and business leaders have experienced no such interplay or far too little of it. These segments
must achieve contact or the race situation in America becomes desperate. Fortunately this is happening. There is a
growing realization that in social effort the co-operative basis must supplant long-distance philanthropy, and that the
only safeguard for mass relations in the future must be provided in the carefully maintained contacts of the enlightened
minorities of both race groups. In the intellectual realm a renewed and keen curiosity is replacing the recent apathy; the
Negro is being carefully studied, not just talked about and
discussed. In art and letters, instead of being wholly caricatured, he is being seriously portrayed and painted. . . .

The particular significance in the re-establishment of contact between the more advanced and representative classes is
that it promises to offset some of the unfavorable reactions of
the past, or at least to re-surface race contacts somewhat for
the future. Subtly the conditions that are molding a New Negro are molding a new American attitude. . . .

Up to the present one may adequately describe the Negro's
"inner objectives" as an attempt to repair a damaged group
psychology and reshape a warped social perspective. Their
realization has required a new mentality for the American
Negro. And as it matures we begin to see its effects; at first,
negative, iconoclastic, and then positive and constructive. In
this new group psychology we note the lapse of sentimental
appeal, then the development of a more positive self-respect
and self-reliance; the repudiation of social dependence, and
then the gradual recovery from hyper-sensitiveness and
"touchy" nerves, the repudiation of the double standard of
judgment with its special philanthropic allowance and then
the sturdier desire for objective and scientific appraisal; and
finally the rise from social disillusionment to race pride,

from the sense of social debt to the responsibilities of social contribution, and offsetting the necessary working and commonsense acceptance of restricted conditions, the belief in ultimate esteem and recognition. Therefore the Negro to-day wishes to be known for what he is, even in his faults and shortcomings, and scorns a craven and precarious survival at the price of seeming to be what he is not. He resents being spoken of as a social ward or minor, even by his own, and to being regarded a chronic patient for the sociological clinic, the sick man of American Democracy. For the same reasons, he himself is through with those social nostrums and panaceas, the so-called "solutions" of his "problem," with which he and the country have been so liberally dosed in the past. Religion, freedom, education, money—in turn, he has ardently hoped for and peculiarly trusted these things; he still believes in them, but not in blind trust that they alone will solve his life-problem. . . .

CLOSING THE RACIAL GAP

More and more, however, an intelligent realization of the great discrepancy between the American social creed and the American social practice forces upon the Negro the taking of the moral advantage that is his. Only the steadying and sobering effect of a truly characteristic gentleness of spirit prevents the rapid rise of a definite cynicism and counter-hate and a defiant superiority feeling. Human as this reaction would be, the majority still deprecate its advent, and would gladly see it forestalled by the speedy amelioration of its causes. We wish our race pride to be a healthier, more positive achievement than a feeling based upon a realization of the shortcomings of others. But all paths toward the attainment of a sound social attitude have been difficult; only a relatively few enlightened minds have been able as the phrase puts it "to rise above" prejudice. The ordinary man has had until recently only a hard choice between the alternatives of supine and humiliating submission and stimulating but hurtful counter-prejudice. Fortunately from some inner, desperate resourcefulness has recently sprung up the simple expedient of fighting prejudice by mental passive resistance, in other words by trying to ignore it. For the few, this manna may perhaps be effective, but the masses cannot thrive upon it.

Fortunately there are constructive channels opening out

into which the balked social feelings of the American Negro can flow freely.

Without them there would be much more pressure and danger than there is. These compensating interests are racial but in a new and enlarged way. One is the consciousness of acting as the advance-guard of the African peoples in their contact with Twentieth Century civilization; the other, the sense of a mission of rehabilitating the race in world esteem from that loss of prestige for which the fate and conditions of slavery have so largely been responsible. Harlem, as we shall see, is the center of both these movements; she is the home of the Negro's "Zionism." The pulse of the Negro world has begun to beat in Harlem.

The West Indian Influence on Harlem

W.A. Domingo

W.A. Domingo was a prominent African American journalist in the 1920s. His articles and essays appeared in such African American journals as the *Messenger* and *Opportunity*. Domingo was an ardent socialist; his essays focused on social equality, often citing as his main argument the assertion that African Americans are entitled, as are whites, the opportunity to pursue the American Dream. In this selection, written specifically for a special edition of the *Survey Graphic* in 1925, Domingo examines the cultural differences between immigrant blacks and American-born blacks. Although Domingo discusses in brief the influence of West Indian black immigration on the cultural atmosphere of other major American cities, he places the most emphasis on the great influx of West Indian blacks to the community of Harlem and their specific influence upon that community. He asserts that immigrants from the Caribbean islands have a stronger desire to succeed. This desire became a point of friction between immigrant blacks and American blacks living in Harlem, but the importance of their contributions to the progress of "the Negro race" as a whole cannot be discounted as it was their efforts at building businesses and buying property that helped to mobilize and to influence other African Americans to pursue these same goals.

Within Harlem's seventy or eighty blocks, for the first time in their lives, colored people of Spanish, French, Dutch, Arabian, Danish, Portuguese, British and native African ancestry or nationality meet and move together.

Excerpted from "The Tropics in New York," by W.A. Domingo, *The Emergence of the Harlem Renaissance*, edited by Cary D. Wintz (New York: Garland Publishing, 1996).

A dusky tribe of destiny seekers, these brown and black and yellow folk, eyes filled with visions of their heritage—palm fringed sea shores, murmuring streams, luxuriant hills and vales—have made their epical march from the far corners of the earth to Harlem. They bring with them vestiges of their folk life—their lean, sunburnt faces, their quiet, halting speech, fortified by a graceful insouciance, their light, loose-fitting clothes of ancient cut telling the story of a dogged, romantic pilgrimage to the El Dorado of their dreams.

Here they have their first contact with each other, with large numbers of American Negroes, and with the American brand of race prejudice. Divided by tradition, culture, historical background and group perspective, these diverse peoples are gradually hammered into a loose unit by the impersonal force of congested residential segregation. Unlike others of the foreign-born, black immigrants find it impossible to segregate themselves into colonies; too dark of complexion to pose as Cubans or some other Negroid but alien-tongued foreigners, they are inevitably swallowed up in black Harlem. Their situation requires an adjustment unlike that of any other class of the immigrant population; and but for the assistance of their kinsfolk they would be capsized almost on the very shores of their haven.

AN INCREASE IN BLACK IMMIGRATION

According to the census for 1920 there were in the United States 73,803 foreign-born Negroes; of that number 36,613, or approximately 50 per cent lived in New York City, 28,184 of them in the Borough of Manhattan. They formed slightly less than 20 per cent of the total Negro population of New York.

From 1920 to 1923 the foreign-born Negro population of the United States was increased nearly 40 per cent through the entry of 30,849 Africans (black). In 1921 the high-water mark of 9,873 was registered. This increase was not permanent, for in 1923 there was an exit of 1,525 against an entry of 7,554. If the 20 per cent that left that year is an index of the proportion leaving annually, it is safe to estimate a net increase of about 24,000 between 1920 and 1923. If the newcomers are distributed throughout the country in the same proportion as their predecessors, the present foreign-born Negro population of Harlem is about 35,000. These people are, therefore, a formidable minority whose presence cannot be ignored or discounted. It is this large body of foreign born who contribute those qualities that make New York so unlike Pittsburgh, Washington, Chicago and other cities with large aggregations of American Negroes. . . .

To the average American Negro all English-speaking black foreigners are West Indians, and by that is usually meant British subjects. There is a general assumption that there is everything in common among West Indians, though nothing can be further from the truth. West Indians regard themselves as Antiguans or Jamaicans as the case might be, and a glance at the map will quickly reveal the physical obstacles that militate against homogeneity of population; separations of many sorts, geographical, political and cultural tend everywhere to make and crystallize local characteristics. . . .

THE BLACK IMMIGRANT'S INFLUENCE ON AMERICAN NEGROES

West Indians have been coming to the United States for over a century. The part they have played in Negro progress is conceded to be important. As early as 1827 a Jamaican, John Brown Russwurm, one of the founders of Liberia, was the first colored man to be graduated from an American college and to publish a newspaper in this country; sixteen years later his fellow countryman, Peter Ogden, organized in New York City the first Odd-Fellows Lodge for Negroes. Prior to the Civil War, West Indian contribution to American Negro life was so great that Dr. W.E.B. DuBois, in his *Souls of Black Folk*, credits them with main responsibility for the manhood program presented by the race in the early decades of the last century. Indicative of their tendency to blaze new paths is the achievement of John W.A. Shaw of Antigua who, in the early 90's of the last century, passed the civil service tests and became deputy commissioner of taxes for the County of Queens.

It is probably not realized, indeed, to what extent West Indian Negroes have contributed to the wealth, power and prestige of the United States. Major-General Goethals, chief engineer and builder of the Panama Canal, has testified in glowing language to the fact that when all other labor was tried and failed it was the black men of the Caribbean whose intelligence, skill, muscle and endurance made the union of the Pacific and the Atlantic a reality.

Coming to the United States from countries in which they had experienced no legalized social or occupational disabilities, West Indians very naturally have found it difficult to adapt themselves to the tasks that are, by custom, reserved for Negroes in the North. Skilled at various trades and having a contempt for body service and menial work, many of the immigrants apply for positions that the average American Negro has been schooled to regard as restricted to white men only with the result that through their persistence and doggedness in fighting white labor, West Indians have in many cases been pioneers and shock troops to open a way for Negroes into new fields of employment.

"THE TROPICS IN NEW YORK"

This poem by Claude McKay shows the influence of the island community on Harlem culture and illustrates the author's desire to return to that simplistic life.

Bananas ripe and green, and ginger-root,
    Cocoa in pods and alligator pears,
And tangerines and mangoes and grape fruit,
    Fit for the highest prize at parish fairs,

Set in the window, bringing memories
    Of fruit-trees laden by low-singing rills,
And dewy dawns, and mystical blue skies
    In benediction over nun-like hills.

My eyes grew dim, and I could no more gaze;
    A wave of longing through my body swept,
And, hungry for the old, familiar ways,
    I turned aside and bowed my head and wept.

Claude McKay, "The Tropics in New York," *Harlem Shadows: The Poems of Claude McKay.* New York: Harcourt, Brace and Co., 1922.

This freedom from spiritual inertia characterizes the women no less than the men, for it is largely through them that the occupational field has been broadened for colored women in New York. By their determination, sometimes reinforced by a dexterous use of their hatpins, these women have made it possible for members of their race to enter the needle trades freely.

It is safe to say that West Indian representation in the skilled trades is relatively large; this is also true of the professions, especially medicine and dentistry. Like the Jew, they are forever launching out in business, and such retail businesses as are in the hands of Negroes in Harlem are largely in the control of the foreign-born. While American

Negroes predominate in forms of business like barber shops and pool rooms in which there is no competition from white men, West Indians turn their efforts almost invariably to fields like grocery stores, tailor shops, jewelry stores and fruit vending in which they meet the fiercest kind of competition.

RESENTMENT OF IMMIGRANT SUCCESS

Ten years ago it was possible to distinguish the West Indian in Harlem especially during the summer months. Accustomed to wearing cool, light-colored garments in the tropics, he would stroll along Lenox Avenue on a hot day resplendent in white shoes and flannel pants, the butt of many a jest from his American brothers who, today, have adopted the styles that they formerly derided. This trait of non-conformity manifested by the foreign-born has irritated American Negroes, who resent the implied self-sufficiency, and as a result there is a considerable amount of prejudice against West Indians. It is claimed that they are proud and arrogant; that they think themselves superior to the natives. And although educated Negroes of New York are loudest in publicly decrying the hostility between the two groups, it is nevertheless true that feelings against West Indians is strongest among members of that class. This is explainable on the ground of professional jealousy and competition for leadership. As the islanders press forward and upward they meet the same kind of opposition from the native Negro that the Jew and other ambitious white aliens receive from white Americans. Naturalized West Indians have found from experience that American Negroes are reluctant to concede them the right to political leadership even when qualified intellectually. Unlike their American brothers the islanders are free from those traditions that bind them to any party and, as a consequence are independent to the point of being radical. Indeed, it is they who largely compose the few political and economic radicals in Harlem; without them the genuinely radical movement among New York Negroes would be unworthy of attention. . . .

ADAPTING TO AMERICAN RACISM

In facing the problem of race prejudice, foreign born Negroes, and West Indians in particular, are forced to undergo considerable adjustment. Forming a racial majority in their own countries and not being accustomed to discrimination expressly felt as racial, they rebel against the "color line" as

they find it in America. For while color and caste lines tend
to converge in the islands, it is nevertheless true that because of the ratio of population, historical background and
traditions of rebellions before and since their emancipation,
West Indians of color do not have their activities, social, occupational and otherwise, determined by their race. Color
plays a part but it is not the prime determinant of advancement; hence, the deep feeling of resentment when the "color
line," legal or customary, is met and found to be a barrier to
individual progress. For this reason the West Indian has
thrown himself whole-heartedly into the fight against lynching, discrimination and the other disabilities from which
Negroes in America suffer.

It must be remembered that the foreign-born black men
and women, more so even than other groups of immigrants,
are the hardiest and most venturesome of their folk. They
were dissatisfied at home, and it is to be expected that they
would not be altogether satisfied with limitation of opportunity here when they have staked so much to gain enlargement
of opportunity. They do not suffer from the local anesthesia of
custom and pride which makes otherwise intolerable situations bearable for the home-staying majorities.

Just as the West Indian has been a sort of leaven in the
American loaf, so the American Negro is beginning to play a
reciprocal role in the life of the foreign Negro communities,
as for instance, the recent championing of the rights of Haiti
and Liberia and the Virgin Islands, as well as the growing resentment at the treatment of natives in the African colonial
dependencies. This world-wide reaction of the darker races
to their common as well as local grievances is one of the
most significant facts of recent development. Exchange of
views and extension of race organization beyond American
boundaries is likely to develop on a considerable scale in the
near future, in terms principally of educational and eco-
nomical projects. Former ties have been almost solely the
medium of church missionary enterprises.

It has been asserted that the movement headed by the
most-advertised of all West Indians, Marcus Garvey, absen-
tee "president" of the continent of Africa, represents the attempt of West Indian peasants to solve the American race
problem. This is no more true than it would be to say that
the editorial attitude of *The Crisis* during the war reflected
the spirit of American Negroes respecting their grievances

or that the late Booker T. Washington successfully delimited the educational aspirations of his people. The support given Garvey by a certain type of his countrymen is partly explained by their group reaction to attacks made upon him because of his nationality. On the other hand, the earliest and most persistent exposures of Garvey's multitudinous schemes were initiated by West Indians in New York like Cyril Briggs. . . .

Prejudice against West Indians is in direct ratio to their number; hence its strength in New York where they are heavily concentrated. It is not unlike the hostility between Englishmen and Americans of the same racial stock. It is to be expected that the feeling will always be more or less present between the immigrant and the native born. However, it does not extend to the children of the two groups, as they are subject to the same environment and develop identity of speech and psychology. Then, too, there has been an appreciable amount of intermarriage, especially between foreign born men and native women. Not to be ignored is the fact that congestion in Harlem has forced both groups to be less discriminating in accepting lodgers, thus making for reconciling contacts.

The outstanding contribution of West Indians to American Negro life is the insistent assertion of their manhood in an environment that demands too much servility and unprotesting acquiescence from men of African blood. This unwillingness to conform and be standardized, to accept tamely an inferior status and abdicate their humanity, finds an open expression in the activities of the foreign-born Negro in America.

African Heritage in the Harlem Renaissance

Sonia Delgado-Tall

One of the driving forces behind the Harlem Renaissance movement was the intense interest in African heritage, a theme that continues to thread itself through modern African American writing. As stereotypes of blacks pervaded white America in the 1920s, many renaissance writers worked to change the African American identity by establishing a deeper connection with Africa. This focus forced black writers to examine their own sense of cultural identity and whether or not this renewed sense of pride in African themes was indeed worthwhile. Roosevelt University professor Sonia Delgado-Tall argues that many writers of the period merely used the African themes as a stepping-stone toward a greater sense of identification with America. She argues that it was this desire to identify with a culture and develop a sense of cultural belonging that shaped the political, historical, and philosophical foundations of the renaissance.

The era of the Harlem Renaissance reversed some of the negative connotations attached to Africa, although we do find Black precursors of a distinctive racial art and history in the 19th century. The new Negro Movement and Pan-Africanism were the two predominant cultural forces of the Harlem Renaissance that initiated the first official rehabilitation of African and Black American cultures in the New World. . . .

This was the time "when Negro was in Vogue," as Langston Hughes mildly put it, which meant in more realistic terms that Blacks were being objectified as exotic icons. This exoticism or primitivism had considerable facets and cultural meanings, but it certainly marked an evolution from the days

Excerpted from "The New Negro Movement and the African Heritage in a Pan-Africanist Perspective," by Sonia Delgado-Tall, *The Journal of Black Studies*, January 2001. Copyright © 2001 by Sage Publications, Inc. Reprinted with permission.

of minstrels and coons. Even if the general lot of Black people had not been improved, these stereotypes were merely masks to Black entertainers, who soon managed to break through the nonthreatening images of Black inferiority. . . .

As for Africa, it still was "the dark continent" in European colonial literature and, consequently, in the White American culture of the 1920s. There was a direct correlation between the inferior status of Blacks in America and that of colonized Africans. Any term evocative of Africa was highly fashionable in Harlem's nightlife: Beale Street was known as Jungle Alley, artificial palm trees decorated the Cotton Club and enhanced the prefabricated exoticism of the stage and performances. Although the literary contributions of the Harlem Renaissance and the cultural implications of Pan-Africanism should be distinguished from the primitivist discourse, there would still be significant interferences. White patrons of the era were so conceited that they had created for Black people this exotic identity, which in dance or literature meant that their distinctive character was their sensuality or, in other words, their closeness to jungle rhythms. Ironically, and from this unique standpoint, we observe that the African heritage was disparagingly imposed upon them. . . .

THE ROLE OF STEREOTYPES

Harlem writers understood the ambivalent role played by stereotypes, and only a careful analysis of each author can reveal their true feelings toward Black arts and the Black heritage or their degree of dependence on White patrons. As early as June 1921, Langston Hughes had his poem "The Negro Speaks of Rivers" published in *The Crisis*, thanks to [W.E.B.] Du Bois's literary editor, Jessie Fauset. Throughout the decade, he would see a variety of his poems and collections in print; most of them—"Danse Africaine," "Negro," "Afro-American Fragment"—echoed that nostalgia and melancholy often seen in Du Bois's autobiographical evocations of the African American heritage. There was no falsity in these poems, yet the same could not always be said of his fiction, as seen in the sensationalism of his short story "Luani of the Jungle." Pressed to be a primitive, he did eventually rebel against his White patron, Charlotte Mason, and her stereotypical views of Black culture:

> She wanted me to be primitive and know and feel the intuitions of the primitive. But, unfortunately, I did not feel the

rhythms of the primitive surging through me, and so I could not live and write as though I did. I was only an American Negro who had loved the surface of Africa and the rhythms of Africa, but I was not Africa, I was Chicago and Kansas City and Broadway and Harlem. And I was not what she wanted me to be.

[Zora Neale] Hurston would be caught in a similar web of dependency on Mason. The main difference between Hughes and Hurston resided in Hurston's emotional detachment vis-à-vis Mason. There is no doubt that the financial support she received from 1927 to 1932 enabled her to do what she liked above anything else: collect Black folklore. . . .

As for Hughes, it is interesting to note that the first phase of his career ended with his Harlem works and the demise of Mason's patronage and of his collaboration with Hurston. But the Pan-Africanist essence of the Harlem Renaissance would continue to provide it impetus during his proletarian phase and beyond. His last work, an anthology of African writers, would be dedicated to the young writers of Africa. Furthermore, as we verify the ubiquity of our subject, we will come to see that it has no better home than Pan-Africanism.

CHANGING THE BLACK IMAGE

By turning to Africa, many African American writers as well as a few White Africanists helped to create a positive identity for Black Americans, yet their itineraries differed greatly, and their views would often be dismissed in the long process of a people in search of their roots, which official history had attempted to suppress. As simple an expression as it seems, the African heritage was far from being identified as a quotidian social or cultural reality by the average Black northerner or migrant, nor was it a deep personal preoccupation for those in pursuit of a literary career. Du Bois emerged as one of the greatest promoters of the New Negro Movement, striving to infuse it with his moral and political conceptions of art and literature. When in 1910 he made *The Crisis*, the organ of the National Association for the Advancement of Colored People (NAACP) and a medium to promote Black achievements, he was encouraging a more self-confident Black personality. By 1915, he set Black humiliation into its international context and laid out new tactics. His purpose was definitely propagandistic in politics as in art. Du Bois, James Weldon Johnson (another tenor of the

Harlem Renaissance), and [Alain] Locke (philosopher and theorist of the New Negro Movement) believed that the cultural high life of Harlem was an integral part of the revitalization of the Black personality that accompanied the repudiation of imperialism. If Locke never actually endorsed the Pan-Africanist credo, his writings and actions evinced his Pan-Africanist ideals in urging Negro artists to embrace the beauty of African art and to create their own distinctive racial art. . . .

In the early days of Black pride and consciousness, taking possession of the African reality often corresponded to a social and political strategy of survival, as in the case of [actors] Bert Williams and George Walker. After centuries of denigration by Whites and Blacks, Africa would provide artistic motifs and economic opportunities even before striking any emotional chord. It was the European interest in African arts that pushed many artists and writers, including Locke and Aaron Douglass, in the direction of the African heritage. In many instances, Douglass revealed his doubts about the African connection; he would write,

> I clearly recall ([white painter] Winold Reiss) impatience as he sought to urge me beyond my doubts and fears that seemed to loom so large in the presence of the terrifying spectres moving beneath the surface of every African Masque and fetish.

Therefore, in spite of Locke's and Du Bois's injunctions to embrace the African arts and Africa's historical grandeur, Africa was merely a stepping stone for poet Countee Cullen and for Douglass, not to mention fine artists such as [composer] Duke Ellington and [singer and actress] Josephine Baker, who carried many "jungle" themes in their repertoire but who knew how to transcend them just like [pantomimist Johnny] Hodgin's Black mask. There is no doubt that they would all partake of the aura of the New Negro and Pan-Africanist philosophies without locking themselves within primitivist or African-oriented aesthetics. . . .

PROBING AFRICAN HERITAGE

As their quest for their remote heritage began through the study of history, by traveling to the continent, or going down home—all had different personal itineraries—Harlemites and Pan-Africanists probed into the significance of their own darkness. Very few of them actually set foot on the African continent, because the heritage had to be redefined within the boundaries of the self if it were to radiate for others. Sometimes, it was only years later that the heritage seekers were indeed able to decipher their expedition, as Hughes himself did. Eurocentricism certainly marked Hughes's, Du Bois's, Locke's, and Nella Larsen's views or depictions of Africa, but when placed in the proper social context, their efforts to recreate the African space can be analyzed separately or collectively as statements of cultural, political, and economic resistance against a growing White hegemonic power.

As we look two centuries back, the idea of possessing a homeland and everything that comes along with it, such as a group identity, cultural pride, and the right to self-government and to the exploitation of one's land, were the essential preoccupations of all back-to-Africa Black proponents. But could the African heritage, the sum of one's forefathers' values, be retrieved from a dreamland or from the acquisition of a new hyphenated identity, as American-Liberians had hoped in the 19th century? And could the trauma of a people having been dispossessed ever be healed through an act of imperialistic conquest?

Even literary or political recognition would be insufficient to appease the spiritual longing for home of a people. Cullen's (1925) question, "What is Africa to me?", seldom raised in the 1920s and before, is startling for the complexity under its formal simplicity. Through a series of beautifully crafted stereotypes, his poem questions the existence of an African heritage per se and goes as far as establishing any belief in it; even those in the White and Black press who lauded *Color* would use Keatsian and Shakespearian comparisons to evaluate his art. Novelist Wallace Thurman, who knew him well, unmasked his short-lived dedication to "the scenes his father loved, / Spicy grove, cinnamon tree" in *Infants of Spring.* In the latter, DeWitt Clinton, a parody of Cullen, exhorts his fellow Negro artist to "go back to his pagan heritage for inspiration and to the old masters for form."

Naturally, Hughes's response to the African/pagan heritage would not be Cullen's, and W.E.B. Du Bois would offer another one. The question was not how rich their knowledge of the African past was or what cultural pride derived from it, for even the most erudite mind was bound to erect pure mental constructions to satisfy that fundamental human need to possess something of one's own as well as to belong somewhere. Du Bois would constantly travel abroad from his early 20s (to Berlin and Paris) until his death (China in the autumn of 1962 and finally Accra, [Ghana,] where he died). Naturally, it indicates his moral and physical commitment to Pan-Africanism; but could this uprootedness not symbolize, as in Hughes's case, that search for home? Did both suffer from the absence of the father? Could Africa and the connection with one's forefathers compensate that paternal separation? In other words, they were not in search of a motherland but of a fatherland. . . .

THE AFRICAN AMERICAN IDENTITY

Africanisms in African American culture have always abounded; unfortunately, centuries of racist propaganda would make any association of the African American with the African sound like an insult well into the 20th century. This was the direct result of the hegemonic historical and philosophical discourses that governed the planter, the politician, and the lawmaker and affected the Black psyche. Two distinct groups developed, with one that would painstakingly hold on to the words and music of their forefathers as Du Bois did to the "heathen melody" of his grandfather's grandmother. Thus, we witness the dynamics of culture when Black people are capable of weaving emotions or values of a remote past into their present lives. The other group had been cut off from their roots or had even dissociated themselves from Black life as victims of the system and out of their own ignorance. . . .

But the Harlem intelligentsia would still be groping to comprehend the nature of their African American identity, because it was far beyond the psychological reality of their two-ness. Cullen, mocked by Hughes, did not want to be acknowledged as a Negro poet. This fact alone illustrates some of the contradictory views about the Black man's racial identity and even Harlem's originality. Locke embraced too many trends in his volume *The New Negro*, which gave an unclear image or, at best, an eclectic one of what the African heritage truly was. In 1940, Melville Herskovitz would revise his judgment expressed in "The Negro's Americanism" in which the African American had first been seen as a passive recipient, as opposed to the active participant he really was in the cultural life of Harlem. The movement of rehabilitation of Black people was initiated in the field of anthropology by [scholar] Franz Boas, who had trained Hurston, Katherine Dunham, and Herskovitz. In *The Myth of the Negro Past*, Herskovitz (1958) countered the racist assumptions of Black and White scholars (including his early ones) who had described the Negro as a man without a past. [Sociologist] E. Franklin Frazier was one of them: "Probably never before in history has a people been so nearly stripped of its social heritage as the Negroes who were brought to America." The fact that these Africanisms remained unseen, unfelt, or unacknowledged for years by African American thinkers was, no doubt, due to the absorption of these men and women into the politics of race. . . .

The majority of Black writers and thinkers of the 1920s were concerned about their visibility as human beings, as a brief analysis of Locke's (1968) *The New Negro* will show. The need for Harlem Renaissance writers to artistically reaffirm their human personalities was acute; it went beyond the question of Negroes begging for humanity, as Richard Wright had ironically put it. Locke's work is a poignant description of his vision of cultural pluralism in America—a pluralism that belied racial inferiority and invited racial interaction for mutual enrichment. He did not advocate separatism but simply the full participation of the American Negroes, with their distinctive culture in the building of American institutions. His cultural program was designed to run counter the effects of a racist society and force full integration into American society.

Despite their strong individualism, Hurston, Hughes, and Nella Larsen spoke for this cultural pluralism. Hughes asserted repeatedly that he, too, was American, and Larsen's neither Black nor White character, Helga Crane, cried out, "I am Negro too." But the notion of cultural pluralism leads us to the question of transcendence of the African heritage. To affirm its validity in America in the 1920s constituted an extraordinary intellectual feat on the part of a number of intellectuals. In effect, the idea of Black cultural distinctiveness in the racist milieu, at the beginning of the century, had been used to justify racial segregation and even immigration restrictions on the grounds that people of African descent could never assimilate. Until today, some Aframericans view the idea of all African heritage as a threat to their social and political integration in the American fabric of society. In reality, the idea of first recognizing Aframericans as complex

human beings illustrated by *The New Negro* anthology reinforced Franz Boas's conclusions that different racial types
were not suited to different types of civilization, consequently dismissing a typical racist argument. Cultural rela-
tivism was born. Viewed in this light, African cultures suddenly became acceptable and useful. From then on, Locke
promoted African Negro art as the "historic art of the
Africana homeland." And he made it the source of the Black
American's distinctive art tradition. Moreover, he classified
African art into different artistic manifestations in accor-
dance with ethnicity; thus, he reveals the plurality of the
African heritage, which he never confuses with African
American art. . . .

SLAVERY'S IMPACT ON AFRICAN HERITAGE

But another neglected issue that globalizes the notion of
African heritage needs to be addressed: Africa was wrenched
from Africans even before the Middle Passage. Unfortunately, few African indigenous texts were preserved to doc-
ument the tragedy of *Arabo-Berber jihads* (Islamic holy wars
in the name of Allah) or of the trans-Saharan slave trade followed closely by the Atlantic slave trade, but we certainly do
possess the crude historical facts of those times and the human gift of empathy to reconstruct these events. So does this
phase of history modify in any way the parameters of our
subject? I strongly contend that it deepens every single
moral, physical, and spiritual suffering associated with the
African heritage that I have just evoked in the context of the
Harlem Renaissance. All these writers and artists unconsciously expressed—in every way society allows them to—
the centuries of despair of a people made to crawl in front of
other men and women in the name of an ideology or a god.
Therefore, Africans in Africa also had a complex role in the
making of the African heritage concept. Too often we view
the African heritage as the exclusive possession/creation of
a single group of people. Cross-cultural studies will no
doubt encourage the recognition of a vast, diverse, historical
heritage common to all peoples of African descent, because
this phase of consciousness is still at its beginnings for the
majority of diasporans. As the drama of racism and neo-
colonialism continues to unfold, resistance to hegemonic
power can successfully be drawn from the act of unearthing
the truth about a people's past. African consciousness—past

and present—or, in other words, the will to preserve a set of
social and cultural values in the face of annihilation, consti-
tutes the soil of a true heritage. It is undoubtedly through the
works of Du Bois and Locke that both Africans and African
Americans have come in the 20th century to understand
many of the connections between Africa and America, but
we cannot dismiss proto-Pan-Africanism or the terrible impact of the slave trade on African worldviews, which have
equally informed the thinking of our mentors. . . .

At this point, we may say that there was indeed a multitude
of political, historical, and even philosophical conceptions of
Africa in the 1920s that had drawn their political legitimacy
from early Black nationalist and Pan-Africanists, but there
were also African cultural forms and worldviews prevalent
in folk forms and language in small all-Black communities
or in self-segregated rural ones, as in Hurston's Eatonsville.
Small shopkeepers, laborers, sharecroppers, artisans, or
even entertainers developed a culture that owed much to
their African roots, spirit, and wit. Theirs was an environment that contained as much good as bad but that they could
claim their own. The African heritage was translated into
feelings and hymns of sorrow caused not only by the sever-
ance from one's land and clan but also from the human race
and consequently from the center. The Black man and
woman had to suffer geographical, social, and ethnic dis-
placement and were, therefore, made to subsist at the pe-
riphery of life and official history. Their raison d'être [reason
for being] was their ultimate link with her, on which the con-
trolling economy and society had stamped out their func-
tional considerations. They had to find the way to her or else
be nonentities. Nevertheless, they were to discover that no
one could deprive them of their ancestral cultural self, which
could be concealed in a name, a word, a story, or a song.

CHAPTER 2

The Black Playwright

Harlem
Renaissance

Early Achievements of Black Theater

Loften Mitchell

In the late 1930s, Loften Mitchell was an aspiring actor who performed regularly with the Rose McClendon Players of New York. Mitchell later studied drama and is now both a playwright and a drama critic. He is the author of *Black Drama: Story of the American Negro in the Theater* (1967), and has written several plays, including *Ballad of the Winter Soldiers, Star of Morning,* and *Ballad of a Blackbird,* which was produced for Broadway in 1967. Written in the late 1960s, Mitchell's essay contends with white critics who saw that decade as the time of the "emerging" black playwright. To refute this claim, Mitchell details the history of African American theater. He asserts that, until the "Negro was in vogue" in the early 1920s, white audiences were simply not interested in venturing into Harlem where the theater thrived with the works of black playwrights. Following the popularity of *Shuffle Along* (1921) with white audiences, black playwrights were able to dramatize a truer sense of Negro life, breaking away from the established black stereotypes that white playwrights had created. Yet until the 1960s, when African Americans fought for and attained more rights and respect in the nation, American history books ignored such achievements, leaving the erroneous impression that black theater was emerging in Mitchell's heyday.

In March, 1957 my play, *A Land Beyond the River,* opened at New York's Greenwich Mews Theatre to unanimously good reviews. My joy over the reviews vanished when I read the columns of praise about the play being entertaining as well as enlightening. One prominent critic lauded my sense of humor and pointed out that I had *not* written a propaganda play. In fact, the critics praised me more for what I had *not* done than for what I had done. That was fair enough, too, but when one reads that I wrote about human beings who were black people, the reason for my displeasure becomes apparent. These reviews, however, brought people to the box office and I decided not to look a gift-horse in the mouth, even when it is long-eared. I had barely made this decision when my press agent scheduled a number of interviews for me. At these I met a charming group of white journalists and they wrote lovely things about me, but what troubled me was the constant reference to the "emerging black playwright."

I cautioned them against its use. For one thing, I did not feel I had just emerged at all. I had been sitting up nights for years, writing and re-writing plays. Two of them—*The Bancroft Dynasty* and *The Cellar* had been successful on New York stages long before I wrote *A Land Beyond the River*. But, what troubled me more than my own plight was the obvious reality that black playwrights have existed longer than many people care to admit. It is obvious that labeling the black playwright as "emerging" is another way the Western world camouflages the realities of cultural trends, particularly in terms of non-white groups. The work of non-white playwrights should be known to anyone who is vaguely familiar with the Chinese and Japanese theatres. If memory serves correctly, it was a man of African ancestry—Alexandre Dumas, *fils*, author of *Camille*—who was responsible for what came to be known as the "well-made play."

In America black people have created for the theatre longer than anyone cares to realize. Sometime during the Eighteenth Century black slaves on southern plantations created the minstrel form. This form—the forerunner of the American musical comedy pattern—was designed by slaves to satirize slavemasters. Minstrelsy was a unique, fast-moving, devastating art form until whites saw it, copied it, and used that form to caricature the black man. The black man's protest was used to destroy his image.

In the Nineteenth Century, specifically in 1821, a black tragedian, James Hewlett, spearheaded the founding of the African Grove Theatre in New York City. This theatre, located at Bleeker and Grove Streets, performed the classics for free black people. It was a source of inspiration for the great Ira Aldridge. The police harassed the company, often arresting the actors in the middle of a performance. The actors returned upon their release from jail and performed again. White hoodlums also created disturbances in the theatre and the management was compelled to post a sign, asking whites to sit in the rear of the theatre because "white people do not know how to behave themselves at entertainment designed for ladies and gentlemen of color."

White hoodlums eventually wrecked the African Grove Theatre. With its destruction the great Ira Aldridge realized that America offered little to the black theatre artist. He sailed for Europe where he was acclaimed by royalty. It is significant to note that less than two years after he left these shores, the shuffling, cackling stereotype of black people was acclaimed on the New York stage—projected by a white man in "blackface."

EARLY SIGNS OF A BLACK THEATER

The black playwright came into a measure of prominence long before the Civil War. William Wells Brown, a former slave, wrote *The Escape, or A Leap to Freedom.* In 1853 William Lloyd Garrison wrote in *The Liberator* of the playwright's power and eloquence.

Minstrelsy, however, remained a dominant theatrical force. After the Civil War black entertainers joined the prevalent minstrel pattern and became, in the words of James Weldon Johnson, a "caricature of a caricature." James Bland, composer of *Carry Me Back to Old Virginny* and *In the Evening By the Moonlight,* was a prominent minstrel man. However, in the latter part of the Nineteenth Century a group of black men set out to destroy the minstrel pattern by putting on musical plays. Among these were: Bert Williams, George Walker, Jesse Shipp, Alex Rogers, Bob Cole, J. Rosamond Johnson, Will Marion Cook and Paul Laurence Dunbar. In doing so they created the multi-million dollar musical comedy pattern.

The black playwright was at work. Bob Cole, along with J. Rosamond Johnson, composer of *Lift Every Voice and Sing,* wrote the operas, *The Red Moon* and *The Shoofly Regiment.* In April, 1898 Mr. Cole was represented by a vehicle known as *A Trip to Coontown,* produced at the Third Avenue Theatre. This multi-talented young man died at an early age and brought despair to black theatre lovers.

Two other outstanding writers for the stage were Paul Laurence Dunbar and Will Marion Cook. Their *Clorindy— the Origin of the Cakewalk* was particularly well received. During this era, too, Jesse Shipp and Alex Rogers were creating works for Bert Williams and George Walker. The Williams and Walker Company, after a number of "road vehicles," crashed Broadway with an original musical called *In Dahomey.* This work went on to London where it played for a year. It was presented at a command performance at Buckingham Palace in the year 1903.

Williams and Walker's next musical, *In Abyssinia,* had a book by Jesse Shipp and Alex Rogers. This musical, incidentally, was called by a New York critic "a little too high brow for a darky show." The work opened with Will Marion Cook's soaring number, *Song of Reverence to the Setting Sun.* The story told of George Walker obtaining some money and taking Bert Williams and some friends to Abyssinia. There the comic, ragged Bert wandered in and out of royal African settings, beautifully contrasting the conditions of the Afro-Americans to those of the Africans.

Williams and Walker's next show, *Bandanna Land,* made even more acid comments about black-white relationships in the United States. This work produced in 1908, told of a group of black people who wanted to get rich quick. They bought up land in a white section of a city and then proceeded to sell it back to the whites at twice the amount they paid for it. If this were not an attack upon the Negro-scare racket, one does not exist.

George Walker became ill during the run of *Bandanna Land.* This led to his retirement and Bert Williams went alone into *Mr. Lode of Kole.* After that, at the invitation of Abraham Erlanger, he went into the *Follies.*

RACIAL BARRIERS

To this writer's knowledge, Bert Williams was the only black artist who worked in the downtown theatre between the years 1910 and 1917. Black people were excluded from Broadway as performers and patrons. Nor was this an accident. It was a product of the sabotaging of the Reconstruction Era, of the same type of backlash faced by black people today in America. The United States Supreme Court was then an oracle for the rights of white people and rampant racism, highlighted by its *Plessy vs. Ferguson* decision in which it upheld the separate-but-equal doctrine. The American power structure had placed a "badge" on color and it became fashionable to attack black people in the press, the pulpit and in public places. Jimcrow laws appeared on the statute books of Southern states and lynch mobs rode the night. Race riots flared in cities as the rape of the black American continued.

Big business assumed control of the American theatre. A powerful group known as the Theatrical Trust Syndicate took control of all bookings, hirings and firings. They punished prominent white stars who failed to cooperate with them, forcing the great Sarah Bernhardt and Mrs. Dwight Fiske to appear in second-rate theatres. This, then, was the tone of the nation of the "Robber Barons."

The attack on black people in New York City was merciless. White hoodlums went into black people's homes and beat women and children. Black men coming home from work had to meet other black men on street corners and walk together. It was this type of terror that made many black people welcome the development of the community known as Harlem.

From 1910 through 1917 black theatrical artists worked primarily in the Harlem area. In 1909 writer-actor-producer Eddie Hunter produced shows at the Crescent Theatre on the site of Lenox Terrace apartments today. Mr. Hunter wrote many of the shows produced at the Crescent, notably, *Going to the Races* and *The Battle of Who Run*. In addition, there were other vehicles presented at the Crescent, among them an opera by Harry Lawrence Freeman called *An African Kraal*. And down the street near Lenox Avenue stood the Lincoln Theatre where Henry Kramer and S.H. Dudley had their plays produced with notable success.

White Americans are strange people. Despite the fact that they want black people off to themselves, whites have a chronic need to race off to black places. And so the whites followed blacks to Harlem to see their shows and sit in their nightclubs. In 1913 when J. Leubrie Hill's *Darktown Follies* opened at the Lafayette Theatre, 132 Street and Seventh Avenue, one critic wrote that "it looked like a Broadway opening." Florenz Ziegfeld bought the Finale of that show for his *Follies*. Another Lafayette show, *Darkydom* by Aubrey Lyles and Flournoy Miller, saw many of its sketches sold to Broadway.

THE DOORS OPEN FOR BLACK DRAMA

In 1921 there came *Shuffle Along* by Aubrey Lyles and Flournoy Miller, with music and lyrics by Noble Sissle and Eubie Blake. It was a smash hit and it launched the period that came to be known as the Black Renaissance. Several editions of the show followed as well as *Blackbirds*. In 1923 Eddie Hunter's *How Come?* was seen on Broadway with that great jazz musician, Sidney Bechet.

Other black playwrights during the Nineteen-Twenties included Willis Richardson, author of *The Chipwoman's Fortune*, Garland Anderson, who wrote *Appearances* and Wallace Thurman, co-author of *Harlem*. And there was work by Eulalie Spence and prolific Randolph Edmonds, author of forty-nine plays.

The *so-called* emerging black playwright *emerged* a long time ago.

The Nineteen-Thirties saw too many fine black writers to be dealt with here. Langston Hughes' *Mulatto* had a long, long Broadway run. Hall Johnson's beautiful *Run, Little Children*, was seen on Broadway and in Harlem. And there was J. Augustus Smith's *Turpentine*, Rudolph Fisher's *The Conjure Man Dies*, and the plays of George Norford, Abram Hill, William Ashley and Ferdinand Voteur, produced by Dick Campbell and the Rose McClendon Players. And the American Negro Theatre produced the plays of Abram Hill, Theodore Browne, Owen Dodson and other black writers. It is said that veteran actor John Proctor practically wrote *Anna Lucasta* for the American Negro Theatre.

In the Nineteen-Fifties there were William Branch's *A Medal for Willie* and *In Splendid Error*, Alice Childress' *Just a Little Simple, Gold Through the Trees* and *Trouble in Mind*, and Theodore Ward's *Our Lan'.* Louis Peterson penned *Take A Giant Step*; Sidney Easton, *Miss Trudie Fair;* Sallie Howard, *The Jackal;* as well as plays by Virgil Richardson, Gertrude Jeanette, Oliver Pitcher, Harold Hollifield, Julian Mayfield, Ossie Davis and this writer.

Broadway saw Charles Sebree's *Mrs. Patterson,* and there were Lorraine Hansberry's two fine plays. And James Baldwin's. And Off Broadway saw LeRoi Jones and Douglas Turner Ward. And C. Bernard Jackson. And this summer I saw the fine work of Ted Shine. And Ed Bullins. And every time I look around I see another black writer—Sara Fabio.

What kind of "emerging" are these folks digging?

I am reminded of an incident during the writing of my book, *Black Drama*. I returned home after a day of research and my wife asked me how things were going. I told of the day's work of documenting the land owned by black people when New York City was called New Amsterdam in the 17th Century. I spoke of the black people who had owned land around City Hall Park, along 23rd Street, on Pell Street and in other areas.

I spoke too, of the artisans and doctors who had been in New Amsterdam. She looked at me and asked: "Where do folks get this nonsense that all black people were slaves?" I snapped at her: "The white folks wrote those history books! And they've been writing plays about us and getting them on while we have to sweat and strain to be heard!"

We had a big argument. Then suddenly we stopped and laughed. We both knew the real enemy had made us argue. It was funny, but it was deadly serious.—It was, in short, America's style of genocide.

The Absence of Negro Drama

Sterling A. Brown

Sterling A. Brown was a social critic and a literary scholar who studied both the social problems of African Americans in the early 1900s and the possible impact that African Americans could have on society through artistic endeavors. He wrote several articles concerning the social conditions of southern African Americans, and he worked closely with such notable scholars as Alain Locke, with whom he developed the *Bronze Book Series,* a showcase of new African American writings. In this selection, Brown comments upon the absence of any significant dramatic writing by a person of color. He cites racism as a contributing factor for this absence. Brown also proposes that white audiences influence the promulgation of negative black stereotypes, thus discouraging young black writers from submitting works worthy of literary merit. Brown challenges young blacks to develop the skills necessary to achieve success as dramatists and thereby infuse the theater with a new vision of the African American.

Now that with the end of August *The Green Pastures* leaves New York, and 'de Lawd wawks 'round de rest uh de country lak a nachal man; and advanced reports of the new ventures come in, one wonders what will be the Negro dramatic success for the coming year. It is a safe enough bet that there will be one, if the hospitable past repeats itself. Paul Green, according to vague rumor, is working on a version of "John Henry," and various other plays of Negro life are in rehearsal. What with the inevitable song and dance shows, there opens up something of promise for the Negro actor. One fears, however, that the Negro playwright won't be there.

ABSENCE OF A NEGRO PLAYWRIGHT

Passing in review *The Emperor Jones, Porgy, In Abraham's Bosom* and *The Green Pastures* [all plays dealing with black life and black characters], one is struck by two facts: one, the hardy longevity of these plays upon the stage, and the other, the absence of the Negro playwright from the list of authors. The second of these facts is more striking than the first, for the artistic stature of Paul Green, DuBose Heyward, Marc Connelly, and Eugene O'Neill is ample warrant for the tenacity with which their plays have held the boards. The absence of the Negro playwright is more noticeable.

The lag of the Negro artist, inevitably bound up with his social conditions, is more obvious in drama than in other branches of writings. The easy explanation—too easy, one believes—is that only a caricatured stereotype is acceptable to the powers that be on Broadway, and that since the self-respecting Negro playwright refuses to create his characters after the fashion of Daddy Rice's Jim Crow and the Christy minstrels, Broadway will have none of him. This complaint would have carried more weight in the first part of the century, when such an artist as Bert Williams could bear witness to the pressure of the stock tradition. But after Porgy, and Brutus Jones, and the Jim of *All God's Chillen Got Wings*, and Abraham McCranie, and the glorious ensemble of saints and sinners in *The Green Pastures*, one must realize that the mould is broken.

Those who still see nothing but a stereotype in character as diverse as these lay themselves open as suspect. One fears that for them the dramatic ideal is race glorification, and any portraiture of Negroes means the betrayal of a race. Unless the world is shown that Negroes too have a Babbitry, absolutely faithful to its white model, smugly going through its paces to a happy ending, the producer is perpetuating the old libels.

The guess of one obtuse person is as good as that of another. It is the chronicler's guess that no army of aspirant Negro playwrights has besieged Broadway. It is his further guess that if any Negro author offered Broadway a play about Negroes that his play would be considered on his merits, and whatever his play said about Negro life whether new or old, would be accepted, *providing that it was dramatically well said.* Of course producers are for the most part in the show business for the same reason that men go into the shoe business, or in bootlegging, i.e. for money. But with the encroachments of the talkies and the revues, the legitimate stage has found that it must interest a smaller but more critical audience and that, therefore, well written plays are good investments. Moreover there are the experimentalists. The New Playwrights have already shown their beliefs in the fruitful possibilities of Negro life for drama. To conclude the guesswork, one doesn't believe that there couldn't be found

OVERTONES OF INFERIORITY IN BLACK DRAMA

In this excerpt, drama critic Randolph Edmonds discusses the inaccurate portrayal of black life by white dramatists.

Turning from the plays themselves to the subject matter, we get a very dismal picture, indeed. Modern naturalistic drama has been often characterized as a "bloody slice of life," and nowhere is this term more befitting than in describing these plays of Negro life. In them we see dark portrayals of human misery silhouetted against a black sky-line of woes. They reveal earthly suffering at its blackest—men and women with skins of night struggling in the anguish and agony of situations that doom them to failure and despair from the very opening of the curtain.

Superstition and voodooism are especially rampant in this part of the theatric world. In one form or another they creep into nearly all of the plays. The intelligent and the city bred react to them in the same manner as the rustics. The entire theme of "Emperor Jones" is woven around the superstitions of Brutus, the usurper. Paul Green's "In Aunt Mahaley's Kitchen" and Ridgley Torrence's "Granny Maumee" have similar themes. Lulu Belle and Abraham have their share, and in one of the dark moments Cordelia, the highly sophisticated vampire in the play "Harlem" buys a love philter from a voodoo doctor. No wonder the average Negro is sceptical about plays that purport to reveal an authentic picture of his life.

I do not contend that the tragic side of life should not be depicted. My point is that it should be grounded in the natural laws of life, and tragedy should come as a result of the fitness or unfitness of a character to perform a task. This piling up of insurmountable obstacles with their overtones of inferiority is very unsatisfactory to those who see something deeper and finer and more dramatic in Negro life, and envisage in it a real contribution to the American theatre.

Randolph Edmonds, "Some Reflections on the Negro in American Drama," *Opportunity*, October 1930.

in New York some producer who would be willing to stage a well written play by a Negro, however courageous, or subversive of the typical American credo on things racial. After such plays *The Last Mile, Once in a Lifetime* and *Roar China* it is hard to believe the New York producer to be nothing but a timid sheep following the ram public opinion over the same old fences.

The chronicler attributes the failure of the Negro dramatist to emerge to the simple fact of the tremendous difficulty of dramatic craftmanship. A man may have ability at characterization, at dialogue, a wide knowledge of life, a deep and sincere humanity and still be a dramatic flop. There is so much of technique to be learned; so arduous an apprenticeship to go through. Obviously a first hand knowledge of the stage is essential—often an absolute prerequisite. To this of course must be added a knowledge of the underlying laws of dramatic construction. A big order obviously.

So far even New York gives our embryonic playwright little enough opportunity for actual contact with the stage. And survey courses of the drama from Aeschylus to Pirandello, or courses on the influence of Beaumont and Fletcher on Restoration drama don't teach technique, whatever else may be their value. The typical audience of our small towns has a confused idea of drama as compounded of a church pageant, a fashion show, and an object lesson in etiquette, and that of our larger towns is sold to Hollywood. Neither furnishes much sustaining interest for the aspirant Ibsen.

The greatest hope lies in the little theatre movements springing up all over the country. Cleveland, New York, and Washington are among the cities boasting community dramatic enterprises; almost every college has its little theatre group. If these will only sponsor the creative efforts of young dramatists as well as the established successes, something of value may come out of them. Eugene O'Neill, Paul Green, according to report, started from such humble beginnings. Lynn Riggs, setting out from a little theatre movement in the Southwest, finally struck Broadway with *Green Grow the Lilacs* in his saddlebags.—The little theatres should serve as laboratories for the Negro dramatist. But they must demand as careful workmanship as they think Broadway demands, or else they will defeat their own end. And Mrs. Grundy and Pollyanna should be locked out. No dramatist has ever got much done with them forever snooping around.

The Slow Progress of Black Drama

Nellie McKay

Several obstacles prevented the development of a significant black theater during the period of the
Harlem Renaissance. First, the black image was
tainted by the idea of minstrelsy, a concept requiring
black actors to play the part of the fool. Second, there
was a severe lack of roles that provided positive black
stereotypes. Even plays like Eugene O'Neill's *Emperor
Jones*, which focused on black themes, often stereotyped blacks as primitive or savage-like. Finally,
black audiences—including the emerging middle-
class blacks—failed to provide financial support for
black drama, forcing playwrights to conform to the
standards of its white audiences. In her 1987 article,
literary scholar Nellie McKay examines these obstacles but also focuses on positive developments within
black theater beginning with the *Crisis* literary contests, the establishment of black dramatic criticism,
and the significance of published anthologies that
showcased one-act plays by black playwrights.

Drama more than any other art form except the novel embodies the whole spiritual life of a people; their aspirations
and manners, their ideas and ideals, their fantasies and
philosophies, the music and dignity of their speech—in a
word, their essential character, and it carries this likeness of
a people down the centuries for the enlightenment of remote
times and races.

Our ideal is a national Negro Theater where the Negro playwright, musician, actor, dancer, and artist in concert shall
fashion a drama that will merit the respect and admiration of
America. Such an institution must come from the Negro himself, as he alone can truly express the soul of his people . . . in
. . . the rich veins of folk-tradition of the past and the portrayal
of the authentic life of the Negro masses of today.

Excerpted from "Black Theater and Drama in the 1920s: Years of Growing Pains," by
Nellie McKay, *The Massachusetts Review*, Winter 1987. Copyright © 1987 by *The Massachusetts Review*. Reprinted with permission.

These statements, the first by Theophilus Lewis, and the second by Montgomery Gregory, both made in 1926, underline the importance that Afro-Americans place on the role of drama in the development of culture, and the predominant attitudes of black critics of the form in the 1920s. In a heritage that spans centuries, from Africa through the Middle Passage, and permeating the diaspora—from the slave community to the rituals of contemporary religious ceremonies—drama has been at the center of day-to-day black activities, meeting the demands of black spiritual life in the face of multiple oppressions.

THE SLOW PROGRESS OF DRAMATIC DEVELOPMENT

Little wonder, then, that literary and cultural historians, as well as critics of black theater and drama unanimously bemoan the poverty of Afro-American formal theater and drama in the first two decades of the twentieth century. Black intellectuals, conscious of the need to strengthen all areas of cultural influences, tried hard but failed to bring a vibrant black theater to birth, and to make that theater a significant part of the history of the Harlem Renaissance. Serious, authentic black theater that attracted public attention did not emerge from the Afro-American community until the 1930s and 1940s with such playwrights as Owen Dodson and Langston Hughes. With the benefit of hindsight, we can point to some of the reasons for the slow progress of black dramaturgical/theatrical development in comparison to other branches of the arts. One was the fact that theater and drama required the collaboration of many people; another, the persistence of negative racial stereotypes of black people; and a third, the economics of theater production. At the same time, concerned critics did their bit to overcome these obstacles by vigorously proposing active directions in which black theater and drama could develop. . . .

Among others, historian/critic Nathan Huggins has noted that while there was no black tradition of theater in America at the turn of the century, for almost a hundred years prior, Afro-Americans "had a very substantial [if distorted and grotesque] place in the American theatrical tradition." Put another way, [critic] Clinton Oliver wrote that the black American "was in American theater long before he was a genuine part of it." "Black" characters—as stereotypes that were the butt of white ridicule—appeared on the American stage as early as 1769, while, for more than half a century, white-originated black minstrelsy was the most popular form of mass entertainment in the country. The black character (on and off stage), defined in the white American mind by minstrelsy—lazy, comic, pathetic, childlike, idiotic, etc.— embodied an image that was disastrous to the advancement of serious black theater, and one not easily reversed. For openers, although there were nineteenth century Afro-American entertainers who repudiated it, many blacks, at all levels in turn-of-the-century theater, continued to accommodate themselves to minstrelsy because it was lucrative. . . .

DEFINING A BLACK THEATER

A large part of the controversy that black intellectuals, dramatists and actors argued in the years leading up to and through the 1920s was connected to disagreements surrounding a definition of black theater, its cultural role and function, and the relationship between black playwrights, producers, actors, and black audiences. [Playwright] Loften Mitchell illustrated the dimensions of the first question in his essay, "Harlem Has Broadway on Its Mind," in which he indicated that more than a dozen major theater groups were formed there between 1910 and 1930. Some groups, like the Lafayette and Lincoln Players, wanted the freedom to perform plays unrelated to the black experience. Others, like DuBois' Krigwa Players and the Negro People's Theater, championed "dignified" plays of Negro life; and a number, like the Rose McClendon Players and the Pioneer Drama Group, wanted to illustrate that, given similar circumstances, blacks and whites reacted alike. Such fundamental differences of opinion do not blur the evidence of ferment, and clearly indicate the interest that many Afro-Americans had in the establishment of "black" theater—however they perceived the nature of the productions they offered their audiences.

THE *CRISIS* CONTESTS

From its beginning in 1910, the *Crisis*, under [W.E.B.] DuBois's editorship, although deeply involved in the politics of race, made clear its support of the arts, including theater and drama. Its influence was large, appealing to a wide black readership with information not otherwise readily available to them. Beginning in 1910 with a circulation of 1,000 copies, by 1919 it reached a peak of 95,000. DuBois set the literary tone in his editorials and essays, blending stories, travel accounts, and character portraits into these different forms, and often using sarcasm, satire, and irony to make his point. In addition, he made the journal easily accessible by publishing works by new as well as already known writers. From 1925 through 1927 the *Crisis* ran annual literary and artistic competitions for first, second, and third place winners in five categories: stories, plays, poetry, essays and illustrations. In 1928, when the readership of the *Crisis* had declined substantially, the contests were discontinued, and instead small prizes were given for the best contributions of each month.

There is little question that the bias of the *Crisis* was toward race pride, and DuBois's attitudes were toward the primacy of the role and function of black art within the Afro-American community. In 1926 he made his now-famous declaration that "all Art is propaganda, and ever must be . . . for gaining the right of black folk to love and enjoy." Not everyone agreed with DuBois, and the differences of opinions on art and propaganda became the legacy for intellectuals of every succeeding generation to debate. The issue for us may be a reconciliation with DuBois's definition of propaganda, and its relationship to Beauty, Truth, and Justice.

Not the least of DuBois's artistic concerns was the representation of Afro-Americans in drama. "As the renaissance of art comes among American Negroes" he wrote, "the theater calls for new birth." He felt that, as minstrels, comedians, singers, etc., Afro-American performers had been trained to entertain white audiences, and black audiences had not demanded authentic black drama of them. Black actors would only do their "best" he noted, when that best was "evoked" by black people who wanted to see their own lives accurately depicted by their own writers and performers. . . .

THE DIRECTION OF THEATER

The 1920s controversy among intellectuals and writers over the merits of propaganda as a function of art is clear in the separate position that DuBois and Alain Locke took on this issue. Still, both men were partly responsible for nurturing the flowering of Afro-American arts in that period. DuBois followed up his strong 1926 statement on black theater by implementing his theories with the Krigwa Players Little Negro Theater. Locke helped to establish a dramatic laboratory at

Howard University in Washington, D.C. His position on black theater and drama is clear in his 1927 essay, "The Negro and the American Theater," originally published in *Theater: Essays on the Arts of the Theater*, edited by Edith J.R. Isaacs.

Like DuBois, Locke called for new directions in the development of an Afro-American tradition in drama, but where the first gave scant information on the steps of the process, Locke unveiled a detailed agenda. Like DuBois, he felt that the "likeliest soil" for an American "dramatic [renaissance]" as in the folk art of Afro-America, but he went farther to suggest the path "should lead back over the trail of the group tradition to an interest in things African. . . . [For] African life and themes," he said, "apart from any sentimental attachment, offer a wonderful field and province for dramatic treatment." In general, he thought, the white American stage was bereft of action, instinct and emotion, qualities that black performers would bring to black drama if it existed as "expression and artistic interpretation," outside of "propaganda," which he called the "drama of discussion and social analysis."

ESTABLISHING ROOTS IN BLACK CULTURE

Like DuBois, Locke's blueprint for a new black drama wedded playwrights and actors to the roots of black culture and the black idiom. He challenged both groups to break with already established dramatic conventions, and to strike out on new experimental ground. Black drama had to "grow in its own soil and cultivate its own intrinsic elements; . . . [in order to] become truly organic, and cease being a rootless derivative." He identified the "art of the Negro actor" as "the free use of body and voice as instruments of feeling," and urged its liberation from old ways (e.g., minstrelsy and buffoonery) in the interests of vibrant artistic revelations. He envisioned the evolution of a truly "great" black drama in two stages. The first, he thought, should look to the folk play, which, realistically and imaginatively, was "drama of free expression and imaginative release . . . with no objective but to express beautifully and colorfully race folk life. . . ." He suggested that "more . . . poetic strain . . . more of the joy of life even when life flows tragically, . . . more of the emotional depth of pity and terror" would give it the vitality it needed. The technical model of this drama would become the foundations for serious black theater.

Locke's second stage in the development of a dramatic tradition was the point at which he broke with DuBois. While both men dismissed the musical comedies as buffoonery and pathos, Locke's disenchantment with Afro-American playwriting revolved around the social problem plays—with what he called their tendency toward "moralistic allegories or melodramatic protests as dramatic correctives and antidotes for race prejudice." Admitting that black dramatists had the advantage of "psychological intimacy" with their subject, he denied them the objectivity that "great art" requires in dealing with these issues, and decried their counter partisanship and propagandistic attitudes. The black playwright, he said, needed to "achieve mastery of a detached, artistic point of view, and reveal the inner stresses and dilemmas of these situations." In time, he hoped for a "race" drama that served as an imaginative channel of escape and spiritual release, and by some process of emotional re-enforcement to cover life with the illusion of happiness and spiritual freedom. . . .

THE FIRST BLACK DRAMA CRITIC

Theophilus Lewis had an entirely different background from Harvard-educated DuBois and Locke, recognized men of great refinement, erudition and letters. In contrast to them, Lewis had little formal education, no claims to fame, and worked in the Post Office. However, even as a child he loved theater, and when he arrived in New York after the war he patronized the Harlem houses. His career as drama critic for *The Messenger* began unexpectedly when he submitted an essay on the subject to that journal and it was accepted (without remuneration). But A. Phillip Randolph, the editor, invited him to join the company of *The Messenger's* regular contributors, and he agreed.

Unlike the *Crisis* and *Opportunity,* with which Locke was closely associated, in its early years (1917–23) the general editors of *The Messenger* had somewhat of a bias against "art." They published verse, but only if it served the social and economic ends of the journal. However, between 1923 and 1928, when Lewis and George Schuyler took over many of the editorial prerogatives of the publication, socialist verse disappeared from its pages in favor of more artistic works by well-known litterateurs like Countee Cullen, Langston Hughes, and Georgia Johnson. From July 1923 to July 1927

Lewis contributed a regular monthly column under the title, "The Theater, The Souls of Black Folks" (echoing DuBois's famous work although never showing any reverence for the older man). In so doing he was not only the first but the only regular black drama critic of that era. As others have noted, he did not simply review plays; like DuBois and Locke he also attempted to evolve an ideology for a national black theater. Unlike them, he based his theories not only on philosophical concepts of a tradition in black drama, but also on analyses of close observations of what was occurring at the grassroots level of popular Harlem theater of the day.

In the 1926 July, September, and October issues of *The Messenger*, Lewis' columns analyzed current conditions of black theater and drama. His most precise definition of black theater did not come until his final "Theater" column in July 1927 in "Main Problems of the Negro Theater." His prescription for black theater and drama was less rigid than DuBois's, but somewhat less flexible than Locke's:

> Negro drama, reduced to a simple statement, is . . . the body of plays written by Negro authors. The kind of life represented in the play is immaterial. The scene may be in Norway or Spain, and the characters presumably natives of one or the other country. Nevertheless it will be a Negro play if it is the product of a Negro mind. Hamlet is not a Danish play. . . . The Phaedra of Euripides is Greek, while the Phaedra of Racine is French. . . . A play is a work of art and . . . to maintain that Negro drama consists merely of plays about Negro life, regardless of who writes them, is to alter the accepted meaning of terms.

DuBois, Locke and Lewis agreed that the responsibility for vital authentic black theater rested with dramatists, players and audiences, perhaps in different proportions, but with each group assuming weighty responsibilities. The stage, said Lewis, was the "vehicle for two important arts— drama and acting," and the black stage "should be a vital force in the spiritual life of the race," delighting and exalting the audience at the same time. . . .

THE LACK OF SUPPORT FOR DRAMA

Lewis blamed the black middle class for three areas of negligence toward promoting authentic Afro-American theater. The first was for its non-support of existing black dramatic activities. While the group freely criticized black theater, it did not support possibilities for change through its presence or financial resources. As a result, the lesser educated audience kept black theater alive. Equally irresponsible was the middle-class lack of critical insight into the economic politics of theater. Theater took on the character of those who supported it, and in this case, since most black theater was economically controlled by whites interested only in profits, promoters catered to those who supported their ends by their presence, applause, and money. In addition, Lewis accused the middle class of ambivalence toward authentic black theater. Instead of promoting serious black drama, the educated classes often demanded a theater that imitated the white American stage. Such a demand, Lewis said, fostered artificiality and did nothing to create a tradition in Afro-American theater. At the same time, black actors and dramatists, anxious for work, often accommodated themselves to the travesty of the economic exploitation of their talents and were also responsible for contributing to the abysmal state of black theater. In the final analysis, it was the lower classes who kept black theater alive, assuring, on some level, an evolution of a tradition. Lewis warned that without economic autonomy the black theater would never become the "medium for the expression of the spirit of Negro people" that everyone wanted it to be. In its failure to develop indigenous drama, said Lewis, black theater contributed nothing to the culture of the race, nor gave it anything to pass on as a gift to the general culture of humanity.

His solution to the problems echoed DuBois and Locke. He called for a national theater and a repertory system that, isolated from the white stage, addressed its appeal to colored audiences. In this theater dramatists would be at home creating race character, which he said was "the real meaning of Negro drama"; and actors would lift their audiences to a "beauty they were not previously conscious of . . . gradually creat[ing even in the lower classes] a demand for a higher standard of entertainment." It is interesting to note that all three critics found most to be optimistic about in the craft of the performers, especially in the energy of their dancing and the rich ribaldry of their comedy.

POSITIVE DEVELOPMENTS IN BLACK DRAMA

Yet, in spite of the bleak picture of the state of the art that emerges from these reports, the situation was not as barren as they suggest. The promotion of all branches of literary endeavor by the *Crisis* and *Opportunity* yielded a number of one-act dramas, including many folk plays. Before the end of the decade, anthologies of drama on black life also appeared, including *Plays of Negro Life* (works not exclusively by black playwrights) edited by Alain Locke and Montgomery Gregory (1923); and *Plays and Pageants from the Life of the Negro,* edited by Willis Richardson (1930). At the University of North Carolina, the *Carolina Magazine* did a "Negro Play Number" with plays of black life in 1929. Notably too, several black women were prominent among the new dramatists of the time. Between 1918 and 1930 eleven black women published twenty-one plays between them, in comparison to no more than half-a-dozen men who saw their works in print during these years. However, this count does not include plays that were performed although never published. . . .

The 1920s were years of growing pains in the development of a tradition in Afro-American theater and drama. As it is often the case, the intellectuals and others who determine trends are often much more advanced in their vision than those who make them come true. By the 1920s there was a solid, urban, educated, sophisticated black middle class, and men like DuBois and Locke felt the responsibility to help to direct the group away from narrow self-interests and into directions that would raise the cultural aspirations of the black masses. Fiction, poetry, painting, music, and sculpture flourished as drama seemed not to, largely because, unlike other areas of the arts, it was not an individualistic venture, but one that required the involvement of many people for its success. The goals of the critics were ambitious: to overturn the almost century-old black public performance tradition as the majority of white and some black people had conceived it. This was the task that they set about to accomplish. If their successes were slow in coming, they were no less significant. It is heartening to know that first they turned to the black experience—to the folk-play, the spirit life of black people—for the model on which to lay the foundations of authentic Afro-American drama. This is a heritage of which we can well be proud.

Women Playwrights of the Harlem Renaissance

Elizabeth Brown-Guillory

Elizabeth Brown-Guillory is both a playwright and a scholar. She wrote the award-winning plays Bayou Relics *and* Snapshots of Broken Dolls. *As an associate professor of English at the University of Houston, Brown-Guillory spends much of her time studying the Harlem Renaissance and the often overlooked role of women within the movement, and she has edited two anthologies of plays and essays regarding black female playwrights of the 1920s. In this selection from her book* Their Place on the Stage *(1988), she points out that women playwrights of the renaissance displayed in their work themes of social injustice and brutality toward African Americans much earlier than their male counterparts. Brown-Guillory's analysis of the playwrights' comments on major inconsistencies within American society are brought to light by elaborating on the works of nine major female playwrights and their development of socially conscious material through a use of folk, historical, and religious narrative forms.*

Two occurrences marked a revolution in black theater in America and ushered in the Harlem Renaissance. First, in 1910, the National Association for the Advancement of Colored People (NAACP) was newly formed, and in that year the first issue of *Crisis* magazine was published. Black artists could now publish their works, and even win literary contests. *Crisis*, edited by W.E.B. Dubois, who insisted that there should be a theater by, for, about, and near Negro people, sponsored annual playwriting contests. This maiden maga-

Excerpted from *Their Place on the Stage: Black Women Playwrights in America*, by Elizabeth Brown-Guillory (New York: Greenwood Press, 1988). Copyright © 1988 by Elizabeth Brown-Guillory. Reprinted by permission of the publisher.

zine served to create a networking of black authors across the country, particularly in New York City, Cleveland, Chicago, and Washington D.C., many of whom were playwrights desperately in need of an audience. *Crisis* served as a laboratory for novice playwrights. Soon the NAACP's Drama Committee of Washington D.C. was established to encourage black playwrights to develop their craft by writing and producing their plays. As a result of support from the NAACP, between 1910 and 1930 blacks owned and operated approximately 157 theaters.

The second occurrence that some critics say sparked the Harlem Renaissance was Ridgely Torrence's New York production in 1917 of *Three Plays for a Negro Theatre*, including *Granny Maumee, The Rider of Dreams*, and *Simon the Cyrenian*. This white playwright's interest in blacks as subject matter on the American stage opened the floodgates and the Negro became popular material for such writers as Eugene O'Neill, William Vaughn Moody, Marc Connelly, and Paul Green. Responsible for the popularization of the primitivistic motif, these playwrights served as an impetus to African American playwrights who began creating their own images of black men and women in an attempt to eradicate stereotypes of well-meaning white playwrights. This emphasis on primitivism and exoticism resulted in the relegation of blacks to the musical rather than to the serious dramatic stage. Both black and white playwrights selected musicals as a medium. Between 1910 and 1940 over eight hundred musicals featuring blacks were produced.

Sterling Brown contends that during the Harlem Renaissance, black playwrights were in the learning stage of their craft. However, playwrights like Wallace Thurman (*Harlem*, 1929), Hall Johnson (*Run Little Chillun*, 1932), and Langston Hughes (*Mulatto*, 1935) made great strides in their craft and had their plays produced for large audiences on Broadway. Too often, however, this burst of dramatic creativity is associated solely with black male playwrights of the period.

The Harlem Renaissance, or as Alain Locke termed it the "New Negro Renaissance," must be reexamined and redefined to include the heart of this movement: its women, particularly its black women playwrights. Plays by early twentieth-century black women are rarely anthologized and are infrequently the subject of critical interpretation. Burns Mantle's *American Playwrights of Today* (1929), which in-

cludes brief discussions of some fifty-odd women dramatists, does not mention any black women playwrights.

It is time that scholars reclaim the sensitive, compassionate, and insightful works of these mother playwrights. These
plays are vital because they supply a unique view of the
black experience during the period between 1910 and 1940,
dates that Arthur P. Davis and Michael W. Peplow, in *The
New Negro Renaissance*, set as the time span for this sun-
burst of writing by and about blacks. Early black women
playwrights offer much to American theater in the way of
content, form, characterization, dialogue, and heart. These
women mavericks who have come from a long and efflores-
cent tradition were instrumental in paving a way for black
playwrights between the 1950s and 1980s.

WOMEN PLAYWRIGHTS SPEAK THEIR MINDS

Before 1940, the suggested cut-off date of the Harlem Renais-
sance, marked by the publication of Richard Wright's *Native
Son*, there was a host of black women playwrights who felt
compelled to speak their minds and to express their hearts.
Like white women playwrights of the period, including
Rachel Crothers, Neith Boyce, Susan Glaspell, Zona Gale, Zoe
Atkins, Edna St. Vincent Millay, Sophie Treadwell, and Ann
Seymour, black women turned to writing about women
whose lives had been blighted by society. Unlike many white
women dramatists, however, "who wrote, like the [white]
men with whom they competed, those serviceable melodra-
mas, farces, mysteries, and [romantic] comedies that made
up the season during the teens and expansive twenties,"
black women playwrights were writing serious drama, characterized most frequently by racial and social protest.

In fact, during the years between 1916 and 1935, [a period
that also gave birth to such significant black women writers
as Regina Andrews, Helen Webb Harris, Ottie Graham, Alvira
Hazzard, and Thelma Duncan], nine black women playwrights captured the lives of black people as no white or
black male playwright could. Angelina Weld Grimke, Alice
Dunbar-Nelson, Georgia Douglas Johnson, May Miller, Mary
Burrill, Myrtle Smith Livingston, Ruth Gaines-Shelton, Eulalie Spence, and Marita Bonner were all original voices that
were unwelcome in the commercial theater of the period.
These authors are crucial to any discussion of the development of black playwriting in America because they provide

the feminine perspective, and their voices give credence to the notion that there was a "New Negro" in America. . . .

The nine black women playwrights previously mentioned are, indeed, the heart of the Harlem Renaissance. They wrote mainly one-act plays about middle class and common folk, about passion and apathy, love and hate, life and death, hope and despair, self-effacement and race pride, oppression and equality of the races and sexes. Most importantly, they wrote with intensity to reach the hearts of black people across the nation. They did not write for a Broadway audience that brought with it monetary remuneration. Eulalie Spence, a daring and vociferous woman playwright who might one day be credited with initiating feminism in plays by black women, after accepting an option given her by Paramount Productions for her full-length play *The Whipping*, commented that the pittance received was the only money that she had ever made by writing plays.

These pioneering spirits seriously impacted black community theater. Many of these women were acquaintances of W.E.B. Dubois who, in a 1926 *Crisis* essay, strongly advocated community theater by saying, "If it is a Negro play that will interest us and depict our life, experience, and humor, it cannot be sold to the ordinary [commercial] theatrical producer, but can be produced by our churches, lodges, and halls." With this admonition in mind, these early dramatists conscienciously wrote for the black community where their plays were produced in black-owned and operated community theaters, churches, schools, social club halls, and homes. Turning to a black audience that desperately needed theater that would teach them how to live better, these mother playwrights developed their craft while supplying their audiences with compassionately drawn, multidimensional characters.

WRITING WITH A SOCIAL CONSCIENCE

These sages wrote for the sheer joy of capturing and preserving the essence of black life for future generations. They were able to turn theaters into nurseries where the black race is given roots, nurtured, tested, healed, and provided with the spirit to survive. They are, indeed, the missing pieces to a multifaceted puzzle of black life during those decades when blacks were becoming aware, and awakening to their own self-worth, and struggling for an identity robbed from them as a result of mutilated African roots.

A close study of these plays reveals seven forms: (1) protest, (2) genteel school, (3) folk, (4) historical (interchangeable with race pride and black nationalism), (5) religious, (6) fantasy, and (7) feminist. One of the limitations of attempting to assign labels is that there are no clear-cut delineations. It is difficult to designate form because many of these early plays contain a balanced blend of protest, folk, and historical elements. Generally speaking, however, the plays contain recognizable, dominant features of one or more of the above mentioned forms.

Following the tradition of William Wells Brown, black women playwrights wrote protest plays. Margaret Wilkerson, in *9 Plays by Black Women*, contends that "the early works of black women were strong protests against these conditions [racism, sexism, and capitalism] and were produced largely within the fold—in churches, lodges, and social halls of the sympathetic few." Mance Williams, in *Black Theater of the 1960s and 1970s*, comments that protest is what characterized the bulk of black drama prior to the 1960s.

Early black women playwrights protested four inconsistencies in American society. First, they were appalled by the dichotomy of Christian doctrine and the actions of white American Christians toward African Americans. In this category, lynching was the principal impetus for protest. Second, they were outraged at the fact that black soldiers fought abroad to keep America safe and free only to return to a land in which their basic constitutional rights were deprived. Third, these women were indignant about the economic disparity between black and white Americans; they felt that poverty was threatening to break the spirit of rural as well as urban blacks. Fourth, miscegenation was a source of fury and was condemned. Several early plays with a dominant element of protest or propaganda are *Rachel* (1916) by Angelina Weld Grimke; *Mine Eyes Have Seen* (1918) by Alice Dunbar-Nelson; *They That Sit in Darkness* (1919) and *Aftermath* (1919) by Mary Burrill; *A Sunday Morning in the South* (1925) by Georgia Douglas Johnson; and *For Unborn Children* (1926), by Myrtle Smith Livingston.

ANGELINA GRIMKE

Angelina Grimke (1880–1958), born to the biracial Grimke family and educated in Boston, spent the bulk of her life writing poetry and teaching English in Washington D.C., a cultural mecca to DuBois' talented tenth. Grimke's *Rachel* is said to be the first play of record by a black, excluding musicals, to be produced and publicly performed by black actors. Alain Locke and Montgomery Gregory, in *Plays of Negro Life* (1927), acknowledge Grimke's contribution to black playwriting when they observe that Grimke's play is "apparently the first successful drama written by a Negro."

Rachel centers around the Lovings, a proud middle-class family that has suffered the lynching of the husband and the eldest son. Mr. Loving was lynched for verbally attacking in a "Colored" newspaper the lynching of another man, and his teenage son was lynched for trying to save his father. The heroine, Rachel, vows never to have any babies after her mother tells her of the lynching and after she learns that her adopted son has been pelted with stones and called nigger.

Grimke protests against the lynching of innocent black people by white Christians. Rachel, when she speaks of the dark mothers who live in terrible, suffocating fear that their husbands and sons might be murdered concludes, "And so this nation—this white Christian nation has deliberately set its curse upon the most beautiful—the most holy thing in life—motherhood!" It is not surprising that lynching should be a subject treated by Grimke and many other writers of the Harlem Renaissance. Davis and Peplow, in *The New Negro Renaissance*, contend that between 1885 and 1919, there were 3,052 lynchings in the United States, methods of torture involving hanging, shooting, burning, drowning, beating, and cutting. . . .

A contemporary audience might find the sentimentality in *Rachel* objectionable, but one must bear in mind that Grimke was born in 1880 and grew up with Victorian influences. . . . Grimke, a gifted poet, uses language eloquently, sensitively, and powerfully to draw the reader into a world that made some black women of the period reluctant to give birth to little black and brown babies. Grimke's protestations do not end with a call for the reciprocity of violence. In fact, there is no call for action; she merely mirrors life for blacks in American society at the turn of the century.

GEORGIA DOUGLAS JOHNSON

Georgia Douglas Johnson (1886–1966), best known for her several volumes of poetry, including *The Heart of a Woman and Other Poems* (1918), *Bronze* (1922), *An Autumn Love Cycle* (1928), and *Share My World* (1960), wrote approximately twenty plays, making her the most prolific of the black women dramatists of the Harlem Renaissance. She spent the bulk of her life in Washington D.C., where her home was christened "Halfway House" and was for four decades a mecca for such intellectual and artistic giants as Langston Hughes, May Miller, Owen Dodson, Sterling Brown, Alain Locke, Angelina Grimke, Zora Neale Hurston, James Weldon Johnson, Claude McKay, and others. As a result of her associations with these leading racially conscious authors, Johnson's later work, which is different from the earlier romantic, raceless pieces, reflects her feelings of protest against injustice and racism.

Johnson's play *A Sunday Morning in the South*, like *Rachel*, levels an indictment against lynching. The play opens with the grandmother, Sue Jones, discussing the recklessness with which whites have been lynching blacks in their town. Johnson makes an appeal for justice when the grandmother says, "I believes in meting out punishment to the guilty but they fust ought to fine out who done it though and then let the law hanel 'em." The grandson, Tom Griggs, chimes in with, "They lynch you bout anything too, not jest women. They say Zeb Brooks was strung up because he and his boss had er argiment. . . . I sometimes get right upset and wonder whut would I do if they ever tried to put something on me." Tom's expressed indignance at the lynchings foreshadows his own victimization. That same day, he is accused of raping a white woman, a crime that supposedly took place two hours after he had been asleep as attested to by his brother and grandmother.

When it is discovered that the weak and confused Southern belle, at the insistence of the mob, participates in the ruination of a young black life, the victim becomes a symbol of black oppression. Though the young white woman can only vaguely recollect what her assailant looks like, Tom is arrested because he comes close to the stated description, "age around twenty, five feet or six, brown skin." Johnson's point here is that a white mob cannot be contained or pacified until black blood is spilled, in spite of the fact that a description of that type fits probably half the black population in America.

Georgia Douglas Johnson's play touches the heart and both angers and pains modern readers. Hatch and Shine argue that *A Sunday Morning in the South* is a protest play by a woman who has a difficult time believing in the judicial system when unjust or unenforced laws provide little or no protection for African Americans. [Literary critic Margaret B.] Wilkerson makes an insightful evaluation of Georgia Douglas Johnson's plays when she says, "Lynching informed most of her works—one-act plays that are spare in dialogue and action based on the very real drama of terrorist acts directed at the Southern black community. . . . The subject matter left no room for humor." Wilkerson, in demonstrating common threads in Johnson's plays, links *A Sunday Morning in the South* to *Safe* (1935–1939), in which a mother strangles her newborn baby [to keep him safe] when she hears the pathetic cries of a black man being dragged away by a lynch mob. Johnson's play starts out like a low murmur and then blossoms into a deafening plea for whites to treat blacks like human beings who possess hearts and souls.

ALICE DUNBAR-NELSON

Alice Dunbar-Nelson (1875–1935), born in New Orleans, Louisiana and a graduate of Straight University (now Dillard University), taught school in West Medford, Massachusetts before marrying Paul Laurence Dunbar and moving to Washington D.C. She spent her last years in Delaware. *Give Us Each Day: The Diary of Alice Dunbar-Nelson,* edited by Gloria T. Hull, chronicles Dunbar-Nelson's extensive travel across the country as poet, journalist, lecturer, and organizer, a factor that provided her with the substance of her writing. In her later years she traveled widely, delivering militant political speeches. Dunbar-Nelson's later writing, like Johnson's, reflects the voice of social protest that was probably shaped by three major factors: a severed attachment to the New Orleans creoles of color, World War I, and the developing Harlem Renaissance.

Dunbar-Nelson's *Mine Eyes Have Seen* (1918) grew out of her work as a member of the Women's Committee on the Council of Defense where she helped organize Southern black women in nine states for the war effort. It is a protest play that centers around a young man, Chris, who has been drafted to fight in World War I, but who debates whether he should honor the draft. Dunbar-Nelson suggests that black men who gladly fight for their country should not have to face degradation when they return to find that the freedom they fought to maintain for America is for white Americans only. Dunbar-Nelson's voice is piercing when Chris comments on blacks and war: "Haven't you had your soul shrivelled with fear since we were driven like dogs from our home? And for what? Because we were living like Christians. Must I go and fight for a nation that let my father's murder go unpunished?"

Not only does this passage indicate Dunbar-Nelson's indignation about soldiers who are forbidden to bask in glory, but it alludes to her disdain for the American lynch mob and, particularly, for the Southern tradition that includes active and overt racism. Chris's reference to his father is poignant because his father was shot in the South while trying to save his home, which was being burned down by a mob.

Dunbar-Nelson will gain stature in years to come because of her depth of perception and her skill at mirroring universal concerns. Ora Williams says that "in all her writings . . . Dunbar-Nelson is always direct. . . . Her concerns about racism, the roles of men and women in society, and the importance of love, war, death, and nature appear as recurring themes. . . . Hers was one of the most consistent, secure, and independent voices of the black community."

MARY BURRILL

Mary Burrill (1879–1946), like Grimke and Dunbar-Nelson, taught English in Washington D.C. Burrill's *Aftermath* (1919), like Dunbar-Nelson's *Mine Eyes Have Seen*, levels an indictment against an American society that forces blacks to fight in foreign wars to protect white Americans while African Americans go unprotected from terrorists who lynch and burn. Set in South Carolina, the play centers around the homecoming of John, a black soldier who earned a medal, the French War Cross, for single-handedly fighting off twenty Germans and thereby saving the lives of his entire company.

Additionally, Burrill protests against lynching. John's glory is short-lived when he returns to discover that his father, who had argued with a white man over the price of cotton, had been burnt to death. Burrill, unlike Grimke, calls for retaliation with violence as John goes out gun in hand to collect retribution. . . .

Burrill's *They That Sit in Darkness* (1919), which is as equally explosive as *Aftermath,* protests against poverty. Burrill very sensitively treats the issue of the poor who, often because of a lack of education and income, bring babies into the world that they can neither feed nor clothe. Additionally, Burrill makes a plea for the government to assist the poor by instructing them in the methods of birth control. . . .

One strong point that Burrill makes is that poverty strips many black parents of the ability to nurture their children, especially spiritually. In very precise and colorful language, Burrill quietly but powerfully levels an indictment against poverty in American society when Mrs. Jasper comments, "We has to wuk so hard to give 'em de lil de gits we ain't got no time tuh look at'er dey sperrits." Mrs. Jasper tells that her husband is unable to guide his children because when he leaves for work and returns, the children are sleeping. She laments that when she gets through with doing laundry for whites all day, "Ah doan wants tuh see no chillern!" Additionally, Burrill calls attention to the inhumanity of the American government, which at that time enforced laws forbidding the distribution of birth control information. The white relief nurse, Miss Shaw, says "When I took my oath as nurse, I swore to abide by the laws of the State, and the law forbids my telling you what you have a right to know."

Another early twentieth-century black woman playwright who provides modern readers with a special window on the black experience in America is Myrtle Smith Livingston (1901–1973), also a graduate of Howard University in Washington D.C. Livingston's subject of protest in *For Unborn Children* (1926) is miscegenation. According to Hatch and Shine, miscegenation is the one racial theme that both black and white playwrights invariably agree upon: mixing is intolerable and degenerative.

For Unborn Children is a taut play that deals with a young black lawyer and a young white woman who plan to circumvent state laws forbidding interracial marriage by fleeing to the North. Parallels can be drawn between Eugene O'Neill and Livingston. O'Neill's *All God's Chillun Got Wings*, written in 1933, just three years before *For Unborn Children*, has as its subject a love relationship between a black law student and a white girl. Just as Jim in O'Neill's play is selfless and risks his life to protect the white woman he loves, so does LeRoy Carlson in *For Unborn Children*.

One twist that does not occur in O'Neill's play is the notion that love between the races must be sacrificed to prevent children from coming into a world that will be hostile, at best. Livingston further complicates the plot by having Grandma Carlson tell LeRoy that he is half white, a product of a marriage that failed desperately because of miscegenation. She tells LeRoy that his white mother could not love him, a black baby, and therefore abandoned him. Grandma Carlson becomes the catalyst for LeRoy's reconsidering his plan to escape to the North when she says, "Think of the unborn children that you sin against by marrying her, baby! Oh, you can't know the misery that awaits them. . . . Every child has a right to a mother who will love it better than life itself; and a white mother cannot mother a Negro baby."

At the end of the play, when the mob reaches the Carlson home, LeRoy triumphantly and defiantly goes to his death. Unlike anything to appear in any play during these decades, LeRoy offers himself up to the mob with great restraint and dignity. Livingston shapes LeRoy into a Christ figure as he goes to the mob, arms outstretched, with these final words: "Don't grieve so; just think of it as a sacrifice for unborn children."

GENTEEL PLAYS

In addition to the preponderance of protest plays written by early black women playwrights, plays of the genteel school of writers managed to appear on the African American stage. Some young writers of the early years of the Harlem Renaissance shied away from the black nationalist approach to literature and were preoccupied with proving to white America that they were just like them, except for the superfluous matter of color. Two types of genteel literature produced by early black women playwrights are "raceless" and "best-foot-forward." These two types, according to [critics Arthur P.] Davis and [Michael W.] Peplow, were written by black writers who felt that literature by and about blacks and in the black dialect might be perceived as limiting, and not good literature.

"Raceless" literature deemphasizes recognizable aspects of black culture. Much of this nonracial, "universal" writing is insipid because it is stripped of the very particulars necessary to constitute universality in any work. Some of the early works of Countee Cullen, James Weldon Johnson, and Claude McKay may be considered raceless literature. In early plays by some black women, race is apparent as an issue, but it is secondary to the issue of humanity and universal good, honor, and decency. This universal literature, which silences the voices and the hearts of blacks, implies that the black experience is not an integral part of the American and human experience. . . .

MAY MILLER

May Miller (1889–), born in Washington D.C., is a graduate of Howard University, where her father was an eminent professor and scholar. Once a student of Grimke and Burrill, May Miller was influenced by her mentors to write. A teacher of speech and drama and a poet, Miller coedited along with Willis Richardson two volumes of Negro plays for school children. [Critics Alvin] Goldfarb and [Edwin] Wilson maintain that Miller, along with Willis Richardson and Randolph Edmonds, "decided that black children needed plays and skits about their own history and heroes . . . and wrote a total of 100 plays and published six books." One of the most prolific of the early black women playwrights, Miller experiments with several different forms, including genteel, folk, historical, and feminist.

Three of May Miller's historical plays contain strong elements associated with the genteel tradition: *Graven Images* (1929), *Samory* (1935), and *Christophe's Daughters* (1935) are set in pre-Christian Ethiopia, the African Sudan, and Haiti, respectively. *Graven Images* is a play in which the black son of Moses suffers abuse because he is different. As the play concludes, he puts his best foot forward and persuades his young enemies that he is very much like them, only tanned. *Samory* presents a culturally sophisticated African general of the same name who fights off French colonizers to protect his family and home. *Christophe's Daughters* shows the courage and strength exhibited by two princesses as their father's throne is being usurped. The language in all three of these plays is artificial, vapid, and saturated with euphemisms, such as when Marion in *Graven Images* politely tells Eliezer, Moses's son, that he is a disgrace to his father. Marion says, "Black one, you had best hide your shame from the followers of your father and not place your complexion where all may see."

In spite of the fact that the voices of black characters in these plays are imagined, at best, and the characters are one-dimensional, positive images of noble or royal blacks, the plays merit serious critical treatment because of their thematic and historical value. Miller comments on sexism,

racism, miscegenation, political backstabbing, reconciliation, gossip, provincialism, illegitimacy, and family loyalty.
Pinkie Gordon Lane contends that Miller is a writer "of deep
personal insight, of unquestioning moral courage and one
who has suffered imbalances of our society yet retained a
grace and wholeness of spirit." Miller's works suggest that
she is perceptive and compassionate.

HISTORICAL DRAMA

Another form popularized by early black women playwrights is the historical drama written to teach blacks, especially the children, about the heroes and heroines of their
race. According to Hatch and Shine, black playwrights write
historical dramas "to liberate the black audience from an
oppressive past, to present a history that provides continuity,
hope, and glory. Such feelings and knowledge have positive
survival value for the race." This emphasis on the black folk
hero represents a new pride in the black person's past, particularly the militant past.

May Miller and Georgia Douglas Johnson are leading figures in the area of historical drama during the Harlem Renaissance. Miller, who devoted much time to anthologizing
historical dramas, gives depth and breadth to such major
African American heroines as Harriet Tubman and Sojourner
Truth in plays of the same titles. *Harriet Tubman* (1935), set
in Maryland, gives an account of one incident when Tubman
helps slaves escape in spite of blockages on land and water.
Miller juxtaposes Tubman's heroism against the disloyalty of
the mulatto house servant, a theme that continues to dominate black literature. Tubman's indomitable will is apparent
when she says, "Trouble or no trouble—thar's two things Ah
got de right to, an' they is death an' liberty. One or de other,
Ah mean to have. No one will take me back into slavery
alive." Miller insightfully comments on slavery as a corrupt
institution, on its engendering mistrust and deception among
an enslaved people, and on the existence of strong black male
and female relationships that have endured in spite of the
shackles of slavery. Miller's Harriet Tubman has a heart that
compels her to reach out to free those in bondage. . . .

THE FOLK TRADITION

Another identifiable form in the plays of early black women
playwrights is the folk tradition, which stresses the lives of

common black people. Some of the historical plays contain folk characters, distinguishable by language, customs, and beliefs, but they are not legendary heroes. Writers of folk plays take great pains to capture the customs, dialect, myths, earthiness and very essence of the down-home black person. . . .

Playwrights before the Harlem Renaissance, such as Ridgely Torrence, Paul Green, Charles W. Chesnutt, and Paul Laurence Dunbar, experimented with folk characters. It was during the Harlem Renaissance, however, that black playwrights, with any degree of frequency, began to take a serious look at and to treat with understanding grass-roots blacks. Langston Hughes' folk play, *Little Ham* (1935), is fairly well known. Few folk plays by black women, however, are a part of the established canon.

EULALIE SPENCE

Eulalie Spence (1894–1981), a West Indian who came to New York City via Ellis Island when she was eight, earned a B.A. from Teacher's College in 1937 and an M.A. in speech from Columbia University in 1939. *Undertow* (1929), Spence's gripping and realistic play about folk life in Harlem, was first published in *Carolina Magazine* in 1929 and has over the years been produced on black college campuses. This jewel of a play focuses on a man and woman who live through a loveless twenty years together after the husband is caught having an affair. The wife, Hattie, spends her whole life nagging and degrading him because of internalized hurt. When Clem, the other woman, returns to rekindle the fire, Hattie and Dan struggle, leaving Hattie dead. This play is saturated with folksy dialect that practically dances across the page. Hattie snaps at Dan, "You ain't gonna tro no dust in mah eyes no second time—not ef Ah know it." Hattie's boldness and streetwiseness, characteristic of folk drama, is evident when she levels verbal blows at her husband's mistress:

> But long's Ah got breaf tuh breathe, Ah ain't gwine say Yes! 'bout no divo'ce. Ef he kin git one 'thout me, let him git it! Yuh hear me? Now ef yuh's tru, yuh better get outa here. Ah ain't sponsible fer what Ah says from now on!

Another element of the folk tradition in *Undertow* is the constant stream of people flowing in and out of Hattie's boarding house. Spence dramatizes tenderly the day-to-day lives of these Harlemites of the twenties.

RELIGIOUS PLAYS

Religious plays, like the folk dramas by early black women playwrights, often center around the Southern, rural poor. Like the Medieval mystery plays that presented the whole scheme of salvation, nearly all of the plays of these mother playwrights contain some reference to God, Christianity, or religion in general. Using religion as a coping mechanism, the characters in many of the plays call on God to help them survive in an oppressive world. Grandma Sue, in Georgia Douglas Johnson's *A Sunday Morning in the South*, turns to God when her grandson is about to be lynched: "Sweet Jesus, do come down and hep us this mornin. Yo knows our hearts and you knows this po boy ain't done nothin wrong. You said you would hep the fatherless and the motherless; do Jesus bring this po orphan back to his ole cripple grannie safe and sound, do Jesus." This gripping plea is characteristic of the bulk of these early religious plays.

RUTH GAINES-SHELTON

A different kind of religious play is one by a woman who chose to experiment with religious allegory. Ruth Gaines-Shelton's (1873–?) play, *The Church Fight* (1925), distinguishes itself on three levels. First, it is a comedy, a rarity during the Harlem Renaissance because of racial unrest, World War I, and an approaching depression. These early black women playwrights, as a rule, did not use humor to effect social change. Second, the play is a religious allegory, wherein the characters in *The Church Fight* are personifications of abstract qualities. Third, the play does not deal with the issue of race. *The Church Fight*, not written in dialect, is a play by, about, and for blacks. . . .

The Church Fight, a play for which Gaines-Shelton won second prize in a *Crisis* contest in 1925, examines church politics. A humorous group of religious leaders, including Investigator, Judas, Instigator, Experience, Take-It-Back, and Two-Face, band together to oust Parson Procrastinator. The problem, however, is that no one can come up with a decent charge against him. Sister Instigator says with enthusiasm, "Well Brother Investigator, we ain't got no charge agin him, only he's been here thirteen years and we are tired of looking at him." When the parson confronts his accusers, they deny that they are plotting to eject him. They each flatter the parson in his presence and can hardly wait for him to adjourn the meeting. Brother Investigator in his prayers, after Parson leaves, mouths the sentiments of the religious leaders: "Lord, smile down in tender mercies upon those who have lied, and those who have not lied, close their lips with the seal of forgiveness, stiffen their tongues with the rod of obedience, fill their ears with the gospel of truth, and direct Parson Procrastinator's feet toward the railroad track."

Gaines-Shelton pokes fun at the fickleness and pettiness of some elders of the church. She seems to be suggesting that it is a waste of time and energy to get involved in church politics because there usually are no resolutions, only a limitless stream of questions and complaints. On another level, Gaines-Shelton demonstrates the power wielded by black religious leaders who are, generally, a driving and persuasive force behind the congregation and the community. *The Church Fight* also illustrates that the black church is a viable gathering place, serving as a social club for the community.

Like Ruth Gaines-Shelton, Marita Bonner experimented with form in the theater. Bonner (1905–1971) was born and educated in Massachusetts. After graduating from Radcliffe College, she went on to teach English in Washington D.C. Bonner's *The Purple Flower*, which first appeared in *Crisis* in 1928, is a fantasy that takes place in a nonexistent world, concerns incredible and unreal characters, and serves as a vehicle for her to make a serious comment on reality in America. Bonner's play, devoid of humor, is a biting, militant fantasy that is every bit as powerful as the radical plays of three decades later.

The Purple Flower is set on a hill called Somewhere inhabited by White Devils (whites) and in the valley called Nowhere peopled by the Us's (blacks). Bonner creatively describes these otherworldly Sundry White Devils as, "artful little things with soft wide eyes such as you would expect to find in an angel. Soft hair that flops around their horns. Their horns glow red all the time—now with blood—now with eternal fire—now with unholy desire." On the other hand, Bonner says of the Us's, "They can be as white as the White Devils, as brown as the earth, as black as the center of a poppy. They may look as if they were something or nothing."

In this fantasy land, the White Devils scheme to keep the Us's off the hill and away from the Purple Flower, which represents the good and the best in life. Several Us's offer suggestions about how to get up the hill: Booker T. Washington's philosophy of hard work and indispensability; W.E.B. DuBois' notion of books and education; or the religion/God, or money philosophies. When all these offerings fail, an old man takes charge and initiates a symbolic destruction of those things that hold the Us's from rebelling against the White Devils. The old man insists that only when the Us's are willing to shed and draw blood will they defeat the White Devils. Bonner's play addresses the issue of revolution. She insists that there will be a bloody revolution. *The Purple Flower*, written three decades before the volatile 1960s, signals change in America. Bonner sets the stage for militant writers like Amiri Baraka, Sonia Sanchez, and Ed Bullins. . . .

TORTURED AND TALENTED WRITERS

These maverick black women playwrights, whose works have for several decades been overshadowed by masculine literature, looked at the world with their feminine hearts and saw much that disappointed and angered them in the American society. In fact, one might conclude that the black women dramatists of the Harlem Renaissance were as much tortured as talented. Each of these women speaks to and for African Americans then and now. Becoming increasingly socially aware of the problems facing African Americans, these women move from the concerns of women to the concerns of Colored women and their families. Sometimes plaintive but always passionate, optimistic, and committed they set out to illuminate the conditions of African Americans with the hopes of bringing about social change. With feeling hearts, they present a slice of United States history from the unique perspective of women who have been both midwives and pallbearers of African American dreamers.

CHAPTER 3

Themes of Significant Writers

Harlem
Renaissance

Claude McKay: Primitive Instinct Versus Black Intellectualism

Michael B. Stoff

Primitivism in literature entailed writers drawing upon ideas and experiences expressing a more simplistic, even primal or savage quality of life. In African American writings of the 1920s, this typically involved authors culling African tribal culture and traditions. The Jamaican-born author Claude McKay gathered his primitivistic themes from Jamaica's peasant life and from the sparseness of the Jamaican landscape. His writings were a constant search for balance between the demands of fast-paced American living and the ease of his native homeland. This essay by literary scholar Michael B. Stoff examines three of McKay's novels: *Home to Harlem, Banjo,* and *Banana Bottom.*

According to Stoff, it is in these three works that McKay addresses the two worlds that both define him as an individual and yet divide his loyalties. As an educated black man, McKay felt robbed of the rustic contentment and primitive virility he associated with island life in Jamaica. Yet as a black man, he also realized his intellectual strength did not necessarily provide access to the advantages of white civilization in America. Stoff argues that McKay's novels are expressions of his longing for a lost homeland while struggling to fit in his newly adopted environment.

When asked why he had never visited Gertrude Stein while they were both in Paris, Claude McKay replied, "I never went because of my aversion to cults and disciples." McKay, a major poet and novelist of the Harlem Renaissance, was less than accurate in expressing a distaste for cults. In his art, he employed the images of the cult of primitivism in vogue among white contemporaries. Similarly, he pursued a primitive life-style as he struggled with the special problems of the black intellectual. McKay's success on the aesthetic level would not be matched in life.

"'The most moving and pathetic fact in the social life of America today,'" wrote Malcolm Cowley about the 1920s, "'is emotional and aesthetic starvation.' And what is the remedy?" The search for that remedy elicited a multitude of responses, all of which seemed motivated by a frantic desire to escape. The physical act of expatriation and the spiritual immersion of the self in art were two mechanisms employed by young intellectuals to flee the materialism and artistic stagnation of modern America. The fear and repugnance engendered by the Machine Age also evoked a third response—the intellectual retreat into the primitive.

The cult of primitivism which gripped many American intellectuals during the 1920s manifested itself in a number of ways. The rising interest in jazz, the study of African art forms, and the examination of tribal cultures were all variations on the theme of the primitive. The Negro as the uncorrupted remnant of preindustrial man became the central metaphor in this cult. Against the background of a tawdry culture stood the instinctive, sensual black man whose "dark laughter" represented a fundamental challenge to the effete civilization of white America. The Negro was transformed into a cultural hero serving as the protagonist in a series of white literary efforts. Eugene O'Neill's *The Emperor Jones* (1920) and *All God's Chillun Got Wings* (1924), Waldo Frank's *Holiday* (1923), Ronald Firbank's *Prancing Nigger* (1924), Sherwood Anderson's *Dark Laughter* (1925), and Carl Van Vechten's *Nigger Heaven* (1926) are merely a sampling of that new genre.

FOCUS ON JAMAICA

The primitivism in Claude McKay's art manifests itself even in his earliest efforts. As a Jamaican youth, McKay composed a series of dialect poems later published in two volumes: *Songs of Jamaica* (1912) and *Constab Ballads* (1912). Both thematically, through their emphasis on everyday peasant life, and stylistically, through their use of native dialect, these poems reveal McKay's fascination with Jamaican folk culture. . . .

McKay's depiction of the Jamaican peasant is integrally related to a stereotyped image of the world's peasantry. His peasants have a universality of condition and reaction which allows them to be exchanged with peasants of any nationality. This conception is consistent with McKay's later claim: "As a child, I was never interested in different kinds of races or tribes. People were just people to me." In describing McKay's image of the Jamaican peasant, the French literary critic Jean Wagner has written:

> All things being equal, McKay's portrait of the Jamaican peasant is in substance that of the peasant the world over. Profoundly attached to the earth, he works the soil with a knowledge gained from age long habit; although a hard worker, the Jamaican, like his counterpart the world over, is condemned to exploitation.

This perception of common qualities among the world's masses later furnished McKay with a theoretical basis for his own peculiar vision of the ideal political state. At this early point in his life, the concept of a "universal peasantry" heightened his sensitivity to folk-art traditions of other cultures. That interest supplied him with a foundation for much of his work.

REFUGE FROM MODERNITY

McKay emigrated from Jamaica in 1912 at the age of twenty-two. He carried with him not only a deep regard for the Jamaican peasantry but also a special vision of the island itself. He retained that vision until his death in 1948. The image of Jamaica as paradise permeates all his recollections of the island. In McKay's first American poems and in his later autobiographical material, Jamaica becomes the metaphorical equivalent of Eden. Its simplicity and freshness offered refuge from the complexities of a modern, industrialized world. Two stanzas from the poem "North and South" are typical of the nostalgic, pastoral strains found in McKay's early work:

> O sweet are the tropic lands for waking dreams!
> There time and life move lazily along,
> There by the banks of blue and silver streams
> Grass-sheltered crickets chirp incessant song;
> Gay-colored lizards loll all through the day,
> Their tongues outstretched for careless little flies.

And swarthy children in the fields at play,
Look upward, laughing at smiling skies.
A breath of idleness is in the air
That casts a subtle spell upon all things,
And love and mating time are everywhere,
And wonder to life's commonplaces clings.

The exotic setting and sensory images give a sensual flavor to the poem. These devices are re-employed in conjunction with themes of innocence and uncorruptibility in other Jamaican poems:

What days our wine thrilled bodies pulsed with joy
Feasting upon blackberries in the copse?
Oh some I know! I have embalmed the days,
Even the sacred moments when we played,
All innocent of passion, uncorrupt,
At noon and evening in the flame-heart's shade.
We were so happy, happy I remember,
Beneath the poinsettia's red in warm December.

McKay did not lose the vision of Jamaica as an undefiled Eden where instinct and sensation reigned supreme. Although he never returned to his island home, he was forever swept back thematically to his preindustrial, peasant origins. In 1947, a year before his death, McKay wrote, "I think of a paradise as something of a primitive kind of place where there are plenty of nuts and fruits and flowers and milk and wild honey. Jamaica has all of this." Recapturing the lost innocence of that Eden provided one of the major themes in McKay's life.

INSTINCTIVE VS. INTELLECTUAL

McKay was also obsessed with describing the social role to be played by the intellectual. His membership in a visible and oppressed minority further complicated matters. In essence, the entire body of his art can be seen as a mechanism through which he sought to transform these personal problems into public issues. Such a transformation entailed an insistent reference to a recurring pattern of images. That pattern was the juxtapositioning of the instinctive black man and the educated Negro. These images defined, with increasing precision, McKay's own concepts and made them salient within a broader cultural context.

McKay's earliest use of this construction came in the first of his three novels, *Home to Harlem*. The book was published in 1928, the sixth year of McKay's expatriation from

America. Its appearance initiated a violent debate among the black literati over the propriety of its theme and subject matter. Many of McKay's peers agreed with Langston Hughes's evaluation. Hughes argued that because it was so "vividly alive," *Home to Harlem* could legitimately be labeled, as "the first real flower of the Harlem Renaissance."

The elder black literary figures and much of the established Negro press were revolted by what they believed to be overtly crude allusions in McKay's book. Claiming the book was not representative of Negro life, this Old Guard expressed its shock and indignation at the lasciviousness of the novel. Its very existence, they suggested, was a calculated affront to the black community. W.E.B. Du Bois's reaction was typical of the initial reviews:

> *Home to Harlem* for the most part nauseates me, and after the dirtier parts of its filth I feel distinctly like taking a bath. . . . It looks as though McKay has set out to cater to that prurient demand on the part of white folk for a portrayal in Negroes of that utter licentiousness which convention holds white folk back from enjoying—if enjoyment it can be labeled.

The controversy enveloping *Home to Harlem* was merely the surfacing of an underlying tension engendered by conflicting visions of the Harlem Renaissance. The Old Guard saw the Renaissance as a vehicle for social amelioration. The Renaissance would not only demonstrate the intellectual achievements of the black man, but would also uplift the masses to some arbitrary level of social acceptability.

BUILDING CULTURE UP FROM THE ROOTS

It was precisely this view of the Harlem Renaissance, this venture in cultural pretension, that McKay's work fundamentally challenged. His notion of a renaissance was an aggregation of ". . . talented persons of an ethnic or national group working individually or collectively in a common purpose and creating things that would be typical of their group." In 1929, McKay defined the problems one faced when speaking of a "racial renaissance." He delineated the tactics and sources to be employed in creating such a movement:

> We educated Negroes are talking a lot about a racial renaissance. And I wonder how we're going to get it. On one side we're up against the world's arrogance—a mighty cold hard white stone thing. On the other the great sweating army—our race. It's the common people, you know, who furnish the bone and sinew and salt of any race or nation. In the modern

race of life we're merely beginners. If this renaissance is going to be more than a sporadic scabby thing, we'll have to get down to our racial roots to create it. . . . Getting down to our native roots and building up from our people is . . . culture.

For McKay, this meant the conscious and studied illumination of a black folk-art tradition whose central themes would be the indestructible vitality of the primitive black man and the inextricable dilemma of the educated Negro.

HOME TO HARLEM

Home to Harlem is a vivid glimpse of the lower depths of black life in urban America. Its peripatetic plot and dialect-oriented style are consistent with its thematic emphasis on the black man as the unrestrained child of civilization. Set in New York's black ghetto, the novel establishes Harlem as a carnal jungle. Our senses are subjected to a barrage of erotic images: "Brown girls rouged and painted like dark pansies. Brown flesh draped in colorful clothes. Brown lips full and pouted for sweet kissing. Brown breasts throbbing with love." At the core of this physical world lies the cabaret Congo, "a real little Africa in New York." Forbidden to whites, the Congo is a distillation of Harlem life. Its atmosphere is filled with the "tenacious odors of service and the warm indigenous smells of Harlem." Its allusions to the unrepressed African culture provide an apt setting for the return of the novel's hero, Jake Brown.

Jake, an Army deserter, is introduced as the natural man whose actions are guided by intuition. He is the instinctive primitive, deeply rooted in the exotic mystique of Africa. As he walks down Lenox Avenue, he is overcome by the pulsations of Harlem life. "His flesh tingled," the narrator tells us, and "he felt as if his whole body was a flaming wave." Jake and Harlem are inexorably bound by a "contagious fever . . . burning everywhere," but burning most fervently in "Jake's sweet blood." That primitive passion sustains Jake and represents a profound threat to the cultural rigidity of modern society.

In contrast to Jake, McKay inserts himself as the Haitian immigrant Ray. Ray represents the cultivated intellect, the civilized black whose education has sensitized his mind but paralyzed his body. Intellectually, Ray can comprehend the cluster of sensations and emotions about him, yet he lacks the naturalness of action and spontaneity of response that are the hallmarks of a Jake Brown. Although envious of

Jake, Ray harbors the obsessive fear that "someday the urge of the flesh . . . might chase his high dreams out of him and deflate him to the contented animal that was the Harlem nigger strutting his stuff."

The result is a vision of the intellectual, and especially the black intellectual, as social misfit. Ray is capable of sensing and recording life, but he is unable to live it. "He drank in more of life," writes McKay, "than he could distill into active animal living." There is no outlet for his immense store of emotional energy. Robbed by his "white" education of the ability to act freely and impulsively, Ray remains little more than a "slave of the civilized tradition." Caught between two cultures, he is immobilized. "The fact is," he tells Jake as he flees to Europe,

> . . . I don't know what I'll do with my little education. I won-der sometimes if I could get rid of it and lose myself in some savage culture in the jungles of Africa. I am a misfit—as the doctors who dole out newspaper advice to the well-fit might say—a misfit with my little education and constant dreaming, when I should be getting the nightmare habit to hog in a lot of dough like everybody else in this country. . . . The more I learn the less I understand and love life.

The implications of Ray's final statement are not only ap-plicable to McKay's personal problems but related to a broader cultural phenomenon. Notions of escape, alienation, and crude commercialism were by no means uniquely black images. They were embraced by intellectuals of varying hues in the twenties. McKay's use of these themes places the black experience into a larger cultural context. Blackness only added a further convolution to the already complex problem of the intellectual's social adaptability.

Ray's expatriation leaves the fundamental questions raised by the novel unresolved. The continuing focus on Jake, and his reunion with the "tantalizing brown" girl Fe-lice, imply that only the instinctive primitive can survive happily in white civilization, its dehumanizing tendencies are irrelevant to his innately free existence. The intellectual, defiled by the process of civilization, is doomed to wander in search of that potency of action he has irrevocably lost.

BANJO

McKay's second novel, *Banjo,* published in 1929, pursues the issues raised in *Home to Harlem.* Although the scene has shifted to Marseille's harbor district, the structural dualism characterizing *Home to Harlem* is present once more. Lincoln Agrippa Daily, familiarly known as Banjo, replaces Jake Brown while McKay again enters as Ray. The dichotomy is now expanded and more lucidly articulated.

In *Banjo* there is a sharpening of figurative focus and a widening of thematic scope. With the character Banjo, McKay adds a new dimension to the earthy black and provides a more concise definition of his own racial conceptions. At the same time, Ray's disposition has progressed from a confused uneasiness with American life to a coherent denunciation of western civilization. This increased clarity of imagery allows McKay to move toward a resolution to the quandary of the black intellectual.

The primitive black is given additional depth in *Banjo*. The loose plot, an account of the lives of a group of beach boys in the port city of Marseille, provides a background for the development of the protagonist, Banjo. He is the same intuitive vagabond originally described in *Home to Harlem*—with one significant difference. While Jake is nebulously characterized as a laborer, Banjo is depicted as an artist. He is a jazzman whose life is the embodiment of his art. Like the songs he plays, Banjo is unrestrained, free-spirited, and vibrantly alive. McKay immediately establishes the intimate relationships between Banjo and his music: "I never part with this instrument," Banjo says in the opening pages of the novel. "It is moh than a gal, moh than a pal; it's mahself.". . .

The instrument is the cultural expression of American Negro folk-art, and Banjo represents the prototype black folk-artist lustily proclaiming the vitality of his race. His music, "the sharp, noisy notes of the banjo," is not derived from a pretentious adaptation of European culture. Drawing inspiration from the "common people," Banjo's art represents the truest expression of black culture.

Again juxtaposed to this earthy, intuitive black man is the intellectual Ray. Recently expatriated from America, Ray comes to Marseille in search of an artistic haven where he could "exist *en pension* prolitarian of a sort and try to create around him the necessary solitude to work with pencil and scraps of paper." Ray has not given up his earlier passion for writing, and although he is occasionally forced to work as a laborer, he never renounces his "dream of self-expression." Once in the Vieux Port, he finds, instead of solitude, a band of beach boys whose free and undisciplined lifestyle is par-

ticularly appealing to Ray's vagabond sensibilities. As a result, he immediately establishes an intimate relationship
with the members of the group and especially with their
leader, Banjo. At this point, the linear progression of the plot
becomes of secondary importance, and the novel is reduced
to a vehicle for the delineation of Ray's (*i.e.*, McKay's) brief
against civilization and the formulation of a solution to his
intellectual quandary.

INDICTMENT OF AMERICAN CULTURE

McKay's condemnation of Western civilization in *Banjo* is
inexorably tied to the psychological problems arising from
his blackness. In 1937 he wrote, "What, then, was my main
psychological problem? It was the problem of color. Color-
consciousness was the fundamental of my restlessness."
And it is color-consciousness which is the fundamental of
Ray's hatred for civilization. "Civilization is rotten," Ray pro-
claims, and in the following passage, McKay defines the sociological basis of Ray's sentiments:

> He hated civilization because its general attitude toward the
> colored man was such as to rob him of his warm human in-
> stincts and make him inhuman. Under it the thinking colored
> man could not function normally like his white brother, re-
> sponsive and reacting spontaneously to the emotions of plea-
> sure or pain, joy or sorrow, kindness or hardness, charity,
> anger, and forgiveness. . . . So soon as he entered the great
> white world, where of necessity he must work and roam and
> breathe the larger air to live, that entire world, high, low,
> middle, unclassed, all conspired to make him painfully con-
> scious of color and race. . . . It was not easy for a Negro with
> an intellect standing watch over his native instincts to take
> his own way in this white man's civilization. But of one thing
> he was resolved: civilization would not take the love of color,
> joy, beauty, vitality and nobility out of *his* life and make him
> like one of the poor masses of its pale creatures.

Although the imagery utilized in the preceding passage is
applied to the peculiar condition of the black man, this vision
of a devitalizing, dehumanizing civilization is part of the
larger, biracial indictment of American culture. While
McKay's attack is rooted in color-consciousness, its targets
remain remarkably similar to those of the general assault.
McKay finds the fraudulence and duplicity of Western civilization in a multitude of situations beyond its psychological
effect on individual black men. The arduous but profitable
exercise of lifting the "white man's burden" was, for McKay,

a particularly noxious undertaking of the civilized world. Under the guise of Judeo-Christian morality, Western civilization succeeded in its drive to commercialize and exploit the "uncivilized" masses of the earth. Furthermore, McKay saw the trend toward cultural standardization as effectively robbing the world of its "greatest charm"—ethnic diversity. . . .

In the closing pages of the novel, Ray explains that he has always wanted "to hold on to his intellectual acquirements without losing his instincts. The black gifts of laughter and melody and simple sensuous feelings and responses." It is in this rather untenable position that his problem lies. Given a world in which the terms intellect and instinct have been assigned opposing definitions, it seems improbable that one figure can plausibly synthesize both qualities. Ray's attempt at such a synthesis is achieved through his decision to join Banjo in the vagabond life. Thematically, this decision represents a rejection of the standardized white civilization and an affirmation of the cultural diversity of the beach boys' existence. . . .

BANANA BOTTOM

In *Banana Bottom*, the third and last of his novels, McKay achieves an aesthetic structure which permits the formulation of a viable resolution to the predicament of the educated black man. This resolution is viable in that it does not contradict any of the definitions set forth in the novel, and it is consistent with McKay's affirmation of the primitive elements of black life. This new form is attained by abandoning the structural dualism of his earlier works in favor of a single protagonist. In this way, McKay frees himself from the limitations imposed by the rigid polarizations of instinct and intellect in separate characters. No longer constricted by Ray's inability to reject even a part of his cerebral existence, or Jake's (and by extension, Banjo's) static, unattainable sensuality, McKay now produces a novel in which the main character can credibly embody both instinct and intellect.

The plot of *Banana Bottom* is relatively simple. Set in the West Indies, the story commences with the rape of a young Jamaican peasant girl, Bita Plant. Following the incident, Bita becomes the ward of the Craigs, a white missionary couple who, with an air of condescension, take pity on the girl. In the best Anglo-Saxon missionary tradition, they see in her the golden opportunity for demonstrating to their peasant flock "what one such girl might become by careful training [and] . . . by God's help." As a result, they send her to a finishing school in England with the hope of "redeeming her from her past by a long period of education." After a six-year absence, Bita returns to Jamaica only to find that, for all her education, she is irrepressibly attracted to the island's peasant life. Despite the Craigs' insistence on her marriage to a black divinity student and on the devotion of her life to missionary work, Bita rejects their civilized world in favor of the simplicity of peasant life.

TWO OPPOSING VALUE SYSTEMS

The novel derives its power from the dynamic tension established between the conflicting value systems of Anglo-Saxon civilization and the Jamaican folk culture. This thematic dichotomy first manifests itself in the contrasting reactions to Bita's rape. Priscilla Craig expresses her shock and indignation with an unveiled sanctimony. The "over-sexed" natives, she comments, are "apparently incapable of comprehending the opprobrium of breeding bastards in a Christian community." On the other hand, the village gossip, a peasant woman named Sister Phibby, reacts with a knowing smile indicating her "primitive satisfaction as in a good thing done early."

McKay expands and sustains the tension of contrary value systems through the ever-present antagonism between the civilized Christ-God of retribution and puritanical repression, and the African Obeah-God of freedom and primeval sensuality. Throughout the novel, the white missionaries and native ministers are constantly troubled with the problem of wandering flocks which "worship the Christian God-of-Good-and-Evil on Sunday and in the shadow of the night . . . invoke the power of the African God of Evil by the magic of the sorcerer. Obi [is] resorted to in sickness and feuds, love and elemental disasters." And although the missionaries struggle desperately to win the native populace, it is the Obeah-God who rules Jamaica, and it is the primitive African value system which is at the core of the peasant culture.

Of peasant origin and possessing a cultivated intellect, Bita Plant represents McKay's first successful synthesis of two cultures. When she finds it necessary to choose a lifestyle, it is a relatively easy decision. As opposed to Ray, she is not fraught with the vague uncertainties and questioning doubts over her ability to survive in either culture. Bita has readily internalized the concept of her blackness and willingly accepted her racial origins. Bearing no warping hatred for white civilization, she is characterized by an assertive self-confidence derived from a sense of her own innate worth:

> . . . a white person is just like another human being to me. I thank God that although I was brought up and educated among white people, I have never wanted to be anything but myself. I take pride in being colored and different, just as any intelligent white person does in being white. I can't imagine

---

A NEW VOICE OF BLACK CONSCIOUSNESS

In this excerpt, author and poet Arna Bontemps recalls the impact that Claude McKay's first book of poetry had on his direction as a writer.

The following year (1922) marked the publication by Harcourt, Brace & Company of Claude McKay's *Harlem Shadows.* This was the first time in about a decade (since Dodd, Mead's publication of Paul Laurence Dunbar's posthumous *Complete Poems*) that a major American publisher had brought out a collection of poems by a Negro. It was the first time in nearly two decades that any such publisher had ventured to offer a book of poems by a living black poet.

I remember it well. I had been a summer school student at UCLA and picked up a copy of the McKay poems in the main public library on the way home. I had not seen a review or heard any mention of the book, but the first sentence of the Introduction made any such announcement unnecessary. "These poems have a special interest for all the races of man," it said, "because they are sung by a pure blooded Negro." Naturally I had to borrow the book that very minute, read it on the yellow Pacific Electric streetcar that day and a second time that night, then begin telling everybody I knew about it.

The responses of black friends were surprising. Nearly all of them stopped to listen. There was no doubt that their blood came to a boil when they heard "If We Must Die." "Harlem Dancer" brought worldly-wise looks from their eyes. McKay's poems of longing for his home island melted them visibly, and I think these responses told me something about black people and poetry that remains true. Certainly it was in my consciousness when I headed for New York two years later.

Arna Bontemps, "The Awakening: A Memoir," *The Harlem Renaissance Remembered.* New York: Dodd, Mead and Company, 1972.

anything more tragic than people torturing themselves to be different from their natural, unchangeable selves.

For Bita, intellect and education are the handmaidens of instinct. Her return to peasant life provides a source of sustenance and vitality for her total existence: "Her music, her reading, her thinking were the flowers of her intelligence, and he [Bita's peasant husband] the root upon which she was grafted, both nourishing in the same soil."

In Bita Plant, McKay at last succeeds in framing an aesthetic solution to the black intellectual's problem of social incongruence. By rejecting not intellect nor education but rather the "civilized" value system in favor of the primitive values of a black folk culture, the intellectual can ultimately escape the stigma of "misfit." On the surface, this solution does not seem to differ from the one developed in *Banjo*. Yet in *Banana Bottom,* McKay makes an important distinction not present in his earlier work. For the first time, McKay distinguishes between education, or the cultivation of the intellect, and the necessary acceptance of the value system implied by that education. Ray's failure to make this distinction is the source of his problem. Believing, on the one hand, that a rejection of civilization implies a rejection of intellect, and at the same time, desiring desperately to hold his intellectual acquirements, Ray is immobilized. He can neither remain in a white world which denies his humanity, nor move into a black world which denies his intellect. However, once the distinction is made, the element of conflict between instinct and intellect is removed. Bita, who rejects the civilized value system but not her intellect, can move easily from one world to another without impairing either instinct or intellect. Unfortunately, it is one of McKay's personal tragedies that although he is capable of making this distinction in his art, he is unable to make it in his life. "My damned white education," he wrote in his autobiography, "has robbed me of much of the primitive vitality, the pure stamina, the simple unswaggering strength of the Jakes of the Negro race."

CONFRONTING THE PRIMITIVE WITH ART

McKay's *art* can be seen as a coherent attempt to articulate and resolve the problems of the black intellectual through an aesthetic retreat into primitivism. His *life,* like the lives of most men, presents a less consistent pattern. If there is any overriding theme, it is found in the vision McKay holds of himself. "All my life," he wrote in 1937, "I have been a troubadour wanderer." The role of artistic nomad is the thread connecting McKay's diverse preoccupations. By choosing this image, he transforms metaphor into reality and captures the elusive elements of instinct and intellect. The primitive, liberated black man, and the sensitive, eloquent artist merge in the vagabond poet who, like Bita Plant, is capable of sensually experiencing and rationally expressing life. However, the image is not the man. It is, rather, a convenient but unsuccessful vehicle through which McKay attempts to realize in life the primitive vision he sought so desperately in art.

Jean Toomer and the Biracial Identity

George Hutchinson

Jean Toomer's *Cane* is considered the first true novel of black fiction to come out of the Harlem Renaissance. In his 1993 article, literary scholar George Hutchinson examines *Cane* as a representation of Toomer's search for a racial identity. Toomer was biracial, and throughout his life he felt unable to identify with either black or white America. Since he was part black, however, the segregated society considered him to be an African American. In his writing Toomer explored the identification that was imposed on him—and other biracial Americans—but ultimately was dissatisfied. Hutchinson illustrates Toomer's inability to identify with black culture through a discussion of the novel's major characters who lack strong ties within the black community of the South. Hutchinson explains that although *Cane* was received well by critics, it failed to receive favorable support from white and black audiences, increasing Toomer's frustration and sense of isolation. Finally, Hutchinson illustrates Toomer's self-exile from the black literary elite in an attempt to identify less with his black heritage.

An undated poem kept in a tin box that no one but the author ever saw in his lifetime bears haunting witness to the great lack of Jean Toomer's existence:

> Above my sleep
> Tortured in deprival
> Stripped of the warmth of a name
> My life breaks madly. . . .
> Breaks against world
> Like a pale moth breaking
> Against sun.

Excerpted from "Jean Toomer and American Racial Discourse," by George Hutchinson, *Texas Studies in Literature and Language*, Summer 1993. Copyright © 1993 by the University of Texas Press. Reprinted with permission.

In their biography of the poet, *The Lives of Jean Toomer*, Cynthia Kerman and Richard Eldridge discuss the relationship of this poem to Toomer's sense of lacking a permanent and certain name, deriving from the fact that his name had changed during his childhood and that different family members called him by different names. His grandfather, for example (the patriarch with whom he lived to young adulthood and who died, Toomer claimed, the day after he completed the first draft of "Kabnis"), would not acknowledge the name he had been given at birth. "Jean Toomer" itself is a later fabrication of the author.

SEARCHING FOR IDENTITY

No doubt it is a fact of the first importance that Toomer was a self-named man. He was also a man who devoted an extraordinary amount of energy to defining himself, authoring some seven autobiographies that never found publishers in his lifetime. In all of his self-definitions, Toomer dwells intensely on his racial identity, which he specifically differentiates from the races now acknowledged and named in the public discourse of the United States. He names his own race, the "American" race, striving to claim the central term of our national discourse to signify an identity which few "Americans" have been willing to acknowledge. If Toomer's family could not agree with each other upon what exactly to call him, thus stripping him of the "warmth" of a name, so far most of those who read his works have equally "denominated" and renamed him, conferring on him the denominations "Negro," "Afro-American," "black." The naming has curiously and ironically empowered his voice by fitting it anew within the very "American" racial discourse whose authority he radically, incessantly disputed. . . .

Toomer's career, the reception of his published texts, and his texts themselves (including *Cane* and contemporaneous works) indicate how the belief in unified, coherent "black" and "white" American "racial" identities depends formally and ethically upon the sacrifice of the identity that is *both* "black" *and* "white," just as American racial discourse depends upon maintaining the emphatic silence of the interracial subject at the heart of Toomer's project. Moreover, the very acts of discursive violence that banish the forbidden terms and thus enable the social fictions by which we live must remain unacknowledged, virtually unconscious gestures—in the case of Toomer scholarship, typically North American "racial" gestures with undertones of the rituals of scapegoating.

TOOMER'S BIRACIAL IDENTITY

Most critics who recognize the nature of Toomer's insistence upon a new "American" racial identity nonetheless perceive *Cane* either as falling into a brief period when the author considered himself a "Negro" or as affirming (regardless of the author's identity) an African American vision, as well as revealing African American expressivity as the "true source" of Toomer's creativity. In the most interesting and sophisticated recent interpretation of *Cane*, Henry Louis Gates, Jr., while seeming to accept Toomer's self-identification, tries ingeniously to evade the problem this identification poses not only by separating intentionality and biographical context from textuality but by defining the "multiracial" text as "black." Hence, because of its "double-voiced discourse," *Cane* is "the blackest text of all." Even if we accept the necessity of separating textuality from biography, however, the trap remains the same: a discourse that allows no room for a "biracial" text (except by defining it as "black") is part of the *same discursive system* that denies the identity of the person who defines himself or herself as both black and white (or, in Langston Hughes's phrase, as "neither white nor black"). . . . Toomer dramatizes, that is, *another* threshold of "racial" difference that he considers to be of a "higher level" than the threshold between black and white, and his "multi-voiced" language aims to bring us to that threshold, to give us a glimpse of what lies beyond. . . .

Other revealing metaphors from the critical tradition suggest that Toomer "disappeared" into "white obscurity" or became "invisible." His "visibility," like his potency, is directly connected to his status as a "black" author. One may well ask whether *Cane* would enjoy whatever canonical status it does today—whether, indeed, it would even be in print—had it not been "rediscovered" and valorized in the late 1960s as a seminal "black" text, comfortably fitting within the North American racial archive. Perhaps the greatest irony of Toomer's career is that at the time modern American racial discourse was taking its most definite shape, "mulattoes"—because they threatened the racial bifurcation—"disappeared" as a group into either the white "race" (through passing) or the

black "race" while the "one-drop rule" [a law stating any relation to a Negro makes a person all black] was defined in increasingly definite terms. The 1920 U.S. census, coinciding
with the beginning of the Harlem Renaissance, was the last
to count "mulattoes." At the same time, "interracial" mating,
and particularly "interracial" marriage, rare as it already
was, drastically declined. By 1990 the census forms, despite
objections, explicitly instructed that all persons who considered themselves both black *and* white, or biracial, must designate themselves "black."

PLACING THE MULATTO

The mutely "tragic," "ghostly" figure of the "mulatto" haunts
our racial ideology as its absent center, the scapegoat whose
sacrifice both signifies the origin of racialist discourse and
sustains it. As René Girard has emphasized, scapegoating
purges a community of the threat of "strange mixtures," first
instituting and then maintaining the system of differences
upon which signification itself depends. Every discursive
system, indeed, depends upon some such sacrifice. Thus, as
Simone Vauthier has written, the biracial character in the literature of the United States, "designates the moment of origins," exposing and undermining "the myth of two discrete
races separated by an impassable gulf." The maintenance of
racial boundaries demands the sacrifice of the "mulatto" either through tragedy or by his or her incorporation into one
of the "fixed" racial groups. . . .

In a preface to one of his unpublished autobiographies—
appropriately called "Book X"—Toomer regrets that he will
have to resort to conventional and distorting terms to get his
racial message across, as our very language allows no other
means of expressing his sense of identity; he has considered
the problem for years and cannot find any adequate solution. "If I have to say 'colored,' 'white,' 'jew,' 'gentile,' and so
forth, I will unwittingly do my bit toward reinforcing the
limited views of mankind which dismember mankind into
mutually repellant factions." Toomer's attempts to explain
himself led to a very precise awareness of the connection between language and ideology, the impossibility of developing an entirely "new" discourse that would be independent
of the inherited one.

The problem was so severe that for a period he stopped
writing, convinced that the more he wrote, the more he re-

inforced the very ideology he was trying to escape.

> This dilemma of the writer happens to strike me with peculiar
> force. It impresses and sometimes depresses me and makes
> me beat my brains almost to the point that I voluntarily seal
> my lips and stop writing. Indeed in the past there was a time
> when I did become mute, owing to a realization of this very
> matter which, as I saw then as I see now, involved the entire
> use of words with reference to any and all aspects of life.

The sense of entrapment in a racialist language founded
specifically upon the denial of his own "racial" name pre-
cipitated an intense realization of the general inadequacy of
language to express "truth." Language, always shaped by oppressive social conventions and more profoundly by what
Michel Foucault would later call the "archive" of the "cultural unconscious," was a hindrance to spiritual development and self-redescription. This rather remarkable insight
of Toomer's helps us understand why, when he, as most
readers would have it, "turned his back on his race"—seeking what countless critics have termed a "raceless" identity
but which he considered the only self-consciously "American" one—he simultaneously turned to mysticism, a route to
knowledge "beyond words.". . .

ANALYZING BIRACIALISM IN *CANE*

A few comments about significant elements in the first two
sections of *Cane* will help to show how the concluding
story/play relates to the volume as a whole. The first section
of the book, which Toomer called a "swan song" for the dying African American folk culture of the South, shows the
enormous contradictions inherent in Southern "racial" culture. Behind all the tragedies of the South lies the repression
of "natural" desires, repression of life itself by conventions
governing all human relations. A chief contradiction (which
Toomer's friend and mentor Waldo Frank would also make
the basis of his novel *Holiday*) is the desire certain members
of each "race" feel for members of the other—and by extension, for incorporation into the "new race"—despite a bru-
tally enforced, "unnatural" segregation. The sexual and
racial codes of the South turn this desire into various per-
verted, stunted, and oppressive manifestations, but interracial desire remains an ineluctable fact.

The text is full of people of "mixed race," episodes revolv-
ing around or emanating from interracial liaisons. The

"biracial" Fern (Jewish and African American) is an erotic-mystical magnet to black and white alike, for example; but one whom, like a vestal priestess, both black and white men leave alone, sensing something "taboo" about her: "She was not to be approached by anyone." The narrator, indeed, draws male readers of both "races" into her spell: "([I]t makes no difference if you sit in the Pullman or the Jim Crow as the train crosses her road,"). The reference to her "weird," mystical eyes as a "common delta," into which both God and the Southern landscape flow, evokes Toomer's consistent trope (from the 1910s through the 1930s) of a river signifying the dissolution of the "old" races into the "New World soul." Moreover, Fern's spiritual "hunger" and frustration as well as her muteness match Toomer's sense of the frustration and inarticulateness of the yet "unawakened" people of his new race.

Interracial desire is denied, thwarted, made a tool of oppression (as in "Blood-Burning Moon"), driven underground, or violently purged throughout section 1 of *Cane*. Manifestations of this desire and denial—this burial, this violence—become sacred, taboo in such pieces as "Becky," "Fern," "Esther," "Blood-Burning Moon," and "Portrait in Georgia." Since women are the objects of a dominating male desire, they often bear the "cross" of this contradiction.

In "Becky," for example, the title character—who has given birth to "mulatto" sons—is ostracized by both black and white communities, each of which "prayed secretly to God who'd put His cross upon her and cast her out". Toomer emphasizes a parallelism in white and black responses to Becky and her unknown lover: "Damn buck nigger, said the white folks' mouths. She wouldnt tell, Common, God-forsaken, insane white shameless wench, said the white folks' mouths. . . . Lowdown nigger with no self-respect, said the black folks' mouths. She wouldnt tell. Poor Catholic poor-white crazy woman, said the black folks' mouths". Blacks and whites together have built her a cabin precisely on an "eye-shaped piece of ground" between a road and the railroad tracks, and she—who has become "invisible"—lives at this boundary line between the white and black sections of town. No one ever sees Becky, and she is utterly silent. Yet people scribble prayers on scraps of paper and throw them toward her house as they pass it, until one day the chimney of her disintegrating cabin caves in and buries her. Returning from church on a Sunday, the narrator and his friend Barlo hear the chimney fall and even enter the home. The narrator thinks he hears a groan, but instead of investigating further and possibly saving her, the two men quickly leave, Barlo throwing his Bible on the mound. Like a true scapegoat, Becky is invested with the sacred aura of the taboo; the food and other objects people leave near her home are distinctly presented as propitiatory offerings for the sign of "pollution," the sacrifice of which sustains racial identities. Even her boys disappear, shouting, "Godam the white folks; Godam the niggers". The mutual decision by blacks and whites to ostracize Becky gives them a commonality: "*We*, who had cast out their mother because of them, could we take them in?" asks the narrator. "They answered black and white folks by shooting up two men and leaving town" (emphasis added). . . .

Toomer's vision of a coming merging of the races makes perfect sense within the framework of the first section of *Cane*: the dystopia of the contemporary South implies a corresponding utopia. Alain Solard's comment on "Blood-Burning Moon" is apt: "To the artist, Bob, Tom, Louisa belong to 'another country' which they feel, but do not know is their own." When desire is freed (as segregation is dismantled), it will cross racial boundaries without violence, embarrassment, or perversion. Those "mixed-race" persons now left in "limbo" will ultimately find home; indeed, the entire country will be transformed in their image. The United States will be a "colored" nation. But at the same time, many elements contributing to the beauty of the South—specifically of the African American folk spirit—will be lost as the conditions of its emergence disappear. "America needs these elements," Toomer wrote in a well-known passage the year he composed *Cane*.

> They are passing. Let us grab and hold them while there is still time. Segregation and laws may retard this solution. But in the end, segregation will either give way, or it will kill. Natural preservations do not come from unnatural laws. . . . A few generations from now, the negro will still be dark, and a portion of his psychology will spring from this fact, but in all else he will be a conformist to the general outlines of American civilization, or of American chaos.

RACE-MIXING AS A SOLUTION TO RACISM

"Race-mixing," in Toomer's view, follows natural laws. If Toomer would hasten the end of racial division and oppression, he would also have to accept the end of that specific sort of folk culture engendered by slavery, a largely preindustrial economy, Jim Crow, and post-Reconstruction peonage. Hence, he is called, in this swan song, to memorialize. "The Negro is in solution," he wrote Waldo Frank.

> As an entity, the race is loosing [sic] its body, and its soul is approaching a common soul. . . . In my own stuff, in those places that come nearest to the old Negro, to the spirit saturate with folk-song: Karintha and Fern, the dominant emotion is a sadness derived from a sense of fading, from a knowledge of my futility to check solution. There is nothing about these pieces of the bouyant expression of a new race. The folk-songs themselves are of the same order.

Toomer implies that if there is nothing in *these* pieces about the "buoyant expression of a new race," the "sense of fading" of the "old races" will be *followed* by such expression. Indeed, *Cane* presupposes such expression. . . .

KABNIS'S REJECTION OF BLACKNESS

Most scholars interpret "Kabnis" as if the failure of the hero is caused by his rejection of his "true" African American identity. This interpretation hinges upon particular views of Lewis, Carrie Kate, and Father John, as well as the title character—upon the idea that the black Christian/folk tradition embodied in Father John and carried on by those such as Carrie Kate will herald a new dawn of African American peoplehood. Too weak to accept the pain of the African American past, Kabnis, so the argument goes, rejects his "true" "black" identity, and this explains his failure to become "whole." Moreover, because of its strong autobiographical echoes, the story is thought to represent Toomer's brief identification of himself as a "black" author. Indeed, just after finishing the manuscript, he wrote Waldo Frank in an intense letter, "Kabnis is *me.*"

The story opens with the haunting lyrics of a song the "night-winds" whisper through cracks in the walls of Kabnis's cabin:

White-man's land.
Niggers, sing.
Burn, bear black children
Till poor rivers bring
Rest, and sweet glory
In Camp Ground

The lines, of course, bring to mind the African American

heritage, specifically the spirituals. But Toomer puts a strange spin on familiar phrases. In a letter to Waldo Frank counseling the latter on how to write the introduction to *Cane*, Toomer wrote that such lines as "I want to cross over into camp ground" (from the spiritual "Deep River") not only signified the desire for salvation but could be translated in social terms as meaning, "my position here is transient. I'm going to die, or be absorbed." Indeed, preposterous as it sounds, Toomer interpreted the lines as prophetically antic- ipating the merging of the "Negro" into the new American race. In "Withered Skin of Berries," the "mulatta" Vera longs to plunge into a river, signifying the merging of black and white races in the "new world soul," intoning, "Lord, I want to cross over into camp ground." She longs for the river to "sweep her under" as she "crosses" over into the "American" identity. Indeed, Toomer frequently uses images of rivers in his work written at this time and later to suggest the current that would dissolve past racial and cultural identities into a new one. . . .

Kabnis suffers inner conflict in great part because of his denial of the pain of the black past and his connection to it. However, the conflict is exacerbated by his "mixed" racial identity. Like Toomer, Kabnis has straight, thin hair, a "lemon" face, brown eyes, and a mustache of "slim silk". He longs to become "the face of the South." Like Toomer's, his ancestors were "southern blue bloods" as well as the black slaves Lewis will not let him deny. The conflict between these identities is precisely the key to Kabnis's difficulty. Lewis charges: "Can't hold them, can you? Master; slave. Soil; and the overarching heavens. Dusk; dawn. They fight and bastardize you. The sun tint of your cheeks, flame of the great season's multi-colored leaves, tarnished, burned. Split, shredded: easily burned. No use". . . .

Ralph Kabnis calls himself a "dream" and regrets that a dream is soft, easily smashed by the "fist" of "square faces." He lacks the "bull-neck" and "heaving body," the strength, to bring his dream to reality. "If I, the dream (not what is weak and afraid in me)," he wonders, "could become the face of the South". Lewis, perceiving the difficulty of "holding" the "sum" of his conflicting "racial" origins, precisely indicates the source of Kabnis's problem in achieving an identity and its adequate expression, an expression that would make him "the face of the [white/black] South" that would realize his dream. In fact, Kabnis longs to achieve an identity by means of verbal expression and is frustrated by his inability to shape the right words, to *name* his reality adequately. Speaking of people of the "expanding type" (i.e., the "new" people), Toomer once wrote, "often they have been so compelled and are now so accustomed to use the dominant, which is to them an alien, language, that they can find no words for even talking to themselves, much less to others."

In striving for an integration of his personality and an adequate expression of his sense of the world, Kabnis is caught between violently antagonistic racial identities, victimized by a history of racial oppression and hatred, a world divided. As a person who physically and culturally embodies the transgression of that division, he is the signifier of "sin," taboo, that which cannot be spoken except in curses—and Kabnis curses profusely. The achievement of "Kabnis," its very language, derives from the sort of tension Kabnis feels—not merely the tension between black and white but, most important, the tension between "black/white" discourse and the dream of an alternative one, a new "American" discourse that would be completely divorced from the old. Toomer came to realize, however, that he would have to borrow terms from the "old" language of race even as he strived to destroy it. This realization is anticipated by the way that Kabnis's violent verbalizations betray the frustrations of a man who hates the very words he speaks. . . .

TOOMER TURNS HIS BACK ON HIS ANCESTRY

Many scholars have charged that Toomer, like Kabnis, finally accepted white dominance and its implications. This conclusion follows from the perception that he denied his African ancestry. But, as David Bradley has suggested, he could be charged more accurately with refusing to deny the rest of his ancestry. His growing frustration with the insistence that he be *either* "black" *or* "white" forced him to a tactic of denying association with any race except the "American" race. Thus, ironically, the demand that he accept a "black" identity drove him away from connection with African American culture, a fundamental source of his art.

Toomer once wrote, in reference to the period of his apprenticeship to writing, "I began feeling that I had in my hands the tools for my own creation"—the tools, we might say, to name himself with "golden words." This brief faith in the power of self-naming, however, was shattered by the reception of *Cane* and Toomer's growing awareness of the impossibility of making himself understood. In the context of the dominant racial discourse, the "American" race could have no name; in the vision which that discourse bespoke, no visible place. Its invisibility, after all, made possible the defining light and shade of the vision. Hence, [critic] Henry Louis Gates's revealing accusation: "To be a human being . . . Toomer felt that he had to efface his mask of blackness, the cultural or racial trace of difference, and embrace the utter invisibility of being an American." Such a statement precisely misses Toomer's point, in a predictable way. It is representative of a pervasive repression of Toomer's idea that, rather than erasing all racial "traces of difference," he envisioned a *new* difference as fundamental—as, indeed, the only (and the inevitable) route out of America's continuing racial nightmare. Toomer felt that his "race" was invisible to other Americans because they had yet to cross the divide in which "black" and "white" could be perceived as elements of the same spiritual, discursive, and social field, a field in which his ideas could only be considered mad, his "race" invisible.

AMERICAN ASSUMPTIONS ABOUT RACE

"New Negro" and not at the same time—North American in the specific conflicts that produce it and in its idiomatic language, its clash of "racial" forms—as we read it *Cane* can, however, make visible the nature of our assumptions about "race" and American identity. In its silences—in Kabnis's failure to find the words to name his soul—it reveals the significant silences of our own deeply racialized social text, the gaps and absences which critics, in turn, have failed to make speak. The rules and structures of our racial "archive"— shaped both for and in reaction against white hegemony, while leaving its foundational discursive violence intact— operate against any acknowledgment of sanity in Toomer's speech. There are certain things that we are ideologically forbidden to say. Toomer's struggle, like Kabnis's, was to break the silence as he brought his "fragments" to "fusion," as he liked to say, a struggle in which he did not, could not, publicly succeed. He became a "mystical irrationalist"; according to the prevailing view he "disappeared." [Critic] Terry Eagleton has well expressed the sort of conundrum Toomer found himself up against:

[T]he languages and devices a writer finds to hand are already saturated with certain ideological modes of perception, certain codified ways of interpreting reality; and the extent to which he can modify or remake those languages depends on more than personal genius. It depends on whether at that point in history, "ideology" is such that they must and can be changed.

By illuminating what, racially speaking, "cannot be said," Toomer's *Cane* . . . poses an ethical challenge. It dramatizes in its own thematic focus and form, enacts in its relation to the crisis of Toomer's literary career, and exemplifies in its interpretive history—its "racial" place in the "canon"—the suppression of the "invisible," "transcendental" signifier upon whose sacrifice our racial discourse ultimately depends. Through his "failure" (to create a language, to be called by his own name) and his subsequent "disappearance" from the literary scene, Toomer revealed the shared contradictions in "black" and "white" American racial ideologies, the violate and tabooed space of miscegenation that, like the black and white citizens who at least can agree to ostracize white Becky for her mulatto sons, we mutually repress and unwittingly sanctify to preserve our racial selves.

Religion, Love, and Social Conscience in Countee Cullen's Poetry

Nicholas Canaday Jr.

Drawing from his own upbringing as the adopted
son of a minister, Countee Cullen relied heavily
upon religious icons and motifs to explore themes of
salvation in relationship to the burdens of the black
experience. In this essay, written in the early 1970s,
critic Nicholas Canaday Jr. examines the scope of
Cullen's work, noting the young writer's progression
from themes of religion and love into poems that
express anger and protest over the discriminatory
treatment blacks have suffered in America. Canaday
also illustrates that Cullen's move toward socially
conscience themes was fueled in part by an era of
controversial court cases that alleged crimes and
denied innocent victims their rights because of their
skin color.

Countee Cullen's first volume of poems, *Color* (1925),
demonstrates convincingly that he is a poet of considerable
scope who handles a variety of ideas and techniques with
ease. The subsequent volumes—*Copper Sun* (1927), *The Ballad of the Brown Girl* (1927), *The Black Christ and Other Poems* (1929), and *The Medea and Some Poems* (1935)—although they do not present marked departures from the
themes he introduces in the first volume, do indeed contain
new variations and complexities within Cullen's major areas of concern. Here we shall demonstrate Cullen at his best,
without regard to chronology, in each of the major thematic
groups, noticing that the groups are by no means mutually

Excerpted from "Major Themes in the Poetry of Countee Cullen," by Nicholas Canaday Jr., *The Harlem Renaissance Remembered*, edited by Arna Bontemps (New York:
Dodd, Mead and Company, 1972). Copyright © 1972 by Nicholas Canaday Jr. Reprinted
with permission.

exclusive because the themes are interrelated. . . .

It should not surprise us that the adopted son of the Reverend Frederick Asbury Cullen of Harlem's Salem African Methodist Episcopal Church should have received from his father an abiding Christian view of the world, which is perhaps the most pervasive element in the younger Cullen's poetry. This faith is not without a countervailing tension of doubt. Many of Cullen's poems quite simply are about religious subjects: this fact in part explains why so many Negro preachers read Cullen's poems from their pulpits and why his poems remain popular as pieces for readings and recitations. Yet Cullen's religious background is also reflected by the frequency and variety of biblical allusion in his poetry, the use of religious imagery even in nonreligious contexts, and a marked tendency to cast poems in parable form. . . .

USE OF RELIGIOUS MOTIFS

Overt religious motifs are found in such poems as "Simon the Cyrenian Speaks," "Pagan Prayer," "The Shroud of Color," the companion pieces "For a Skeptic" and "For a Fatalist," "Judas Iscariot," and "Gods"—all from his first volume, *Color.* "Simon the Cyrenian Speaks" is a dramatic monologue delivered by a black follower of Christ, drafted to carry his cross, who accepts his calling when he understands his Master's dream transcends race, that he is not simply being asked to bear another burden as a black man. "Pagan Prayer" is a short poem, the meaning of which relates to the central tension of Heritage.

> Our Father, God; our Brother, Christ,
> Or are we bastard kin,

the poet asks prayerfully. He speaks of his "pagan mad" heart and prays that all "black sheep" be retrieved, a nice irony given both the obvious biblical values associated with straying sheep, as well as what the phrase "black sheep" usually means. "The Shroud of Color" is the poem that first gained Cullen important attention; it was published in the November 1924 issue of H.L. Mencken's *American Mercury.* It begins:

> "Lord, being dark," I said, "I cannot bear
> The further touch of earth, the scented air;
> Lord, being dark, forewilled to that despair
> My color shrouds me in, I am as dirt
> Beneath my brother's heel . . ."

And the answer seems to be:

> *"Dark child of sorrow, mine no less, what art*
> *Of mine can make thee see and play thy part?*
> *The key to all strange things is in thy heart."*

This poem, too, is a kind of parable, with its dialogue between the poet and the divine voice. The poet's resolve is to go on living, even in the shroud of color, living anxiously, to be sure, close to nature, in a kind of trembling but joyful hope.

In the epitaphs "For a Skeptic"—which points out that the skeptic may have more faith than he knows but in the wrong thing—and "For a Fatalist"—which holds that such a person has his ship wrecked even before he can hoist his sail—two irreligious postures are rejected. "Judas Iscariot" is a sentimental poem depicting Judas as having willingly played the destined role of betrayer, taking the "sorry part" out of great love and being thus forever scorned by unknowing people. Finally, "Gods" is an interesting short poem because it shows paganism again in conflict with Christianity. The poet says:

> I cannot hide from Him the gods
> That revel in my heart,
> Nor can I find an easy word
> To tell them to depart . . .

Just as "gods" is not capitalized—they are the idols of a pagan impulse—neither is "word" capitalized. But the allusion to the Word that dispels such gods seems unmistakable. Yet the poet says he cannot find "an easy word," and thus the tension remains. . . .

LOVE LYRICS

Traditional lyric poets traditionally deal with love and death, and Countee Cullen is no exception. This second category of thematic concern contains the largest group of his poems, including many love lyrics of one mood or another. Let an early example stand for his frequent verses in the *carpe diem* tradition. In "To a Brown Girl" Cullen says it this way:

> What if no puritanic strain
>   Confines him to the nice?
> He will not pass this way again,
>   Nor hunger for you twice.
>
> Since in the end consort together
>   Magdalen and Mary,
> Youth is the time for careless weather:
>   Later, lass, be wary.

The inconstancy of love is also a traditional theme Cullen treated many times. The poems "There Must Be Words" and "Nothing Endures" from the 1929 volume may serve as examples. In the first he writes of love departing, leaving no external sign of its former presence:

After a decent show of mourning I,
As once I ever was, shall be as free
To look on love with calm unfaltering eye,
And marvel that such fools as lovers be.

And from the second:

Nothing endures,
Not even love,
Though the warm heart purrs
Of the length thereof.

Though beauty wax,
Yet shall it wane;
Time lays a tax
On the subtlest brain.

Let the blood riot,
Give it its will;
It shall grow quiet,
It shall grow still.

Claims made for paganism in love lyrics have been traditional through many centuries of English poetry, but since Cullen writes out of the black experience, this strand has an added weight in his poems. We have already seen the opposing Christian/Pagan claims in his religious poetry. His advice in "To a Brown Boy" is:

Lad, never dam your body's itch
    When loveliness is seen.

And the word "dam" probably contains a deliberate ambiguity: neither condemn it nor attempt to obstruct its natural force. There is bliss, the poem continues, in "brown limbs,"

And lips know better how to kiss
    Than how to raise white hymns.

The imagery here, typical in Cullen's poems, opposes brown/sensuality/paganism to white/spirituality/Christianity. At the same time a cold sterility is also a connotation of the latter. Cullen does not honor an ascetic purity. . . .

THE THEME OF DEATH

One poem may stand as the best example of Cullen on death. His poem "The Wise" echoes his master, John Keats, "half in love with easeful death." In a quiet, contemplative mood appropriate to the title, Cullen presents in rhymed triplets the several reasons why death is to be desired, what in fact are the elements of wisdom. In the first place, knowledge is gained through the dark glass, literally, of the earth, knowledge of ultimate natural mysteries:

> Dead men are wisest, for they know
> How far the roots of flowers go,
> How long a seed must rot to grow.

This knowledge is perhaps not commanding in an emotional sense, but in the second stanza the senses are stilled and there is no feeling of joy or pain. This aspect of death is emotionally more satisfying to the weary:

> Dead men alone bear frost and rain
> On throbless heart and heatless brain,
> And feel no stir of joy or pain.

Thirdly, the soul is at rest because the raging of love and hate is quieted:

> Dead men alone are satiate;
> They sleep and dream and have no weight,
> To curb their rest, of love or hate.

Thus the dead are the wise, and indeed a good definition of wisdom for the living would include the elements of knowledge, detachment, and peace. The poem concludes with a neat paradox:

> Strange, men should flee their company,
> Or think me strange who long to be
> Wrapped in their cool immunity.

In the concluding phrase "cool immunity" we have a particularly felicitous expression—appropriate to the tone, insightful, suggestive.

POEMS OF BLACK EXPERIENCE

As we would expect of a lyric poet, Countee Cullen takes as his province the larger categories of religion, love, and death. Many of Cullen's poems, however, and here is added a new dimension of subject matter, are solely concerned with what he would call "color" or "race" and what we would call the black experience. Yet these divisions, as we have seen, are wholly arbitrary, for almost every poem already considered comes out of the black experience in one way or another. Many of them overtly refer to racial matters. Thus critics who assert that Cullen was not activist enough in orientation—

and some are even harsher—would seem to have a rather narrow view of what a poet ought to be doing. . . .

Of the poems that deal primarily with the black experience, it is appropriate to begin with two poems of initiation, both dramatic anecdotes presented in verse, one obviously based on an early experience in life and the other a later incident. The first is called "Incident." The subject matter of this poem is loss of innocence, and the impact of the poem depends partly on an incongruity between the subject matter and the form, as well as within the subject matter itself. Here is a smiling, friendly black boy eight years old—and to use the phrase "black boy" is to place it within context as part of a major motif in Afro-American literature—an innocent black boy who has an encounter with ugliness, evil.

> Once riding in old Baltimore,
>   Heart-filled, head-filled with glee,
> I saw a Baltimorean
>   Keep looking straight at me.

> Now I was eight and very small,
>   And he was no whit bigger,
> And so I smiled, but he poked out
>   His tongue, and called me, "Nigger."

There is, then, an incongruity between what a childhood experience ought to be and what it is. There is now a sad awareness in the last stanza; it was then shock.

> I saw the whole of Baltimore
>   From May until December;
> Of all the things that happened there
>   That's all that I remember.

What happened there wiped out all other memories; it is as though a portion of innocence were destroyed. The tension between innocence and experience is also reflected in the ambiguity between subject matter and verse form. It is a child's verse, highly regular in rhyme and meter, simple in diction. It could be a poem in "A Black Child's Garden of Verse." By way of comparison, hear one of Robert Louis Stevenson's poems from *his* collection. No doubt Cullen would have known Stevenson's poems, perhaps even this one called "Singing":

> Of speckled eggs the birdie sings
>   And nests among the trees;
> The sailor sings of ropes and things
>   In ships upon the seas.

> The children sing in far Japan,
>   The children sing in Spain;

> The organ with the organ man
>   Is singing in the rain.

Children sing in Baltimore, too, and, sadly, one thing they sing is "Nigger." Speckled eggs and birds and ropes and things and ships upon the seas—these should be the stuff of childhood. Cullen's "Incident" is all about finding a spider in the Rice Krispies. The sadness of the last stanza is not unwarranted.

Another poetic anecdote recounts an experience with a bitter, pipe-smoking black uncle, who says only, "White folks is white," and waits for the poet to understand and to feel the meaning of the statement. The poem "Uncle Jim" begins:

> "White folks is white," says Uncle Jim;
> "A platitude," I sneer;
> And then I tell him so is milk,
> And the froth upon his beer.
> His heart welled up with bitterness,
> He smokes his pungent pipe,
> And nods at me as if to say,
> "Young fool, you'll soon be ripe!"

At the end of the poem the poet is in the company of a white friend, who shares deeply his joys and sorrows and his interest in poetry, but still the poet's thoughts return to Uncle Jim. He wonders why. The unspoken implication is that there is an impassable gulf between the white and the black experience, however intimate the friendship. So the poem as initiation experience deals with separation as a fact of life, Cullen would say a sad fact of the present. Whether inevitable or forever is a question I think not answered in Cullen's poetry.

THREADS OF ANGER AND PROTEST

Anger and ominous warning is the theme of Cullen's "From the Dark Tower," a poem that he places first in his second volume of poetry, *Copper Sun*. Another sonnet of considerable accomplishment, its octave reads:

> We shall not always plant while others reap
> The golden increment of bursting fruit,
> Not always countenance, abject and mute,
> That lesser men should hold their brothers cheap;
> Not everlastingly while others sleep
> Shall we beguile their limbs with mellow flute,
> Not always bend to some more subtle brute;
> We were not made eternally to weep.

The poetic diction—"bursting fruit" and "mellow flute"— makes the poem seem removed from reality, but the last line above—sad, angry, prophetic—is a sweeping line of ringing militancy: "We were not made eternally to weep." Ominous warning is also the theme of "Mood," a poem that captures an angry mood in the black experience. It begins:

I think an impulse stronger than my mind
May some day grasp a knife, unloose a vial,
Or with a little leaden ball unbind
The cords that tie me to the rank and file.
My hands grow quarrelsome with bitterness,
And darkly bent upon the final fray;
Night with its stars upon a grave seems less
Indecent than the too complacent day.

What are these cords that keep him from violence, that restrain him and his mass of brothers? Who controls them? Are they good restraints on an impulse toward destructive savagery or are they chains? And the ambiguous "final fray" may mean Armageddon. But who will win, or will all be destroyed? Such questions are implicit in this heavily suggestive poem. . . .

The last poem in this last volume (not including, of course, the posthumously published *On These I Stand* of 1947) is perhaps the most militant protest poem that Cullen wrote. It is called "Scottsboro, Too, Is Worth Its Song," and it is dedicated to "American Poets." The clear but unspoken criticism in the poem is that the American poets who wrote eloquently about Sacco and Vanzetti[1] (including Cullen himself) failed to notice the Scottsboro incident.[2] It is appropriate that Cullen should choose to close his last volume of new poems with "Scottsboro." Cullen is the representative and symbolic figure of the Harlem Renaissance, and the Scottsboro tragedy of 1931 was the traumatic experience in the black community that ended this literary flowering. A few lines will reveal the tone of the poem:

I said:
Now will the poets sing,—
Their cries go thundering
Like blood and tears
Into the nation's ears,
Like lightning dart
Into the nation's heart.

And these were his reasons:

1. Two Italian immigrants, Nicola Sacco and Bartomeo Vanzetti were falsely accused of robbery and murder in 1927. They were convicted of the crime, most likely because both were anarchists.   2. In Scottsboro, Alabama, nine black youths were falsely accused of raping white women. They were convicted by an all-white jury in 1931.

Here in epitome
Is all disgrace
And epic wrong,
Like wine to brace
The minstrel heart, and blare it into song.

We know the nation was not called to account by its poets.
Here is Cullen's ironic conclusion:

Surely, I said,
Now will the poets sing.
  But they have raised no cry.
  I wonder why.

. . . Thus many of the aspects of the black experience are
reflected in Countee Cullen's poetry: awareness of a dehumanizing racism, uniqueness, and separatism, yearning for
freedom, anger, and militant protest. And there is one thing
more that adds to his scope. As the representative artist of
the Harlem Renaissance, he may well have written the best
poem about Harlem. It is called "Harlem Wine." It begins:

This is not water running here,
  These thick rebellious streams
That hurtle flesh and bone past fear
  Down alleyways of dreams.

The wine is a narcotic and at the same time a symbol of a
dark race. All this is said in the poem: Whatever is running
in Harlem is darker and more intoxicating, more vital than
white water. It is rebellious because Harlem is a place apart,
representing values other than those in white America. The
wine gives courage when there may be fear; it represents a
deep and dreamlike racial heritage. The primitivism of the
poem concludes with the joy of music and dance presented
in the imagery of lovemaking. All this is summarized in a
place symbolizing human communication, personal relations, identity—the place is Harlem.

Nigger Heaven and the Van Vechten Vogue

Hugh M. Gloster

Carl Van Vechten was one of the few white patrons of
the Harlem Renaissance who was viewed more as a
friend of the Negro artist rather than as a patron of
Negro art. Van Vechten traveled in African American
circles and considered most of his closest friends to
be those very individuals who achieved artistic
prominence in Harlem. Many of the black intelligentsia of the renaissance felt somewhat betrayed by
Van Vechten, however, when his novel, *Nigger
Heaven*, was published in 1926. White audiences
read the novel as an exposé of the Harlem nightlife
but many African Americans felt that it focused too
heavily on sex and debauchery, themes that catered
to the white interest in primitivism. In the following
essay, literary critic Hugh M. Gloster agrees that Van
Vechten, like others who capitalized on the fad of
primitivism, overglamorized the sex and the cabaret
lifestyle instead of offering a truer representation of
the African American community. But Gloster maintains that the images of blacks in these writings were
an improvement over the heinous stereotypes that
persisted through earlier periods of black history.

Perhaps the most popular novel of Negro life during the
1920's was Carl Van Vechten's *Nigger Heaven* (1926), a work
which not only dramatized the alleged animalism and exoticism of Harlem folk but also influenced the writings of Negro Renaissance authors. Appearing at the proper time,
when the Negro was making considerable headway as a
stellar performer in the entertainment world as well as
when white Americans were inordinately curious about so-
called picturesque and primitive facets of Harlem society,

Excerpted from "The Van Vechten Vogue," by Hugh M. Gloster, *Phylon*, December
1945. Copyright © 1945 by *Phylon*. Reprinted with permission.

Nigger Heaven enjoyed widespread popularity and became a sort of guidebook for visitors who flocked uptown seeking a re-creation of the African jungle in the heart of New York City. The songs and blues selections by Langston Hughes which Van Vechten incorporated in the novel not only augmented the appeal of the book but also drew general attention to the rising young *literati* of Manhattan's black ghetto.

As a framework for his presentation of the Harlem *milieu* Van Vechten provides a slender plot tracing the rather mediocre romance of Mary Love, a respectable librarian, and Byron Kasson, an unstable and extremely race-conscious young Philadelphian who comes to New York City to seek success as a writer. Everything goes moderately well with the couple until Lasca Sartoris, "a gorgeous brown Messalina of Seventh Avenue," completely bewitches the would-be author and then deserts him for Randolph Pettijohn, the Bolito King. Rendered insanely vengeful by being jilted, Byron impulsively fires two bullets into the body of Pettijohn, who has previously been fatally wounded by a pimp called the Scarlet Creeper, and thereafter helplessly surrenders to police.

EMPHASIZING THE CABARET LIFESTYLE

On the crowded canvas of *Nigger Heaven* Van Vechten presents many colorful aspects of Harlem life. He gives an account of a lavish week-end party at the Long Island estate of Adora Boniface, an ex-music hall diva who also maintains a luxurious residence on Striver's Row on West 139th Street. He essays to present *bourgeois* respectability in the life of Mary Love, who associates with young writers and other professional men, frequents dinner and bridge parties, attends plays and musical entertainments, reads the best books (including Gertrude Stein's *Three Lives*, which made a deeper impression than any of the others), and appreciates African sculpture. He describes the Charity Ball, a mammoth paid dance sponsored annually by a group of socially prominent colored women, and gives the opinions of Negroes concerning Harlem sightseers, passing, miscegenation, inter- and intra-racial color prejudice, and many other subjects.

But, with more gusto than he does anything else, Van Vechten paints Harlem cabaret life. He is particularly fascinated by the barbaric rhythms of Negro jazz, the tom-tom beat of the drum in the band, and the melting bodies of intoxicated dancers swaying to sensuous music. Contemplating the cabaret, Van Vechten surmises that Negroes are essentially primitive and atavistic. In the singing of spirituals and jazz, black folk are described as "recognizing, no doubt, in some dim, biological way, the beat of African rhythm.". . .

PRIMITIVE THEMES

Ever the painter of the exotic and fantastic, Van Vechten took particular delight in emphasizing—even in exaggerating and distorting—the primitive aspects of his *milieu.* To him the Harlem cabaret was a transplanted jungle, and Negroes were creatures of impulse and emotion, atavistically yearning for the animalistic exhibitions of Africa. This stress upon the Negro as a child of nature did at least three things: first, it increased the influx of white visitors to upper Manhattan; second, it created a furious controversy among Negro intellectuals; and, third, it made American publishers and readers eager for more works with a similar emphasis.

In the metropolitan dailies *Nigger Heaven* usually received favorable reviews—e.g., that of Carl Van Doren in "The New York Herald Tribune" (August 22, 1926), and that of Harry Hansen in "The New York World" (August 28, 1926)—which stimulated a wide reading of the novel and a hegira of white folk to Harlem. In "The Ebony Flute," a monthly column in "Opportunity," Gwendolyn Bennett records, during the same year, the power of *Nigger Heaven* to attract outsiders to Black Manhattan. Placed on the stands in August, the book was so popular by October, as Miss Bennett notes, that sightseers, visitors and other strangers were "said to be 'van vechtening' around." Intrigued by the portrayal of the Negro in the book, whites from downtown and elsewhere temporarily neglected Greenwich Village in order to explore Harlem and enjoy the Negro. During this time the Cotton Club became one of the most celebrated night clubs in the country.

CONTROVERSY AMONG BLACK INTELLECTUALS

While *Nigger Heaven* was generally received with favor by white critics and readers, it aroused a storm of controversy among Negro intellectuals. Reviews of commendation were given by Wallace Thurman in "The Messenger" (September, 1926); by Charles S. Johnson in a letter to Van Vechten published in "The Pittsburgh Courier" (September 4, 1926); by James Weldon Johnson in "Opportunity" (October, 1926);

and by George Schuyler in "The Pittsburgh Courier" (November 6, 1926). Unfavorable reactions were expressed by Hubert Harrison in "The Amsterdam News" (October 9, 1926); by Floyd Calvin in "The Pittsburgh Courier" (November 6, 1926); by Dewey R. Jones in "The Chicago Defender" (November 24, 1926); and by W.E.B. DuBois in "The Crisis" (December, 1926). Voicing nearly all of the dissenting reactions to the novel, DuBois argued that *Nigger Heaven* is "a blow in the face," "an affront to the hospitality of black folk and to the intelligence of white," "a caricature," "a mass of half-truths," and "an astonishing and wearisome hodge-podge of laboriously stated facts, quotations and expressions, illuminated here and there with something that comes near to being nothing but cheap melodrama." Reflecting the sentiments of Negroes who liked the novel, James Weldon Johnson insisted in his review, "Romance and Tragedy in Harlem," published in "Opportunity," that *Nigger Heaven* is "an absorbing story," "comprehends nearly every phase of life from dregs to the froth," and ranks as "the most revealing, significant and powerful novel based exclusively on Negro life yet written." Johnson held that the book "is all reality" and "does not stoop to burlesque or caricature." In his opinion, Van Vechten is "the first white novelist of note to undertake a portrayal of modern American Negro life under metropolitan conditions" and "the only white novelist who has not viewed the Negro as a type, who has not treated the race as a unit, either good or bad."

CAPITALIZING ON A VOGUE

The modern critic, viewing *Nigger Heaven* nineteen years after it was published, submits that the novel's proper evaluation is at a point somewhere between the appraisal of DuBois and that of Johnson. In stylizing the primitivism of the Negro and the jungle atmosphere of the Harlem cabaret, Van Vechten was doing no more than Langston Hughes had done a year earlier in *The Weary Blues* (1925.) In the jungle pose Langston Hughes wrote such poems as "Nude Young Dancer," "Dream Variation," "Our Land," "Lament for Dark People," "Afraid," "Poem for the Portrait of an African Boy after the Manner of Gauguin," and "Danse Africane." However, when a wealthy patron expressed dissatisfaction because he wrote "Advertisement for the Waldorf-Astoria," Hughes explained in *The Big Sea*:

She wanted me to be primitive and know and feel the intuitions of the primitive. But unfortunately, I did not feel the rhythms of the primitive surging through me, and so I could not live and write as though I did. I was only an American Negro—who had loved the surface of Africa and the rhythms of Africa—but I was not Africa. I was Chicago and Kansas City and Broadway and Harlem.

Van Vechten, who knows or should know that the Negro is no more primitive and atavistic than any other racial group in America, was merely a literary faddist capitalizing upon a current vogue and a popular demand. In an article, "The Negro in Art: How Shall He Be Portrayed," released in *The Crisis* shortly before the publication of *Nigger Heaven*, he expressed his interest in the literary possibilities of the wretchedness, immorality, and exoticism of Negro life:

> The squalor of Negro life, the vice of Negro life, offer a wealth of material to the artist. . . . The question is: Are Negro writers going to write about this exotic material while it is still fresh or will they continue to make a free gift of it to white authors who will exploit it until not a drop of vitality remains?

He probably did not deserve the vitriolic criticism of DuBois, for he frankly set out to exploit what he considered to be the exotic and animalistic elements in Harlem life. At the same time, however, he did not merit the high praise of Johnson, who called *Nigger Heaven* a mosaic of Harlem and the first work by a white novelist in which the Negro is considered as an individual rather than as a type. There were many significant phases of Harlem life which Van Vechten did not apparently know and therefore could not describe; and surely Gertrude Stein, T.S. Stribling, Waldo Frank, DuBose Heyward, and several other white predecessors of Van Vechten in the use of Negro subject-matter made departures from the stereotyped presentation of colored characters.

THE IMPACT OF *NIGGER HEAVEN*

All these considerations notwithstanding, the Van Vechten Vogue exerted profound influence upon literature by and about American Negroes. In 1927 Countee Cullen produced *Copper Sun*, a volume of poetry which shows the imprint of the Dark Continent in its title. Partly in awareness of "the traditional jazz connotations," James Weldon Johnson called his versified sermons *God's Trombones* (1927). Wallace Thurman collaborated with William Jordon Rapp in 1929 to produce *Harlem*, a play dealing with life in the black

ghetto. But the emphasis upon jazz, sex, atavism, and primitivism is much more pronounced in novels and short stories than in poetry and drama. Fictional works that stress
some or all of these elements are Claude McKay's *Home to
Harlem* (1928), *Banjo* (1929), and six narratives in *Gingertown* (1932); Wallace Thurman's *The Blacker the Berry*
(1929) and *Infants of the Spring* (1932); and Arna Bontemps's
God Sends Sunday (1931). All of these works, except *Banjo*
and *God Sends Sunday*, are laid chiefly in New York City; but
even in these two variant novels there is the same preoccupation with sensual pleasures and instinctive living. Like
Nigger Heaven, the Harlem-centered works ordinarily depict
cabaret scenes, interracial social gatherings, and Negro
literati. The low-life characters of these books are primarily
concerned with the pleasures of the hour—food, intoxicants,
and sex. They unapologetically follow their natural impulses
and have no such moral codes as those of the respectable
Philadelphia *bourgeoisie* delineated by Jessie Fauset. Moreover, unlike the heroes of the propaganda novels, they do not
undertake to effect racial reforms.

Being primarily a fad, the Van Vechten Vogue was doomed
to fall before the first violent shock or the next new rage. The
inevitable reaction came in the form of the Wall Street *deba-
cle* of 1929 which, as Langston Hughes wittily remarks, "sent
Negroes, white folks and all rolling down the hill toward the
Works Progress Administration."

The fatal mistake of the Van Vechten school was to make
a fetish of sex and the cabaret rather than to give a faithful,
realistic presentation and interpretation of Harlem life. In
spite of this error, however, the Van Vechtenites helped to
break away from the taboos and stereotypes of earlier years,
to make self-revelation and self-criticism more important
considerations in fiction by Negroes, and to demonstrate to
publishers and readers that Negro authors have an important contribution to make to the nation's cultural life.

The Theme of Harlem in Langston Hughes's Poetry

Arthur P. Davis

Langston Hughes is one of the most notable poets of the Harlem Renaissance. Although he had traveled the world and lived in Paris as an American expatriate, Harlem remained a constant and major theme within his poems and other writings. In this essay written in the early 1950s, Arthur P. Davis, a literary scholar and critic, explores the evolution of Harlem as it is traced throughout Hughes's work. Harlem begins as an intellectual enclave and exotic destination for white thrill seekers, but transforms into a somber, more serious community as Hughes traces the effect of the depression era on the neighborhood and its residents. The transition reveals the underlying instability of the community when white patronage evaporates, leaving the residents of Harlem with no false pretenses about America as an all-inclusive society.

In a very real sense, Langston Hughes is the poet-laureate of Harlem. From his first publication down to his latest, Mr. Hughes has been concerned with the black metropolis. Returning to the theme again and again, he has written about Harlem oftener and more fully than any other poet. As Hughes has written about himself:

> I live in the heart of Harlem. I have also lived in the heart of Paris, Madrid, Shanghai, and Mexico City. The people of Harlem seem not very different from others, except in language. I love the color of their language: and, being a Harlemite myself, their problems and interests are my problems and interests.

Knowing how deeply Langston Hughes loves Harlem and how intimately he understands the citizens of that community, I have long felt that a study of the Harlem theme in

Hughes' poetry would serve a twofold purpose: it would give us insight into the growth and maturing of Mr. Hughes as a social poet; it would also serve as an index to the changing attitude of the Negro during the last quarter of a century.

When Mr. Hughes' first publication, *The Weary Blues* (1926), appeared, the New Negro Movement was in full swing; and Harlem, as the intellectual center of the movement, had become the Mecca of all aspiring young Negro writers and artists. This so-called Renaissance not only encouraged and inspired the black creative artist, but it served also to focus as never before the attention of America upon the Negro artist and scholar. As a result of this new interest, Harlem became a gathering place for downtown intellectuals and Bohemians—many of them honestly seeking a knowledge of Negro art and culture, others merely looking for exotic thrills in the black community. Naturally, the latter group was much the larger of the two; and Harlem, capitalizing on this new demand for "primitive" thrills, opened a series of spectacular cabarets. For a period of about ten years, the most obvious and the most sensational aspect of the New Negro Movement for downtown New York was the night life of Harlem. The 1925 Renaissance, of course, was not just a cabaret boom, and it would be decidedly unfair to give that impression. But the Harlem cabaret life of the period was definitely an important by-product of the new interest in the Negro created by the movement, and this life strongly influenced the early poetry of Langston Hughes.

HARLEM AS "JAZZONIA"

Coming to Harlem, as he did, a twenty-two-year-old adventurer who had knocked around the world as sailor and beachcomber, it was only natural that Hughes should be attracted to the most exotic part of that city—its night life. The Harlem of *The Weary Blues* became therefore for him "Jazzonia," a new world of escape and release, an exciting never-never land in which "sleek black boys" blew their hearts out on silver trumpets in a "whirling cabaret." It was a place where the bold eyes of white girls called to black men, and "dark brown girls" were found "in blond men's arms." It was a city where "shameless gals" strutted and wiggled, and the "night dark girl of the swaying hips" danced beneath a papier-maché jungle moon. The most important inhabitants of this magic city are a "Nude Young Dancer," "Midnight

Nan at Leroy's," a "Young Singer" of *chansons vulgaires*, and a "Black Dancer in the Little Savoy."

This cabaret Harlem, this Jazzonia is a joyous city, but the joyousness is not unmixed; it has a certain strident and hectic quality, and there are overtones of weariness and despair. "The long-headed jazzers" and whirling dancing girls are desperately trying to find some new delight, and some new escape. They seem obsessed with the idea of seizing the present moment as though afraid of the future: "Tomorrow . . . is darkness / Joy today!" "The rhythm of life / Is a jazz rhythm" for them, but it brings only "The broken heart of love / The weary, weary heart of pain." It is this weariness and this intensity that one hears above the laughter and even above the blare of the jazz bands.

There is no daytime in Jazzonia, no getting up and going to work. It is wholly a sundown city, illuminated by soft lights, spotlights, jewel-eyed sparklers, and synthetic stars in the scenery. Daylight is the one great enemy here, and when "the new dawn / Wan and pale / Descends like a white mist," it brings only an "aching emptiness," and out of this emptiness there often comes in the clear cool light of morning the disturbing thought that the jazz band may not be an escape, it may not be gay after all:

> Does a jazz-band ever sob?
> They say a jazz-band's gay . . .
> One said she heard the jazz-band sob
> When the little dawn was gray.

THEMES OF DISILLUSIONMENT

In this respect, the figure of the black piano player in the title poem is highly symbolic. Trying beneath "the pale dull pallor of an old gas light" to rid his soul of the blues that bedeviled it, he played all night, but when the dawn approached:

> The singer stopped playing and went to bed
> While the Weary Blues echoed through his head.
> He slept like a rock or a man that's dead.

It is hard to fool oneself in the honest light of dawn, but sleep, like dancing and singing and wild hilarity, is another means of escape. Unfortunately, it too is only a temporary evasion. One has to wake up sometime and face the harsh reality of daylight and everyday living.

And in the final pages of *The Weary Blues*, the poet begins to sense this fact; he realizes that a "jazz-tuned" way of life is not the answer to the Negro's search for escape. The last poem on the Harlem theme in this work has the suggestive title "Disillusionment" and the even more suggestive lines:

> I would be simple again,
> Simple and clean . . .
> Nor ever know,
> Dark Harlem,
> The wild laughter
> Of your mirth . . .
> Be kind to me,
> Oh, great dark city.
> Let me forget.
> I will not come
> To you again.

Evidently Hughes did want to forget, at least temporarily, the dark city, for there is no mention of Harlem in his next work, *Fine Clothes to the Jew*, published the following year. Although several of the other themes treated in the first volume are continued in this the second, it is the only major production in which the name Harlem does not appear.

But returning to *The Weary Blues*—it is the eternal emptiness of the Harlem depicted in this work which depresses. In this volume, the poet has been influenced too strongly by certain superficial elements of the New Negro Movement. Like too many of his contemporaries, he followed the current vogue, and looking at Harlem through the "arty" spectacles of New Negro exoticism, he failed to see the everyday life about him. As charming and as fascinating as many of these poems undoubtedly are, they give a picture which is essentially false because it is one-dimensional and incomplete. In the works to follow, we shall see Mr. Hughes filling out that picture, giving it three-dimensional life and being.

HARDSHIPS OF THE DEPRESSION ERA

The picture of Harlem presented in *Shakespeare in Harlem* (1942) has very little in common with that found in *The Weary Blues*. By 1942 the black metropolis was a disillusioned city. The Depression of 1929, having struck the ghetto harder than any other section of New York, showed Harlem just how basically "marginal" and precarious its economic foundations were. Embittered by this knowledge, the black community had struck back blindly at things in general in the 1935 riot. The riot brought an end to the New Negro era;

the Cotton Club, the most lavish of the uptown cabarets, closed its doors and moved to Broadway; and the black city settled down to the drab existence of WPA and relief living.

In the two groups of poems labeled "Death in Harlem" and "Lenox Avenue," Hughes has given us a few glimpses of this new Harlem. There are no bright colors in the scene, only the sombre and realistic shades appropriate to the depiction of a community that has somehow lost its grip on things. The inhabitants of this new Harlem impress one as a beaten people. A man loses his job because, "awake all night with loving," he cannot get to work on time. When he is discharged, his only comment is "So I went on back to bed . . ." and to the "sweetest dreams" ("Fired"). In another poem, a man and his wife wrangle over the family's last dime which he had thrown away gambling ("Early Evening Quarrel"). Harlem love has lost its former joyous abandon, and the playboy of the cabaret era has become a calculating pimp who wants to "share your bed / And your money too" ("50-50"). In fact all of the lovers in this section—men and women alike—are an aggrieved lot, whining perpetually about being "done wrong." Even the night spots have lost their jungle magic, and like Dixie's joint have become earthy and sordid places: "Dixie makes his money on two-bit gin;" he also "rents rooms at a buck a break." White folks still come to Dixie's seeking a thrill, but they find it unexpectedly in the cold-blooded shooting of Bessie by Arabella Johnson, in a fight over Texas Kid. As Arabella goes to jail and Bessie is taken to the morgue, Texas Kid, the cause of this tragedy, callously "picked up another woman and / Went to bed" ("Death in Harlem"). All of the fun, all of the illusion have gone from this new and brutal night life world; and as a fitting symbol of the change which has come about, we find a little cabaret girl dying forlornly as a ward of the city ("Cabaret Girl Dies on Welfare Island").

THEMES OF SELF-PITY

There is seemingly only one bright spot in this new Harlem—the spectrum-colored beauty of the girls on Sugar Hill ("Harlem Sweeties"); but this is only a momentary lightening of the mood. The prevailing tone is one of depression and futility:

Down on the Harlem River
Two A.M.

Midnight
By yourself!
Lawd, I wish I could die—
But who would miss me if I left?

We see here the spectacle of a city feeling sorry for itself, the most dismal and depressing of all spectacles. Hughes has given us a whining Harlem. It is not yet the belligerent Harlem of the 1943 riot, but it is a city acquiring the mood from which this riot will inevitably spring.

The Harlem poems in *Fields of Wonder* (1947) are grouped under the title "Stars Over Harlem," but they do not speak out as clearly and as definitely as former pieces on the theme have done. The mood, however, continues in the sombre vein of *Shakespeare in Harlem*, and the idea of escape is stated or implied in each of the poems. In the first of the group, "Trumpet Player: 52nd Street," we find a curious shift in the African imagery used. Practically all former pieces having an African background tended to stress either the white-mooned loveliness of jungle nights or the pulse-stirring rhythm of the tom-tom. But from the weary eyes of the 52nd Street musician there blazes forth only "the smoldering memory of slave ships." In this new Harlem even the jazz players are infected with the sectional melancholy, and this performer finds only a vague release and escape in the golden tones he creates.

In "Harlem Dance Hall" there is again an interesting use of the escape motif. The poet describes the hall as having no dignity at all until the band began to play and then: "Suddenly the earth was there, / And flowers, / Trees, / And air." In short, this new dignity was achieved by an imaginative escape from the close and unnatural life of the dance hall (and of Harlem) into the freedom and wholesomeness of nature and normal living.

Although it is rather cryptic, there is also the suggestion of escape in "Stars," the last of these poems to be considered here:

O, sweep of stars over Harlem streets . . .
Reach up your hand, dark boy, and take a star.

DESIRE FOR EQUALITY

One Way Ticket (1949) and *Montage of a Dream Deferred* (1951), especially the latter work, bring to a full cycle the turning away from the Harlem of *The Weary Blues*. The Harlem de-

picted in these two works has come through World War II, but
has discovered that a global victory for democracy does not
necessarily have too much pertinence at home. Although the
Harlem of the 1949–51 period has far more opportunity than
the 1926 Harlem ever dreamed of, it is still not free; and the
modern city having caught the vision of total freedom and total integration will not be satisfied with anything less than the
ideal. It is therefore a critical, a demanding, a sensitive, and
utterly cynical city.

In *One Way Ticket*, for example, Harlem remembers "the
old lies," "the old kicks in the back," the jobs it never could
have and still cannot get because of color:

So we stand here
On the edge of hell
In Harlem
And look out on the world
And wonder
What we're gonna do
In the face of
What we remember.

But even though Harlem is the "edge of hell," it still can be
a refuge for the black servant who works downtown all day
bowing and scraping to white folks ("Negro Servant"). Dark
Harlem becomes for him a "sweet relief from faces that are
white." The earlier Harlem was a place to be shared with
fun-seeking whites from below 125th Street; the new city is
a sanctuary from them.

So deep is the unrest in this 1949–51 Harlem it may experience strangely conflicting emotions. Like aliens longing
sentimentally for the "old country," it may feel momentarily
a nostalgia for the South, even though it has bought a one
way ticket from that region. In "Juice-Joint: Northern City,"
we find sad-faced boys who have forgotten how to laugh:

But suddenly a guitar playing lad
Whose languid lean brings back the sunny South
Strikes up a tune all gay and bright and glad
To keep the gall from biting in his mouth,
   Then drowsy as the rain
   Soft sad black feet
   Dance in this juice joint
   On the city street.

The deepest tragedy of a disillusioned city is the cruelty it
inflicts on its own unfortunates, and this bitter Harlem
wastes no pity on a poor lost brother who was not "hep":

Harlem
Sent him home
In a long box—
Too dead
To know why:
The licker
Was lye.

The longest and most revealing Harlem poem in *One Way Ticket* is the thumping "Ballad of Margie Polite," the Negro girl who "cussed" a cop in the lobby of the Braddock Hotel and caused a riot when a Negro soldier taking her part was shot in the back by a white cop. In these thirteen short stanzas, Langston Hughes has distilled, as it were, all of the trigger-sensitiveness to injustice—real or imagined; all of the pent-up anti-white bitterness; and all of the sick-and-tired-of-being-kicked-around feelings which characterize the masses of present-day Harlem. It is indeed a provocative analysis of the frictions and the tensions in the black ghetto, this narrative of Margie Polite, who

Kept the Mayor
And Walter White
And everybody
Up all night!

"A DREAM DEFERRED"

In *Montage of a Dream Deferred*, Mr. Hughes' latest volume of poems, the Harlem theme receives its fullest and most comprehensive statement. Devoting the whole volume to the subject, he has touched on many aspects of the city unnoticed before. His understanding is now deep and sure, his handling of the theme defter and more mature than in any of the previous works. In this volume, the poet makes effective use of a technique with which he has been experimenting since 1926—a technique he explains in a brief prefatory note:

In terms of current Afro-American popular music . . . this poem on contemporary Harlem, like be-bop, is marked by conflicting changes, sudden nuances, sharp and impudent interjections, broken rhythms, and passages sometimes in the manner of the jam session, sometimes the popular song, punctuated by the riffs, runs, breaks, and disctortions [*sic*] of the music of a community in transition.

According to this scheme, we are to consider the whole book of ninety-odd pieces as really one long poem, marked by the conflicting changes, broken rhythms, and sudden interjections characteristic of a jam session. This "jam session" technique is highly effective because, tying together as it does fragmentary and otherwise unrelated segments in the work, it allows the poet, without being monotonous, to return again and again to his overall-theme, that of Harlem's frustration. Like the deep and persistent rolling of a boogie bass—now loud and raucous, now soft and pathetic—this theme of Harlem's dream deferred marches relentlessly throughout the poem. Hughes knows that Harlem is neither a gay nor healthy but basically a tragic and frustrated city, and he beats that message home. Because of the fugue-like structure of the poem, it is impossible for the reader to miss the theme or to forget it.

A HARLEM OF UNREST

This 1951 Harlem is a full and many-sided community. Here one finds the pathos of night funerals and fraternal parades: "A chance to let / the whole world see / old black me!"; or the grim realism of slum-dwellers who like war because it means prosperity; or the humor of a wife playing via a dream book the number suggested by her husband's dying words. This is the Harlem of black celebrities and their white girl admirers, the Harlem of vice squad detectives "spotting fairies" in night spots, the Harlem of bitter anti-Semitism, and the Harlem of churches and street corner orators, of college formals at the Renaissance Casino and of Negro students writing themes at CCNY. It is now definitely a class-conscious Harlem, a community of dicties and nobodies; and the Cadillac-riding professional dicties feel that they are let down by the nobodies who "talk too loud / cuss too loud / and look too black." It is a Harlem of some gaiety and of much sardonic laughter; but above all else, it is Harlem of a dream long deferred; and a people's deferred dream can "fester like a sore" or "sag like a heavy load."

Whatever else it may or may not believe, this Harlem has no illusion about the all-inclusiveness of American democracy. Even the children know that there is still a Jim Crow coach on the Freedom Train.

> What don't bug
> them white kids
> sure bugs me;
> We knows everybody
> ain't free.

Perhaps the dominant over-all impression that one gets from *Montage of a Dream Deferred* is that of a vague unrest. Tense and moody, the inhabitants of this 1951 Harlem seem to be seeking feverishly and forlornly for some simple yet apparently unattainable satisfaction in life: "one more bottle of gin"; "my furniture paid for"; "I always did want to study French"; "that white enamel stove"; "a wife who will work with me and not against me." The book begins and ends on this note of dissatisfaction and unrest. There is "a certain amount of nothing in a dream deferred."

These then are the scenes that make up the Harlem of Langston Hughes' poetry. The picture, one must remember, is that of a poet and not a sociologist; it naturally lacks the logic and the statistical accuracy of a scientific study, but in its way the picture is just as revealing and truthful as an academic study. As one looks at this series of Harlems he is impressed by the growing sense of frustration which characterizes each of them. Whether it is in the dream fantasy world of *The Weary Blues* or in the realistic city of *Montage of a Dream Deferred*, one sees a people searching—and searching in vain—for a way to make Harlem a part of the American dream. And one must bear in mind that with Langston Hughes Harlem is both place and symbol. When he depicts the hopes, the aspirations, the frustrations, and the deep-seated discontent of the New York ghetto, he is expressing the feelings of Negroes in black ghettos throughout America.

CHAPTER 4

Challenging Racism Through Literature

Harlem
Renaissance

White Patronage in the Harlem Renaissance

Bruce Kellner

Literary scholars do not dispute that white patronage played a major role in the success of the Harlem Renaissance as a legitimate movement for art, literature, drama, and music. What is not commonly discussed is the extent to which white financial control influenced the topics and themes of African American writers during this period. This is not to suggest that positive financial contributions did not aid the movement during this period, as the influence of financiers and patrons such as Carl Van Vechten and Albert C. Barnes cannot be ignored. Writing in the 1970s, literary critic and scholar Bruce Kellner suggests in the following essay that white patronage, no matter how well intentioned, often influenced the direction of artistic development through financial dependency. Kellner examines four major patrons from white society, their relationships with the literati of Harlem, and the impact of each on the creative development of the Harlem literary movement.

Despite their good intentions, white intellectuals and philanthropists bestowed mixed blessings in support of black artists and writers during the Harlem Renaissance. Their involvement contributed indirectly to the Black Arts Movement of the 1960s, yet the cost to the 1920s is undeniable. The black writer both thrived and suffered, torn between well-meant encouragement from the white race to preserve his racial identity (usually described as "primitivism") and a misguided encouragement from his own race to emulate the white one. Madame C.J. Walker's products, designed to straighten hair, and surely those of her competitors, designed to lighten skin, as well as the regular practice of black come-

Excerpted from "Refined Racism: White Patronage in the Harlem Renaissance," by Bruce Kellner, *The Harlem Renaissance Re-examined: A Revised and Expanded Edition*, edited by Victor A. Kramer and Robert A. Russ (Troy, NY: The Whitston Publishing Company, 1997). Copyright © 1974 by Bruce Kellner. Reprinted with permission.

dians wearing blackface makeup, are extreme examples at opposite ends of this appalling scale. Nevertheless, at the time of the Harlem Renaissance, that "renaissance" would never have progressed beyond Harlem without the intervention and support of white patrons. Inevitably, such support manifested itself in action which in retrospect seems patronizing, but to deny its positive aspects is intellectually indefensible. White patronage, for good as well as ill, was merely an unavoidable element in getting from the past to the present, and the roles of people like Albert C. Barnes, for example, Charlotte Mason, all the Spingarns—Joel and Amy and Arthur—and Carl Van Vechten, make a strong supporting cast. Some were bad actors; some were better.

Alphabetical order is a reasonable approach to such a list; coincidentally, it is an order leading from the weakest to the strongest involvement with the Harlem Renaissance, although quantity and quality are rarely equal.

ALBERT C. BARNES AND AFRICAN ART

Albert C. Barnes . . . might begin either list. This brash and opinionated Philadelphia millionaire began to collect impressionist and post-impressionist art around 1907, and fifteen years later he founded the Barnes Foundation in Merion, Pennsylvania, with what was then the most important collection of work by Henri Matisse in America, along with substantial representations of Renoir, Dégas, Picasso, Cézanne, and dozens of other celebrated painters. During the years Barnes was amassing these holdings, he rescued African art from ethnology, "stripping [art] of the emotional bunk," he declared, "[with] which the long-haired phonies and that fading class of egoists, the art patrons, have encumbered it." He extolled the aesthetics of African art, even though he could define it only in abstract terms, unable to get far beyond vague references to color and line and space. But he saw himself with the "emotional intensity of a moral reformer. . . . as one of the few true friends of black Americans, . . . beleaguered by misinformed and even racist others," as historian Mark Helbling put it. In 1923, when Barnes was trying to write an essay called "Contribution to the Study of Negro Art in America," he called on the influential black educator Alain Locke for assistance. Locke, in turn, sensing possibilities for financial as well as emotional support for young black artists, encouraged a friendship by introducing Barnes to several figures who would shortly become active in the Harlem Renaissance, among them Walter White, already a powerful gadfly in the NAACP [National Association for the Advancement of Colored People]. White himself was trying to do an article about black art in America just then and sought help from Barnes; but White had cited several of those "long-haired phonies" as his authorities, and not surprisingly Barnes damned it. Then, when white editor H.L. Mencken turned down Barnes's article to consider White's for publication in *The American Mercury*, the "terrible tempered Barnes" began to court the Urban League's Charles S. Johnson, hoping that an issue of the organization's magazine *Opportunity* might be devoted to African art, featuring his own article, of course, and offering his Foundation as bait since it exhibited black and classical Greek and Egyptian sculpture side by side. Like Locke, Johnson welcomed Barnes's knowledge, his own decorum able to hold in check his reactions to the paranoid outbursts that emanated regularly from Merion, Pennsylvania. *Opportunity* did run a special issue on African art, with Barnes's essay, but his impact was not felt fully until the following year when the white periodical *Survey Graphic* gave over its March 1925 issue to "The New Negro." That title was used for Locke's impressive anthology eight months later, with Barnes's article expanded, and reproductions of various works of African art in the Barnes Foundation.

Albert C. Barnes was an important voice in attempting to give to both races a sense of what negligence had lost, but he tried to focus the reconciliation of a primitive African art and a new cultural spirit among the emerging black intellectuals of the Harlem Renaissance, and Alain Locke was dissatisfied with his questionable analysis. . . . Of the white American, Barnes wrote in *The New Negro*: "Many centuries of civilization have attenuated his original gifts and have made his mind dominate his spirit. He has wandered too far from the elementary human needs and their easy means of natural satisfaction. The deep and satisfying harmony which the soul requires no longer arises from the incidents of daily life." The imagination of the black American, on the other hand, he contended, had been intensified by the existence of racism. The "daily habit of thought, speech, and movements of Afro-Americans," he continued, "are flavored with the picturesque, the rhythmic, the euphonious." As for African art, Barnes was only able to say that the "renascence of Negro art" was as "characteristically Negro as are the primitive African sculptures." What that "characteristic" was, however, Barnes could never make clear, so it is not surprising that Alain Locke wrote an essay of his own on the subject for *The New Negro*, even though his argument was similar—that African art was at the root of Afro-American artistic expression. . . .

By 1925, Albert C. Barnes's emphasis on form and abstract content in African art and his innocent physical descriptions of what he had squirrelled away in Merion, Pennsylvania, do not really come to terms with the influence of primitivism at all. His concern with the cultural identity of black Americans, however, the African collection in the Barnes Foundation, and certainly his money, speak to that cultural awakening during the twenties.

CHARLOTTE MASON'S PURSE STRINGS

Money seems to be the only contribution made to the movement by Mrs. Rufus Osgood Mason, born Charlotte Louise Vandevere Quick, and called "godmother" by her protégés when she could get her way. She got it most of the time, because the purse strings she controlled were like tentacles. They gave rein to young black writers; they could strangle. As Agatha Cramp in Rudolph Fisher's *The Walls of Jericho*, as Dora Ellsworth in Langston Hughes's *The Ways of White Folks*, and, indeed, as Godmother in Zora Neale Hurston's *Dust Tracks on a Road*, Charlotte Mason has been immortalized, but with marked ambivalence.

Widowed at fifty-one when her physician husband died at seventy-three, Mrs. Mason first used her vast wealth in some preliminary anthropological studies of American Indians, even making some field trips at the turn of the century. She was interested as well in psychology and psychic phenomena, through her husband's influence, but by the twenties her interests had shifted to the primitive and therefore innocent elements (or so she judged them) in Afro-American arts and letters.

From her regal penthouse on Park Avenue, surrounded by Indian and African artifacts, minor though respectable European paintings, eighteenth-century French furniture, a staff of servants, and a retinue of white toadies, this old dowager ruled over a stable of young Afro-American artists and writers. At one time or another during the Harlem Renaissance, she considered as her personal property both Hughes and Hurston, as well as Aaron Douglas, Richmond Barthé, Hall Johnson, Claude McKay, Louise Thompson, and especially Alain Locke. None of them was permitted to divulge her identity as the source of their good fortune, even though one or another of them served as escort on several occasions. Langston Hughes remembered her white chauffeur driving him home to Harlem after these outings to the theater, and Louise Thompson remembered similar discomfort. When Godmother wished to communicate with her godchildren by mail, she employed the services—without pay presumably— of white sometime poet Katherine Garrison Chapin and her sister, sometime sculptor Cornelia, members of an artistic circle that included muralist George Biddle and his wife Helene Sardeau. To young and inexperienced black writers, the power of that white world, not to speak of its glamour, must have been somewhat intimidating, but they were privy to it so long as they fulfilled Charlotte Mason's expectations. They were to live in Harlem; they were to emphasize in their work what she identified as folk culture or primitivism, and they were to eschew subjects she judged as didactic or smacking of social reform. Plenty of those letters the Chapin sisters were obliged to write for her to Alain Locke, after all, expressed her open hostility toward organizations designed to improve relations between the races.

She paid Langston Hughes's living expenses while he was writing his first novel, *Not Without Laughter.* She underwrote the single performance on Broadway of Zora Neale Hurston's musical drama *The Great Day.* She picked up the monthly rental for Richmond Barthé's Greenwich Village studio so he could devote all his time to sculpture. She financed research trips, college tuition, rehearsal time in concert halls; she doled out pocket money for shoes, winter coats, bus fares; and she called each of her protégés "my child." She invested today's equivalent of about half a million dollars in young black artists and writers, but she broke off the alliances when her charges proved disloyal by abandoning what she considered the purity in their work, its "primitivism." Because she believed in "primitivism" with cult fervor and disapproved of social protest, the breaks were frequent and the value of the support, as Nathan Irvin Huggins suggested, was questionable: "Whatever other burdens Negro artists carried, this arrangement stigmatized Negro poetry and prose of the 1920s as being an artistic effort that was trying to be like something other than itself."

Langston Hughes was still a Lincoln University student when Alain Locke took him to Mrs. Mason's apartment. As was her wont, she sat on a dais at one end of the drawing room *in* rather than *on* a chair best described as a throne, and before Hughes left she slipped him a fifty dollar bill. To Zora Neale Hurston, Mrs. Mason delivered a monthly $200 stipend for two years. At today's rate of exchange that pushes $30,000. Both rewarded her in their autobiographies: Hurston claimed that she and her godmother were mystically tied together, pagans spiritually joined; Hughes wrote in awe of her power that he didn't "know why or how she still found time" for him, since she moved in circles far removed from his own. Both broke with her when their work was less than what she considered "beautiful," which is to say "primitive." By that time, however, the stock market had fallen, and Harlem's plight replaced its popularity. Hughes's poems began to reflect a world in which Mrs. Mason had no interest, and he asked to be released, to remain a friend but without the onus of financial obligation. In turn, in venom apparently, she berated his talent and his character. . . .

THE SELFLESS SPINGARN BROTHERS

The most selfless of these white philanthropists were surely the Spingarn brothers, Arthur and Joel. They devoted their lives to racial equality as the leading twentieth-century abolitionists and constant supporters of the National Association for the Advancement of Colored People and its interests, motivated by the indifference of the white race, the despair of the black race, and the driving need they felt for integration. Both were involved in the founding of the NAACP, and as early as 1914 both were touring at their own expense to picket in the South against Jim Crow laws. Arthur was the NAACP's lawyer from its beginnings, its vice-president from 1911, and its president from 1940 until his retirement in 1966, as well as its unpaid legal counsel until his death in 1971. His first of several legal successes for the race came in 1927, when the Supreme Court upheld his challenge to the all-white Democratic primary election in Texas, and that one was succeeded by many others. At the beginning of his career, Arthur Spingarn's law practice suffered because of his racial sympathies, but he believed in later years that his racial sympathies actually increased it. Like his brother, he believed unquestioningly in the theory of the "talented tenth," sharing with W.E.B. Du Bois and many others the idea that within any group there would be ten percent capable of extraordinary achievement, gifted by the gods or by circumstances to speak for the rest. If white America could be awakened to that "talented tenth" in black America, they reasoned, segregation would diminish, conditions would improve, and in time prejudice would disappear. Hindsight tells us that the theory was too firmly grounded in idealism ever to survive the dream. The advocates of art as well as its practitioners do not, alas, populate the "untalented ninetieth" in either race.

Arthur Spingarn's brother Joel, three years his elder, began his career as a professor of comparative literature at Columbia University with a formidable reputation as a scholar—he was an authority on the Italian philosopher and art critic Benedetto Croce—but that lasted less than a decade. A colleague had been dismissed because of a breach-of-promise suit against him; when Joel Spingarn rose in defense of academics being allowed their private lives, he was fired too, although he seems not to have mourned long. Twenty-five years later he celebrated the anniversary with a cocktail party for his friends, many of them, perhaps most, Afro-Americans.

Long before he left Columbia, Joel Spingarn had been deeply involved with the race. Already, he had dismissed politics, failing in a bid for a congressional seat in 1908 and resigning from the Republican party in 1912 because it had no black delegates. By that time, from his family home, Troutbeck, New York, he was editing his suffragist newspaper *The Amenia Times* and was deeply committed to the NAACP. He served as its chairman of the board until 1919, its treasurer until 1930, and its president until his death. His wife, Amy, completed his final term of office. Joel Spingarn's long tenure was not entirely smooth. Black newspapers like the *New York Age* regularly complained because of too many whites in influential positions in the NAACP, and W.E.B. Du Bois, who respected Spingarn's commitment as well as his intellect, inevitably and understandably resented what was at that time a practical necessity. At the same time, he recognized Joel Spingarn's contributions and paid them strong tribute. In 1914, as I observed earlier, the Spingarn brothers barnstormed to protest segregation practices. In 1915, Joel

Spingarn attempted to stop showings of D.W. Griffith's racist film epic *The Birth of a Nation*. In 1916, he organized the first Amenia Conference, with many influential blacks in attendance, to formulate official policy combatting racial inequities. In 1917, he drafted the first deferral anti-lynching legislation. In 1918, as a major in the army, he laid aside his anti-separatist stand long enough to force the establishment of a black officers' training school.

Independently wealthy after 1919, he devoted the majority of his time to the NAACP, and he was in part responsible for its 300 branches by 1921. Both Joel Spingarn and his wife, Amy, regularly contributed funds to the NAACP throughout their lives and spent a good deal of time soliciting funds from others for its various causes. In 1925, when the literary contests in *The Crisis* and *Opportunity* were at their height, Amy Spingarn established financial awards of her own, voted by a committee to Rudolph Fisher for fiction, Marita Bonner for drama, and Countee Cullen for poetry (Frank Horne and Langston Hughes placing second and third in the latter category). Joel Spingarn himself had long before established the most prestigious award for the race, the Spingarn Medal, and he insured its continuance by setting up a trust fund in his will. The gold medal was to be awarded annually for "the highest and noblest achievement of an American Negro during the preceding year or years." The cover of the June 1914 issue of *The Crisis* carried a drawing of the medal's design. . . .

THE CONTROVERSIAL CARL VAN VECHTEN

The last white patron in this brief catalog, Carl Van Vechten, is probably the most controversial, the one about whom white as well as black scholars feel strong prejudice. Nathan Irvin Huggins's conclusions in his book on the period of the Harlem Renaissance do not underestimate Van Vechten's contributions, but, he contends, "it is open to question how well, or in what way, Van Vechten served Harlem and the Negro" and equally important to question how well they "served him." In *When Harlem Was in Vogue*, David Levering Lewis allows that Van Vechten "praised everything artistically good or promising with enthusiastic good sense, balanced by sympathetic dismissal of whatever Harlem produced that was clearly mediocre," but he allows for the possibility "that Van Vechten was a literary voyeur, exploiting his Harlem connections in order to make himself even richer." On the other hand, James Weldon Johnson said Van Vechten was "one of the most vital forces in bringing about the artistic emergence of the Negro in America," and the assessments of Van Vechten's contemporary biographers reinforce that judgment.

By the time Carl Van Vechten had become addicted to black arts and letters during the twenties, he was already well established as a music critic of considerable perception and, on the strength of four highly popular novels, a successful writer hardly in need of being "served," at least not financially. But he certainly seems to have discovered the potential for artistic excellence in the race before the race had fully realized that for itself, and he announced it with the same enthusiasm he had brought to any number of other matters labeled *avant-garde* in their own time. It is not difficult, however, to understand why others—white as well as black—might misinterpret Van Vechten's motives, assuming, on the basis of his reputation as a dandy and a dilettante, that he was not only self-serving but slumming.

His interest was of long standing, however. At the turn of the century, Van Vechten had fallen under the spell of ragtime and, before the first world war, of jazz, about which he wrote in *Red* (from the mid-twenties), it "may not be the last hope of American music, nor yet the best hope, but at present, I am convinced, it is its only hope." Even before he had praised the music of Igor Stravinsky, Erik Satie and George Gershwin, the operas of Richard Strauss, the dancing of Isadora Duncan and Anna Pavlova, the writings of Gertrude Stein—all in advance of anybody else in America—he had begun his campaign. In 1914, he was advocating in print the formation of a Negro theater organization, with black actors and black playwrights.

In the mid-twenties he met Walter White through their mutual publisher and, through him, he came to know the entire set of Harlem literati, including his greatest friend, James Weldon Johnson. If Van Vechten needed a catalyst for his growing enthusiasm for black arts and letters, he found it in that remarkable figure. He met the young poets Langston Hughes and Countee Cullen, and eventually Eric Walrond, Wallace Thurman, and Zora Neale Hurston—the latter responsible for having coined the term "niggerati" to describe the young black intellectuals of the period, and for having dubbed Carl Van Vechten the first "Negrotarian." Shortly, he had arranged for the work of Cullen and Hughes to appear in the pages of the prestigious *Vanity Fair*, and through his instigation Alfred Knopf published Hughes's first collection of poems *The Weary Blues* as well as novels by Nella Larsen and Rudolph Fisher. For *Vanity Fair*—as popular and influential in the twenties, apparently, as any magazine in recent history—Van Vechten wrote several articles himself: about the spirituals, about the blues, about blues singers Bessie Smith and Ethel Waters, about black theater. He wrote dozens of reviews of books by black writers; he financed Paul Robeson's first recitals of spirituals in New York; and he became, in Nathan Irvin Huggins's apt phrase, "the undisputed downtown authority on uptown life." Although he devoted an inordinate amount of time to shabby pursuits—getting drunk regularly in speakeasies, collecting handsome Harlem sycophants about him, unconsciously propagating stereotypes through his own delight in Harlem's exotic elements—there is nothing in any of his work to suggest that his respect and admiration were not genuine, and it is clear that his desire to share his discoveries resulted in a cultural interchange unique at the time. In their glamorous apartment, Van Vechten and his wife, the Russian actress Fania Marinoff, entertained frequently and lavishly, always with fully integrated guest lists. The parties were eventually reported as a matter of course in some of the black newspapers of the city, and Walter White called their West 55th Street address "the mid-town office of the NAACP."

A NOVEL OF QUESTIONABLE VALUE

And then Carl Van Vechten wrote *Nigger Heaven*. The title alone guaranteed controversy, but readers were violently split in their reactions to the content, and despite the support of several influential black writers, there was widespread feeling that he had used his Harlem acquaintances badly. *Nigger Heaven* is no great novel, but it certainly created a large white readership for black literature, and it popularized Harlem and brought plenty of money into the cabarets north of 125th Street. Whether those two influences are close enough in value to be mentioned in the same sentence is open to question. *Nigger Heaven* is usually criticized because of its preoccupation with Harlem's seamy side, although only about a third of the action takes place in speakeasies and bedrooms. Those passages surely are rough and erotic, and blacks espousing the theory of a "talented tenth," eager to put a best foot forward in Harlem, did not enjoy seeing it depicted as frequently engaged in the Charleston, or otherwise tangled up in the bedsheets of pimps and courtesans. The other two-thirds of the novel is about Harlem's black intelligentsia, with a pedantic heroine and a feeble hero locked in a pathetic little romance that ends in melodramatic violence more appropriate for the silent movies of the period. W.E.B. Du Bois wanted to burn the book, but Wallace Thurman suggested that a statue of the ofay author be erected in Harlem. The real problem with *Nigger Heaven* is not a question of either its sincerity or its scandal-mongering, but the fact that it is consciously didactic, a deliberate attempt to educate Van Vechten's already large white reading public by presenting Harlem as a complex society fractured and united by individual and social groups of diverse interests, talents, and values. The scandalous drinking and sleeping around in *Nigger Heaven* goes on in all of Van Vechten's novels; such vagaries are hardly limited to the white race. In his afterword to a subsequent paperback edition of *Nigger Heaven,* Van Vechten declared, "Negroes are treated by me exactly as if I were depicting white characters, for the very excellent reason that I do not believe there is much psychological difference between the races." As a consequence—though it is probably true that this only proves itself to somebody willing to read Van Vechten's other novels—*Nigger Heaven* is best understood as the one of his books which has characters who happen to be black. But who could have known that, or have even cared to, faced with a title like *Nigger Heaven*?

Whatever its limitations, the novel strengthened Van Vechten's ties with the race—certainly he lost no friends because of it—and increased his loyalty. Through the rest of his long career, he devoted his time and substantial funds from his million-plus inheritance beginning in 1927, to a wider recognition of black achievement, first, by making documentary photographs of virtually every celebrated black person. The list is staggering, in quality as well as quantity, and especially in the number of people photographed before their talents were generally recognized; but Van Vechten's eye and ear had been fairly unerring since the turn of the century, so it is not surprising to discover

Shirley Verett at 24, Leontyne Price at 23, Lena Horne at 22, Diahann Carroll at 18, and about thirty years ago such subjects as James Baldwin, Alvin Ailey, Harry Belafonte, James Earle Jones, Chester Himes, LeRoi Jones, and Arthur Mitchell. Second, Van Vechten established the James Weldon Johnson Memorial Collection of Negro Arts and Letters at Yale University, surely one of the greatest repositories for black studies, and he specified in his will that any money ever realized from reprints of his own books and photographs be donated to the collection's endowment fund. It is difficult to conceive of the books written since Van Vechten's death, on various black figures and subjects, without the materials he amassed and collected and supported.

None of the preceding discussion addresses itself to the subtle distinction between patronage and patronizing. From the vantage point of the 1990s, it is difficult to embrace without strong reservation the naiveté and paternalism of the twenties as faultless when sincere, or forgivable when devious. It is doubtless easy for the one to become the other, but it may be almost as easy for the one to *seem* to become the other—blanket judgments are always dangerous—because of black dismay over the circumstances that led to white patronage in the first place.

Charles S. Johnson and the Emancipation of Black Artists

Ralph L. Pearson

The role of Charles S. Johnson in the development of the Harlem Renaissance's literary movement is often overlooked. Johnson was a black entrepreneur who was troubled by the lack of control that blacks had over their own creative projects. Since critical, editorial, and publishing fields were operated and controlled by whites, blacks had little opportunity to determine how and if their work would be presented to audiences. In an effort to change this, Johnson became the editor of *Opportunity* magazine in the 1920s and used the publication as a springboard for the creative development of black talent. In this essay, literary critic Ralph L. Pearson cites the influence of *Opportunity*'s writing contests as a way of breaking down the racial barriers that had prevented black voices from finding a deserving audience. Although white America was predisposed to ignore black achievements, Johnson was able to shrewdly use the magazine's contests to combat racism as well as promote new black artists. In doing so, Johnson helped to shape a new, positive black self-image.

Until the appearance of Patrick Gilpin's essay, "Charles S. Johnson: Entrepreneur of the Harlem Renaissance," the important role of Johnson as a cultivator of the Harlem Renaissance was described in a paragraph or two by historians and literary critics. In his recent analysis of the Renaissance as a cultural movement encompassing all the arts, Nathan Irvin Huggins merely cites Johnson as editor of *Opportunity* and then comments on the role of *Opportunity* in the Re-

Excerpted from "Combating Racism with Art: Charles S. Johnson and the Harlem Renaissance," by Ralph L. Pearson, *American Studies*, Spring 1977. Copyright © 1977 by *American Studies*. Reprinted by permission of the publisher.

naissance, ". . . even more than the others [*Crisis; The Messenger*], *Opportunity* believed its motto—'Not Alms but Opportunity'—to apply to the arts. It sponsored a literary contest in the 1920s that became a major generating force in the renaissance."

Describing Johnson's entrepreneurial activities such as the Civic Club dinner of May 21, 1924, which brought "together the black literati and the white publishers," and the *Opportunity* contests, Professor Gilpin argues persuasively that it was "in reporting and promoting black culture in the United States and the world at large that Johnson and *Opportunity* found their forte." He reveals also Johnson's concern with "placing the New Movement into historical and sociological perspective." This observation leads to provocative suggestions of the importance Johnson ascribed to "the serious development of a body of literature about Negroes" for blacks as an "ethnic group"; and to literature as "a great liaison between races." But Gilpin never develops the sociological and historical implications of these observations for Johnson's role as entrepreneur of the Renaissance. This essay proposes to fill the gap by analyzing how Johnson expected the revelation of black artistic talent to be a liaison between the races, as well as to affect the self-image of blacks as an ethnic group.

EXPOSING CONDITIONS OF BLACK LIFE

A major source of racial antagonism in America, Johnson believed, was the misunderstanding and ignorance of the two races about one another. Johnson's opinion was shared by Alain Locke, who wrote in 1925;

> It does not follow that if the Negro were better known, he would be better liked or better treated. But mutual understanding is basic for any subsequent cooperation and adjustment. The effort toward this will at least have the effect of remedying in large part what has been the most unsatisfactory feature of our present stage of race relationships in America, namely the fact that the more intelligent and representative elements of the two race groups have at so many points got quite out of touch with one another.

Johnson spent much of his life as a sociologist, first with the National Urban League and later at Fisk University, engaging in sociological studies that exposed the conditions of black life in America. As his friend Edwin Embree wrote, his role was one of interpreting "colored people to whites and white people to Negroes, Southerners to Northerners, rustics to city dweller, analyzing people's problems so that they can understand themselves."

But interpreting the races to one another meant more than exposing the inferior social and economic conditions to which blacks were condemned by white discrimination and prejudice. As important for altering race relations was emphasis upon black achievements. "There are facts of Negro progress as well as handicaps that should be known not only for the stimulation which comes from recognition," Johnson wrote, "but as an antidote to a disposition not infrequently encountered to disparage unjustly the capacities and aspirations of this group."

OPPORTUNITY CONTESTS

The Harlem Renaissance provided just the opportunity for blacks to reveal their capacities as artists. Gilpin suggested, but never developed, Johnson's conception of the Renaissance as a tool for altering racial patterns when he wrote, "Johnson's motivation in beginning the *Opportunity* contests appears to be that of a skilled, shrewd and pragmatic entrepreneur who saw a flourishing of black culture as but another road for combatting white racism while aiding black people."

In September, 1927, Johnson himself described the *Opportunity* contests as a way to stimulate "not merely an interest in Negro life and in the work of the artists of the race, but work of a character which stands firmly and without apology along with that of any other race." Artistic work that equalled the quality of any other race would surely undermine white arguments of innate black inferiority. Johnson assumed, of course, that whites would react to evidence of black artistic talent as an argument for racial equality. This assumption, Huggins notes, was widespread among black intellectuals in the 1920's: "Inequities due to race might best be removed when reasonable men saw that black men were thinkers, strivers, doers, and were cultured, like themselves. Harlem intellectuals, with their progressive assumptions, saw themselves as the ones most likely to make this demonstration."

Johnson feared, of course, that the use of art to combat racism would fail because whites were predisposed to ignore black achievements. Occasionally this frustration turned to cynicism. Referring to *Ebony and Topaz*, a collection of black art, fiction, poetry and essays he edited, Johnson chided, "It is not improbable that some of our white readers will arch their brows or perhaps knit them soberly at some point before the end. But this is a response not infrequently met with outside the pages of books. There is always an escape of a sort, however, in ignoring that which contradicts one's sense, even though it were the better wisdom to give heed." In a less cryptic moment Johnson told a friend what he hoped white reaction would be to evidence of black talent: "The best use of the volume is in its presentation to some white person who needs a succinct, face value presentation of Negro competence. . . ."

Equally in need of "a succinct, face value presentation of Negro competence" were blacks themselves. Johnson was among the earliest sociologists to emphasize the psychological toll discrimination and segregation had taken on blacks and to combat the behavioral adjustments the race made to survive and function in American society. He fought the resulting sense of inferiority so many of his race had lived with because he knew that until blacks conceived of themselves as equals with other races they could not begin to relate, and so be treated, as equals. . . .

ALTERING THE BLACK SELF-IMAGE

Johnson sought to alter the self-image of many blacks not with demands or accusations that would further alienate the races, but with ideas and programs that were achievable within the racial atmosphere of the 1920's. He remained constantly aware of the social milieu in which he was seeking to reorient race relations. Publishing *Opportunity* magazine, he wrote in 1928, was one way to encourage Negroes to think more objectively about their role in the race problem, as well as "to effect an emancipation from their sensitiveness about meaningless symbols, and . . . [to] inculcate a disposition to see enough of interest and beauty in their own lives to rid themselves of the inferior feeling of being a Negro."

Who better than black artists themselves could capture the "interest and beauty" of black lives that could emancipate much of the race from feelings of inferiority. Here, then, is the framework for understanding how the Harlem Renaissance became for Johnson a means to change the self-image of many blacks and, in the end, to alter race relations. Evidence of black talent equal to that of other races could be an important step in the direction of race pride. Nathan Huggins describes the effect of black literary publications in *The Messenger, Liberator, Crisis* and *Opportunity* in just this way: "The tone and the self-assurance of these magazines were the important thing. They gave a sense of importance to blacks who read them. They gave answers that always had failed the porter, the barber, the maid, the teacher, the handyman. They were the Negro's voice against the insult that America gave him."

But to succeed as artists and, consequently, as uplifters of the race's image, Johnson argued, blacks must use their own experiences as the basis for their creativity. They had to free themselves from the hold white cultural values exercised upon their art, just as white artists had found it imperative to reject European standards as the arbiter of their work:

> It was the dull lack of some idealism . . . that held America in a suspended cultural animation until it sought freedom thru self-criticism and its own native sources of beauty. In the same manner, American Negroes, born into a culture which they did not wholly share, have responded falsely to the dominant patterns. Their expression has been, to borrow a term which Lewis Mumford employs in referring to Americans in relation to Europe, 'sickly and derivative, a mere echo of old notes.' There has been the same self-deception of 'boasting and vain imagination[,]' the same indifference to the spiritual refinement of the beautiful, the same dull seeking of an average level, and the same mystifying sense of an imponderable shortcoming which led inevitably to inferior feeling and apology. The form of expression merely has been different.

A NEW FREEDOM

The lives of black men and women were replete with deeds and words worthy of being captured in poetry and story, in music and portrait. Survival itself, while trapped in the snares of slavery and Jim Crow, could provide inspiration for creativity. "There is a thrilling magnificence and grandeur," Johnson wrote, ". . . in the thread of unconquerable life thru two centuries of pain." The folk life of the race included untapped sources for creative inspiration. "The vast sources of this field for American literature," Johnson reminded aspiring black artists, "cannot be escaped. . . . There is here a life full of strong colors, of passions, deep and fierce, of struggle, disillusion—the whole gamut of life free from the wrapping of intricate sophistication."

So important was the black artists' use of black experiences to Johnson that he described their utilization of folk material as "a new emancipation." Gone was the "sensitive-ness" that only a decade before denied the existence "of any but educated Negroes" and opposed Negro dialect, folk songs or anything that "revived the memory of slavery." Black artists were now sensitive "to the hidden beauties" of the black experience and expressed "a frank joy and pride in it."

The emancipation of black artists was the means for a "new freedom" for the entire race. Addressing a graduating class of black students in 1928, Johnson argued, ". . . that the *road to a new freedom for us* lies in the discovery of the sur-rounding beauties of our lives and environment, and in the recognition that beauty itself is a mark of the highest ex-pression of the human spirit." Black artists of the Renais-sance were capturing the beauty of black lives. In their work blacks could discover countless reasons for pride in their race. Simultaneously white men and women could experi-ence the revelation of a long suppressed race with artistic talent, a history and culture equal to that of other races.

Johnson's race relations philosophy dictated, however, that racial pride be not a tool for further racial separation or for a Garveyite dream of African glory [Marcus Garvey was a black leader who advocated that blacks return to Africa], but a lever for achieving equality in American society. His sense of realism convinced him that there was no value in pursuing a separatist course. Blacks were a distinct minor-ity segment of American life and institutions. Those institu-tions were givens in their environment. The racial injustices of American society would not be eliminated by seeking to create another society, but by altering the racial habits of functioning institutions through such tools as research and education, negotiation and persuasion, confidence and achievement within the race itself.

Equality within American society did not mean the loss of racial identification or "becoming a black Anglo Saxon," as Gilpin phrased it. Indeed, a careful reading of Johnson's published and unpublished writings conveys his conception of black Americans as a separate ethnic group within Amer-ican society—an ethnic group that could contribute to, as well as draw upon, the society's cultural mainstream. . . .

BLACK CULTURAL AUTONOMY

The conception of the Renaissance as a tool for fostering black cultural autonomy, which could then contribute to the nation's cultural life, has been seriously questioned by Huggins. Rather than contributing to the national culture as a distinct ethnic group, he argues, "black men and American culture have been one—such a seamless web that it is impossible to calibrate the Negro within it or to ravel him from it." These divergent views underscore differing conceptions of the relationship between blacks and the remainder of American society, not the benefit of historical perspective allowed by the passage of decades. Johnson himself reflected on the meaning of the Renaissance in the mid-1950's and spoke again in terms of a distinct "self conscious and race conscious" movement that "could be incorporated into the cultural bloodstream of the nation."

If black artists were to contribute to the nation's "cultural bloodstream" and simultaneously make art a liaison between the races, they would have to produce works equal in quality to those produced by artists of other races. Being the best Negro author in a particular genre benefited neither the artist nor the race. "As Negro writers come into their estate it is expected that what they produce shall approach the standards set by the accepted writers of the country." Not only would failure to meet accepted standards of quality perpetuate the widely held opinion that blacks were innately inferior, but it would also threaten interest in what black authors wrote. Furthermore, the possibility existed that authors with a polished style but little information might usurp the audience interested in literature about the black experience. Therefore, Johnson told *Opportunity* contest entrants, ". . . the cult of competence must be courted assiduously. We must write to be known; we must write well to be heard at all."

And when black men wrote so well that their excellence achieved recognition in literary anthologies, Johnson applauded the achievement as more than an individual accomplishment: ". . . to the glory of their skill, it speaks for Negroes." This articulation of the significance of individual success for an entire race underscores the importance of the Harlem Renaissance for Johnson's race relations philosophy—for surely this display of artistic skill called into question traditional white attitudes about blacks, as well as the image blacks had of their own race.

During the past decade several scholars have questioned the meaning of the Harlem Renaissance for black independence and/or equality. As noted, Nathan Huggins rejects the Renaissance as an expression of black cultural autonomy. The autonomous ethnic culture Johnson and others saw expressed in the Renaissance had little independent ballast to support it. Huggins concedes that blacks did achieve a maturity of racial conceptualization and an appreciation of folk roots and culture which permitted partial emancipation from the "embarrassment of past conditions" as a result of the Renaissance. But these achievements led to a "naive faith in the possibility of creating an ethnic culture." When, in fact, black artists were unable to free themselves from emulation of white values.

THE SINCERITY OF WHITE PATRONS

In his study of *Harlem: The Making of a Ghetto* Gilbert Osofsky questioned the sincerity of whites who seemed genuinely attracted to black art—individuals to whom the meaning of black creativity for race relations should have been most obvious. The attraction of the New Negro and the Renaissance, Osofsky contends, was the challenge they represented to traditional American values. That generation of Americans who discovered "newness" all around it—New Humanism, New Criticism, New Masses, New Poetry and so on—"also found a 'New Negro'; and the concept became a cultural weapon: 'Another Bombshell Fired into the Heart of Bourgeois Culture.'"

The traditional view of the Negro as Sambo did not change, Osofsky argued. Instead new characteristics were attributed to him that made him exciting. He was "expressive," "primitive," "exotic," possessing an "innate gayety of soul." Such characteristics were captivating when compared with the puritanical and repressed culture of white America. Still, the black man remained a toy with which the players would tire. What remained was a degraded, suppressed race.

Charles Johnson was not unaware of the artificiality which attached itself to what he considered to be a genuine cultural expression of black life and experiences. He was sensitive to the shallowness which could overtake an artistic movement such as the Renaissance once it appeared to have captivated public attention. Concerned that the Renaissance was moving in that direction he wrote in 1997,

> The public has recently given a sudden ear to the submerged voices of dark Americans; hearing has brought a measure of

interest and this interest, in characteristic American fashion has catapulted itself into something very much like a fad.

EXPLOITING THE RENAISSANCE

In a March, 1926, *Opportunity* editorial he had enumerated the dangers to the legitimacy of the Renaissance: the "short-sighted exploiters of sentiment"; the "immediate and pre-maturely triumphant ones who think that Negro writers have fully arrived"; and the "superficial ones, inebriated with praise and admission to the company of writers, who are establishing by acceptance, a double standard of compe-tence as a substitute for the normal rewards of study and practice, and in many instances, lack talent." Unless the ex-ploiters of public interest were curbed, Johnson feared the Renaissance would indeed be a fad "to be discarded in a few seasons" instead of a "sound wholesome expression of [artistic] growth.". . .

Even if the assumption of ethnic distinctiveness is ques-tionable, there is no doubt of his awareness of the economic and social realities of the society in which black artists la-bored. Johnson's entrepreneurial activities reveal a clear understanding of which groups and individuals controlled opportunities in the arts and of their past attitudes about black artists.

And if blacks were unable to emancipate themselves from the values of white society, as Johnson occasionally felt they had or were doing, he was realistic enough to see in the Re-naissance a tool for altering the black self-image. His most unrealistic social goal for the movement was that it might af-fect white attitudes toward the black race. It was an unrealis-tic goal not because only a relatively few whites knew of black art, but because whites were not prepared to grant blacks the same distribution of talent and mediocrity that characterizes other races. No rational proof would convince whites that the black race included individuals with abilities and capabilities equal to those of individuals from other races.

The Negro Artist and the Racial Mountain

Langston Hughes

Langston Hughes, one of the first poets to be heralded by critics of the Harlem Renaissance, is the author of several books of poetry, including *The Weary
Blues*. He also wrote several plays and was well
known for his stories and novels about an allegorical
character named Jessie B. Simple. In this essay, submitted to *The Nation* in 1926, Hughes expresses dismay that many black writers—and black people in
general—seek to embrace white society at the expense of their own racial identity. He states that the
lifestyle of "high-class Negroes" as well as white
concepts of black identity have very little to offer the
average African American. Instead, he suggests that
young writers draw upon the experiences and tribu-
lations of average black folk, as this common pool of
identifiable issues and experiences will provide
enough creative material for African American
writers to establish a better sense of cultural identity.

One of the most promising of the young Negro poets said to
me once, "I want to be a poet—not a Negro poet," meaning,
I believe, "I want to write like a white poet"; meaning sub-
consciously, "I would like to be a white poet"; meaning behind that, "I would like to be white." And I was sorry the
young man said that, for no great poet has ever been afraid
of being himself. And I doubted then that, with his desire to
run away spiritually from his race, this boy would ever be a
great poet. But this is the mountain standing in the way of
any true Negro art in America—this urge within the race toward whiteness, the desire to pour racial individuality into
the mold of American standardization, and to be as little Negro and as much American as possible.

Excerpted from "The Negro Artist and the Racial Mountain," by Langston Hughes, *The Nation*, June 23, 1926.

But let us look at the immediate background of this young poet. His family is of what I suppose one would call the Negro middle class: people who are by no means rich yet never uncomfortable nor hungry—smug, contented, respectable folk, members of the Baptist church. The father goes to work every morning. He is a chief steward at a large white club. The mother sometimes does fancy sewing or supervises parties for the rich families of the town. The children go to a mixed school. In the home they read white papers and magazines. And the mother often says "Don't be like niggers" when the children are bad. A frequent phrase from the father is, "Look how well a white man does things." And so the word white comes to be unconsciously a symbol of all the virtues. It holds for the children beauty, morality, and money. The whisper of "I want to be white" runs silently through their minds. This young poet's home is, I believe, a fairly typical home of the colored middle class. One sees immediately how difficult it would be for an artist born in such a home to interest himself in interpreting the beauty of his own people. He is never taught to see that beauty. He is taught rather not to see it, or if he does, to be ashamed of it when it is not according to Caucasian patterns.

DISDAIN FOR BEING BLACK

For racial culture the home of a self-styled "high-class" Negro has nothing better to offer. Instead there will perhaps be more aping of things white than in a less cultured or less wealthy home. The father is perhaps a doctor, lawyer, landowner, or politician. The mother may be a social worker, or a teacher, or she may do nothing and have a maid. Father is often dark but he has usually married the lightest woman he could find. The family attend a fashionable church where few really colored faces are to be found. And they themselves draw a color line. In the North they go to white theaters and white movies. And in the South they have at least two cars and a house "like white folks." Nordic manners, Nordic faces, Nordic hair, Nordic art (if any), and an Episcopal heaven. A very high mountain indeed for the would-be racial artist to climb in order to discover himself and his people.

But then there are the low-down folks, the so-called common element, and they are the majority—may the Lord be praised! The people who have their nip of gin on Saturday nights and are not too important to themselves or the community, or too well fed, or too learned to watch the lazy world go round. They live on Seventh Street in Washington or State Street in Chicago and they do not particularly care whether they are like white folks or anybody else. Their joy runs, bang! into ecstasy. Their religion soars to a shout. Work maybe a little today, rest a little tomorrow. Play awhile. Sing awhile. O, let's dance! These common people are not afraid of spirituals, as for a long time their more intellectual brethren were, and jazz is their child. They furnish a wealth of colorful, distinctive material for any artist because they still hold their own individuality in the face of American standardizations. And perhaps these common people will give to the world its truly great Negro artist, the one who is not afraid to be himself. Whereas the better-class Negro would tell the artist what to do, the people at least let him alone when he does appear. And they are not ashamed of him—if they know he exists at all. And they accept what beauty is their own without question.

Certainly there is, for the American Negro artist who can escape the restrictions the more advanced among his own group would put upon him, a great field of unused material ready for his art. Without going outside his race, and even among the better classes with their "white" culture and conscious American manners, but still Negro enough to be different, there is sufficient matter to furnish a black artist with a lifetime of creative work. And when he chooses to touch on the relations between Negroes and whites in this country with their innumerable overtones and undertones, surely, and especially for literature and the drama, there is an inexhaustible supply of themes at hand. To these the Negro artist can give his racial individuality, his heritage of rhythm and warmth, and his incongruous humor that so often, as in the Blues, becomes ironic laughter mixed with tears. But let us look again at the mountain.

A prominent Negro clubwoman in Philadelphia paid eleven dollars to hear Raquel Meller sing Andalusian popular songs. But she told me a few weeks before she would not think of going to hear "that woman," Clara Smith, a great black artist, sing Negro folksongs. And many an upper-class Negro church, even now, would not dream of employing a spiritual in its services. The drab melodies in white folks' hymnbooks are much to be preferred. "We want to worship the Lord correctly and quietly. We don't believe in 'shouting.' Let's be dull like the Nordics," they say, in effect.

No Encouragement for Black Artists

The road for the serious black artist, then, who would produce a racial art is most certainly rocky and the mountain is high. Until recently he received almost no encouragement for his work from either white or colored people. The fine novels of Charles W. Chesnutt go out of print with neither race noticing their passing. The quaint charm and humor of Paul Laurence Dunbar's dialect verse brought to him, in his day, largely the same kind of encouragement one would give a sideshow freak (A colored man writing poetry! How odd!) or a clown (How amusing!).

The present vogue in things Negro, although it may do as much harm as good for the budding colored artist, has at

"I, Too, Sing America"

In this poem, Langston Hughes expresses the frustration that accompanies the search for a cultural identity.

I, too, sing America.

I am the darker brother.
They send me to eat in the kitchen
When company comes,
But I laugh,
And eat well,
And grow strong.

Tomorrow,
I'll be at the table
When company comes.
Nobody'll dare
Say to me,
"Eat in the kitchen,"
Then.

Besides,
They'll see how beautiful I am
And be ashamed—

I, too, am America.

Langston Hughes, "I, Too, Sing America," from *The Collected Poems of Langston Hughes.* New York: Knopf and Vintage Books, 1994.

least done this: it has brought him forcibly to the attention of his own people among whom for so long, unless the other race had noticed him beforehand, he was a prophet with little honor. I understand that Charles Gilpin acted for years in Negro theaters without any special acclaim from his own, but when Broadway gave him eight curtain calls, Negroes, too, began to beat a tin pan in his honor. I know a young colored writer, a manual worker by day, who had been writing well for the colored magazines for some years, but it was not until he recently broke into the white publications and his first book was accepted by a prominent New York publisher that the "best" Negroes in his city took the trouble to discover that he lived there. Then almost immediately they decided to give a grand dinner for him. But the society ladies were careful to whisper to his mother that perhaps she'd better not come. They were not sure she would have an evening gown.

The Negro artist works against an undertow of sharp criticism and misunderstanding from his own group and unintentional bribes from the whites. "O, be respectable, write about nice people, show how good we are," say the Negroes. "Be stereotyped, don't go too far, don't shatter our illusions about you, don't amuse us too seriously. We will pay you," say the whites. Both would have told Jean Toomer not to write *Cane*. The colored people did not praise it. The white people did not buy it. Most of the colored people who did read *Cane* hate it. They are afraid of it. Although the critics gave it good reviews the public remained indifferent. Yet (excepting the work of W.E.B. Du Bois) *Cane* contains the finest prose written by a Negro in America. And like the singing of Paul Robeson, it is truly racial.

FUTURE ACCEPTANCE OF BLACK THEMES

But in spite of the Nordicized Negro intelligentsia and the desires of some white editors we have an honest American Negro literature already with us. Now I await the rise of the Negro theater. Our folk music, having achieved world-wide fame, offers itself to the genius of the great individual American Negro composer who is to come. And within the next decade I expect to see the work of a growing school of colored artists who paint and model the beauty of dark faces and create with new technique the expressions of their own soul-world. And the Negro dancers who will dance like flame and the singers who will continue to carry our songs

to all who listen—they will be with us in even greater numbers tomorrow.

Most of my own poems are racial in theme and treatment,
derived from the life I know. In many of them I try to grasp
and hold some of the meanings and rhythms of jazz. I am
sincere as I know how to be in these poems and yet after
every reading I answer questions like these from my own
people: Do you think Negroes should always write about Negroes? I wish you wouldn't read some of your poems to
white folks. How do you find anything interesting in a place
like a cabaret? Why do you write about black people? You
aren't black. What makes you do so many jazz poems?

But jazz to me is one of the inherent expressions of Negro
life in America: the eternal tom-tom beating in the Negro
soul—the tom-tom of revolt against weariness in a white
world, a world of subway trains, and work, work, work; the
tom-tom of joy and laughter, and pain swallowed in a smile.
Yet the Philadelphia clubwoman is ashamed to say that her
race created it and she does not like me to write about it. The
old subconscious "white is best" runs through her mind. Years
of study under white teachers, a lifetime of white books, pic-
tures, and papers, and white manners, morals, and Puritan
standards made her dislike the spirituals. And now she turns
up her nose at jazz and all its manifestations—likewise almost
everything else distinctly racial. She doesn't care for the
Winold Reiss portraits of Negroes because they are "too Negro." She does not want a true picture of herself from anybody.
She wants the artist to flatter her, to make the white world believe that all Negroes are as smug and as near white in soul as
she wants to be. But, to my mind, it is the duty of the younger
Negro artist, if he accepts any duties at all from outsiders, to
change through the force of his art that old whispering "I want
to be white," hidden in the aspirations of his people, to "Why
should I want to be white? I am a Negro—and beautiful!"

So I am ashamed for the black poet who says, "I want to
be a poet, not a Negro poet," as though his own racial world
were not as interesting as any other world. I am ashamed,
too, for the colored artist who runs from the painting of Negro faces to the painting of sunsets after the manner of the
academicians because he fears the strange un-whiteness of
his own features. An artist must be free to choose what he
does, certainly, but he must also never be afraid to do what
he might choose.

Let the blare of Negro jazz bands and the bellowing voice of Bessie Smith singing Blues penetrate the closed ears of the colored near-intellectuals until they listen and perhaps understand. Let Paul Robeson singing *Water Boy*, and Rudolph Fisher writing about the streets of Harlem, and Jean Toomer holding the heart of Georgia in his hands, and Aaron Douglas drawing strange black fantasies cause the smug Negro middle class to turn from their white, respectable, ordinary books and papers to catch a glimmer of their own beauty. We younger Negro artists who create now intend to express our individual dark-skinned selves without fear or shame. If white people are pleased we are glad. If they are not, it doesn't matter. We know we are beautiful. And ugly too. The tom-tom cries and the tom-tom laughs. If colored people are pleased we are glad. If they are not, their displeasure doesn't matter either. We build our temples for tomorrow, strong as we know how, and we stand on top of the mountain, free within ourselves.

The Alienation of Negro Literature

Charles I. Glicksberg

Categorizing African American writings during the scope of the Harlem Renaissance as "Negro Literature" was perpetuated by white Americans to alienate black achievement from that of society as a whole. Writing during the 1950s but referring to the achievements brought on by the renaissance, sociologist Charles I. Glicksberg points out that the label of "Negro Literature" is inherently racist and attempts to classify works by their supposed primitive themes and black subject matter. Glicksberg then acknowledges that black writers who attempt to expose white racism through their writing unwittingly reinforce the separateness of "Negro Literature" since these themes of protest are registered by white audiences as just another aspect of that distinct category. Thus, to Glicksberg, black authors face a dilemma in writing, namely how to draw upon their own racial history and not appear cut off from America at large.

Even in the republic of letters, Negroes work under a crippling handicap. The poison of racial prejudice subtly pervades the cultural atmosphere so that even the language of criticism is influenced by unconscious but nonetheless invidious value-judgments which set the colored people apart from the American folk and its native culture. The brutal lynching of the Negro has given way to a more refined form of cultural segregation. Negro writers are praised and encouraged for possessing talent that is authentically "Negroid." They are not *American* writers. They are Negroes, and that makes all the difference. Only those elements of their work which differentiate it *racially* from "white" art are praised and encouraged, and since the whites for the most part control the aesthetic norms of appreciation as well as the channels of public recognition, they have helped to lay the foundation of what has been called "Negro literature."

There would be little objection to such a designation if it were nothing but a descriptive label. The connotations of the label, however, are more significant than the denotative aspect. What is usually implied by the term? It is hard to say, since no two "white" critics would agree *in toto,* but the prevailing theme seems to be that "Negro literature" is racial at heart, a "primitive" product. "Negroid" in substance and spirit, Negro literature and art gives expression to the soul of the black folk: their exuberance, their earthy sensuousness, their childlike mind and innocent eye, their African sense of rhythm. It is the art of a separate race within America.

Thus the term "Negro literature" reveals the pattern of cultural segregation in which Negro writers are being confined. Since they are Negroes, not Americans, their work must somehow be identified as "alien." The linguistic impasse springs from a contradiction in the mind and heart of the whites. Everything is either honorifically white or damnably black. There is American literature and "Negro literature." There is American culture, and an alien sector reserved exclusively for Negroes. The reservation is not altogether exclusive. The whites hold a mortgage even on this segregated sector and dictate the terms of the lease. (Not *all* whites to be sure, but that is where the difficulty comes in: the sharp black-white dualism distorts the perspective of discourse.) They decide what is unique in Negro genius: the blues, the spirituals, jazz, primitive music, neo-African art, racial poetry and fiction. If a Negro poet were to write on universal rather than specifically racial themes he would most likely be ignored by the whites, and the colored folk would probably regard him as a traitor, trying to "pass." It is rare to find a Negro novelist dealing with anything but themes of racial conflict and oppression. Even the Negro social scientists are obsessed with this subject.

Remarkable indeed is the fact that Negro writers have adjusted themselves to this state of affairs. In fact, they have transformed it into a militant crusade. Cultural alienation manifests itself as racialism, the Negro writers betraying an almost pathological pride in their separateness, their "difference," their achievements as a people. Racialism is a fetish, a source of inspiration and strength, a philosophy of aesthetics, a creative religion.

INTENSE IN FEELING BUT NARROW IN SCOPE

The race war is on. Because the "whites" exalt "whiteness" as the mark of superiority, the source and standard of all that is truly excellent in the world of letters, the Negroes are constrained to take exaggerated pride in the contrasting fact of "blackness." "Color" thus becomes a category of culture, and Negro writers are driven into a cultural Black Belt. As a result of being thus segregated and of segregating themselves, they find it extremely difficult to reach the plane of the universal. Too much Negro fiction and poetry is of an aggressive racial cast, dealing obsessively and often monotonously with the theme of racial discrimination. This is the basic reason for the limitations of Negro literature in the United States. That it why, alas, it so often falls short of greatness. It cannot view the condition of humanity objectively, only through the "colored" lens of the racial problem. . . . It is not without considerable aesthetic significance that those who are able to see beyond the racial motif are, by and large, those who have been deeply influenced by the philosophy of Communism. As a result of serving his literary apprenticeship in left-wing groups and identifying himself with the struggles of the proletariat, white and black, [novelist] Richard Wright came to perceive that injustice and exploitation are not confined to the Negro masses but are the logical evolution and inevitable outcome of a particular economic system.

For the great majority of Negro writers, however, Communism is no solution. They must work out their creative salvation in terms of the American scene. Recoiling from the painful experience of rejection, they return with intensified love to the security offered by their own racial group, focusing their hatred against the "white" oppressor. The price of cultural alienation is racial identification. Since they are judged as a race rather than as individuals, as Americans, they will ally themselves unreservedly with their own people. Creative Negroes voice the aspirations and resentments, the hurts and traumatic hatreds, the desires and dreams and terrible frustrations, of their own race. They know what it means to be a Negro in "white America," and they protest with all the force of their being against the myth of innate racial inferiority.

Consequently, they attack the vicious stereotypes the whites have created about their race, by endeavoring to prove that Negroes are uniquely talented in this or that artistic field. This belief, namely, that in music, rhythm, and in spirituals, the Negro is exceptionally well endowed by virtue of his primitive African ancestry, deepens and confirms his cultural alienation. The whites are delighted to welcome any contribution which can be conspicuously and generically labeled "Negroid." By stressing the "Negroid" quality of his art, the whites strengthen the dualism in the heart of the Negro writer. After pushing him into a Black Ghetto, they say: "Go to it, boy. That is your distinctive racial talent. You will succeed best to the extent that you are most truly yourself: a Negro." Buell G. Gallagher, who in *American Caste and the Negro College* has written sanely on this aspect of cultural alienation, points out that the reversion of the Negro to "specifically 'Negroid' themes and modes of expression is in a sense a tacit admission that the Negro is giving up the struggle for acceptance as part of a white world—he is accepting cultural segregation, a symbol of social status as well." There is the inexorable dilemma: if the Negro writer retreats into himself and develops his "racial" potentialities he is departing from the norms of "American" culture; if he imitates that culture, he may cease to be himself and destroy both his uniqueness and his creative vitality.

Negro literature is thus handicapped by its very virtues. It is a literature of passionate protest, intense in feeling but narrow in scope. Its hatred of racial injustice assumes at times the shrill, incoherent character of an obsessional neurosis. The writer has his eyes fixed broodingly on one sector of experience, the suffering of his people, the fatality of "color," and he can think and write of nothing else. He must drink this cup of gall and wormwood to the lees. In novel and drama and lyric, the Negro writer voices in bitter and poignant accents the Golgotha [wasteland of bones] his folk must tread. . . .

Hemmed in as they are by a psychological as well as physical Black Ghetto, for the Negro writers race is fate. Everything that happens to the Negro is interpreted in the light of the racial struggle. The individual scarcely appears in all his uniqueness and emotional complexity. Instead he appears almost invariably as a race man, his conflicts and his personal development conditioned by his environment and the persecutory hostility of the whites. The Negro who becomes a killer is a cultural product, fighting against overwhelming odds, filled with ineffectual resentments that explode in hot murderous impulses.

LACKING CULTURAL IDENTITY

Then, too, Negro writers have been so preoccupied with the immediate racial issue that they have failed to develop a true historical sense. As a rule, their work reveals little trace of their native cultural past. It is singularly deficient in historical perspective. This arises from the curious circumstance that the Negro regards himself in a sense as a man without a history. Since he is treated not as an American but as a Negro, he feels himself cut off from the cultural heritage of this land. True, he is a most earnest believer in the American Creed, but he is forced to view the American past with a divided mind. Fundamentally he is ashamed of the past of slavery and ashamed to confess that he is ashamed. He simply keeps silent about it. There are few Negro novels or poems or dramas which deal realistically and yet understandingly with this extraordinary phase of the American past. Yet here is epic material for those with the imaginative courage and the talent and the fierce insight to develop it to the full.

If one sought a common denominator in Negro poetry he would find it in its single-minded preoccupation with the racial problem. When Paul Laurence Dunbar first came on the American scene, few critics recognized the creative potentialities of the Negro. The publication of Dunbar's poetry was therefore an event of considerable importance. Here was Negro humor, here was Negro dialect. Here was a writer blazing a new tradition, writing about the experiences of his own people in their own "peculiar" tongue. Dunbar's aesthetic philosophy was basically sound, even though his poetic strategy was mistaken. He strove scrupulously to attain the ideal of universality. For him there was but one road to salvation: the Negro must be acklowledged as a man. Only after his humanity was recognized did the secondary identifying characteristics of color and race enter in.

Admirable as such a theory is when considered in the abstract, it was unfortunately out of alignment with the facts of life as they then functioned in American society. As Benjamin Brawley points out in his study of Dunbar, this was a way of blinding himself to the truth of social reality. Dunbar hypnotized himself into the belief that he was primarily a man when the rest of the world continued to look upon him only as a Negro. Because of this contradiction, his poetry, written for a predominantly white audience and completely divorced from the racial conflict, was born of a divided will and a split personality. He once told a reporter: "For two hundred and fifty years the environment of the Negro has been American, in every respect the same as that of all other Americans." His great hope was that his people would in time be permitted to share as equals in the cultural life of this country. Yet he unwittingly lent himself to the writing of poetry in dialect, which popularized many of the ugly stereotypes concerning the Negro. It is poetry steeped in sentimentality, nostalgic, romantically idealized.

Contemporary poetry has tended to steer away from dialect verse, since it fails to do justice to the spirit of the Negro folk and is out of touch with the facts of modern life. James Weldon Johnson saw that no matter how sincere the Negro poet writing in the conventionalized dialect might be, he was really expressing "only certain conceptions about Negro life that his audience was willing to accept and ready to enjoy," and that audience consisted of whites who knew what they wanted. That is it precisely: dialect for the Negro writer is a trap. He thinks he is being "racial" whereas he is in reality conforming to white stereotyped conceptions of Negro life and speech, Negro character and sentiment. Dialect poetry has had to be discarded by poets who wished for freedom in their choice of subject matter and mode of treatment. It is James Weldon Johnson's considered opinion that *"traditional* Negro dialect as a form for Aframerican poets is absolutely dead." Whatever compromises Paul Laurence Dunbar had to make, he was definitely on the right track in asserting that the Negro was first and foremost an American, and that he must write as an American, not as a segregated Negro with a peculiar, caste-conditioned culture of his own.

DEFINING A CULTURAL PAST

No writer can function vitally without sinking his roots deep into native soil. The past is always with us; the Negro writer is the organic summation of his past. Whatever the Negro people are now is the evolutionary result of all they have been. If they fight for full freedom today, it is because they were once denied freedom in the American past. But what

past should the Negro writer resurrect? If human beings
trace their biological evolution back far enough, they come
to the primordial slime. The past exists for the writer only in
so far as it is viable. Shall the Negro rediscover Africa and
make common cause with black people the world over or
shall he confine himself to his cultural past in the United
States so that eventually he may become creatively and culturally identified with America? If he chooses the former alternative, he is doomed. If the latter, the question arises, how
shall this be accomplished?

For the Negro writer is not permitted to sink his roots into
the cultural soil of his native land. He cannot identify himself with what passes for American culture because it is a
"white" man's culture, just as he has failed in his attempts to
transcend discrimination within the heart of Christianity by
creating images of a "black" Christ and "black" saints.
Whereas Negro writers still appeal to the tradition embodied
in the Declaration of Independence and the Bill of Rights,
the work of John Brown and Abraham Lincoln and Thad-
deus Stevens, and the writings of the Abolitionist poets, their
usable past must be sought elsewhere. It is to be found in the
history and martyrdom of their own people, in the insurrec-
tions of poorly armed and loosely organized slaves who attempted to break the chains that bound them. The Negroes
need no longer be ashamed of their past; their primary need
as writers is to understand it and put it creatively to use.

Dangerous in its implications is the tendency to amalga-
mate with African culture, to return to primitive fountain-
heads of feeling, tradition, and myth. If "white" America rejects Negroes, they will look for salvation to their ancestral
"homeland." On the cutural plane, this back-to-Africa movement represents the sublimated equivalent of the old discarded plan to have Negroes transplated to Africa. That way
is forever closed to American Negroes. True enough, investi-
gations of life in Africa at the time the Negroes were brought
to these shores point to the existence of a rich ancient culture and disprove the Southern stereotype that the imported
Negro slaves were ignorant savages. They had been part of a
proud, flourishing native culture. But what ideological cas-
tles can be built on such historical foundations? The Negro,
after all, belongs to America. His art is genuinely American
in inspiration and content, untutored and underivative, un-
influenced by African as well as European models. As Gun-

nar Myrdal concludes in *An American Dilemma*: "Negro art will continue to be American because its creators are American and American influences continually mold it."

Negro writers cannot have it both ways: if they oppose racialism as a meaningless as well as dangerous term when applied to politics, they must, if they are to remain consistent in their thinking, oppose it with equal firmness when they encounter it, however camouflaged, on the cultural front. They cannot, on the one hand, maintain that they are American born and bred, native sons of this land, and, on the other, propose to alienate themselves from the American cultural tradition on the ground of racial solidarity with the people of Africa or black folk throughout the world. As Countee Cullen asks in troubled introspection, what is Africa to the American Negro? How much does he know of its history, tribal composition, folklore, collective life, indigenous culture? Even if he studied it, what creative value would it have for him as a writer? What is it he hopes to find in Africa that is denied him in America? Nothing but the hope that in this land and among these people, his ancestors, he will discover the sources of a pure, primitive, autochthonous art.

That hope is foredoomed to failure. As the result of his acculturation in America, he is as much a stranger to Africa as the African is a stranger to America. By spiritually migrating to Africa, he abandons the struggle for freedom and equality in order to retreat to a mythical paradise in the tropics, an idyllic jungle of primitivism. He repudiates his creative citizenship in the body of Western culture for the sake of a pseudo-primitivism which fundamentally has no appeal and no meaning for him. There is no reason why he must make such a choice. He can still support the cause of the colored people, whether in India or Indonesia or China or Africa, without seeking artistic inspiration and cultural roots in the heart of Africa. He will not find them there. . . .

AN AMERICAN LITERATURE

What then is the Negro writer to do? To imitate the "white" American culture is damnable, a confession of a lack of originality. To exploit his unique "racial" soul is to cut himself off from the taproot of universality and the culture of his own land. Negro literature is American literature or it is nothing. Langston Hughes once argued earnestly that the assimilative tendency was the mountain standing in the way of true Negro art in America—"this urge within the race toward white-ness, the desire to pour racial individuality into the mold of American standardization, and to be as little Negro and as much American as possible." Though Hughes speaks of racial individuality, this is different from postulating a racial creative spirit, a racial mentality. Even at that the statement is fallacious. Why this false antithesis between "Negro" and "American"? Why can't the Negro write as a full-fledged American and still retain his individuality, the precious amalgam of all his experiences, intuitions, and insights?

On this issue the Negro writer cannot afford to compromise. By surrendering uncritically to the insidious appeal of "Negroid" or "racial" art, he is in effect accommodating himself to the ethics and aesthetics of a "segregated" literature; he is impoverishing his art and deepening his sense of alienation, confining the Negro genius within the dark and narrow walls of caste. The major task of the Negro writer at present is to destroy the stereotypes that keep him in mental as well as physical bondage. He must break down both the practice of cultural exclusion and the barriers of economic discrimination. At all costs he must find a way out of the trap of cultural alienation if he is to take his rightful place in American literature. All of life, all that is distinctively human, should be included within his creative province. Then Negro comedy as well as tragedy will be born: the gift of irony and laughter. Is it not significant that the Negroes have not yet produced an outstanding humorist? That will surely come in the fullness of time, and when it does Negro literature, having come of age, will cease to be "Negroid" or racial; it will be truly American in spirit and substance, instinct with overtones of the universal.

CHAPTER 5

The Legacy of the Movement

Harlem
Renaissance

The Origin of Modern Black Expression

Mbulamwanza Mudimbe-Boyi

Mbulamwanza Mudimbe-Boyi is a professor of literature studies and has taught at several universities
throughout Africa and France. Writing in the early
1980s, Mudimbe-Boyi contends that the Harlem Renaissance was the foundation of the modern movement to explore black cultural identity. To Mudimbe-
Boyi, America in the 1920s and 1930s provided black
writers with the unique experience of being part of
the American experience and yet being divorced from
its culture because of racial discrimination. Mudimbe-
Boyi argues that these black literati were not able to
express themselves fully until they joined the Expatriate Movement and relocated to Paris, France. Once
out of the restrictive American society, authors such
as Langston Hughes and Richard Wright were free to
critique America's shortcomings and develop their
ideas on the uniqueness of being black.

According to Mudimbe-Boyi, these authors inspired black writers first in France and then
throughout the world to meditate on their own
unique situations. Eventually, black authors and
other artists worldwide noticed similar threads in
their experiences. Coupled with a burgeoning interest in their African heritage, blacks gained a grander
sense of shared cultural identity that continues to
pervade black communities in every nation. And, in
Mudimbe-Boyi's view, it all can be traced back to the
Harlem Renaissance.

One of the most important moments of self-assertion and
emergence for the black personality in the world was the
Negro Renaissance or, as it is also called, the Harlem Re-

Excerpted from "African and Black American Literature: The 'Negro Renaissance'
and the Genesis of African Literature in French," by Mbulamwanza Mudimbe-Boyi,
translated by J. Coates, *For Better or Worse: The American Influence in the World*,
edited by Allen F. Davis (Westport, CT: Greenwood Press, 1981). Copyright © 1981 by
Mbulamwanza Mudimbe-Boyi. Reprinted by permission of the publisher.

naissance. It was the reflection and the remarkable expression not only of a peculiar culture but also the living proof of a particular cultural longing. This literary movement demonstrates the integration of black American culture with American society and, to a very great degree, with the black world as a whole.

It was [scholar] Margaret Butcher who noted with some force that:

> By setting up an inveterate tradition of racial differences in the absence of any fixed or basic differences of culture and tradition on the Negro's part, American slavery introduced into the very heart of American society a crucial dilemma whose resultant problems, with their progressive resolution, account for many fateful events in American history and for some of the most characteristic qualities of American culture. On all levels, political, social, and cultural, this dilemma has become the focal point, disruptive as well as constructive, of major issues in American history. In the pre-Civil War period, the issue was slavery versus anti-slavery; in the Reconstruction era it was discrimination and bi-racialism versus equalitarian nationalism. In the contemporary era, it is segregation and cultural separatism versus integration and cultural democracy.

Summed up in this passage we find the most important points of contradiction in American society, which essentially boil down to certain basic modes of life and dynamics in the American context.

Yet what was the point of making appeals if one was black and living in the America of Lothrop Stoddard and Madison Grant, who were adopting and revising the racial theories of Gobineau, Schultz, Wagner, and Chamberlain? And what was the point of making demands if, just at the very moment when the purity and power and beauty of New Orleans music [i.e., jazz,] was bursting upon the world, the ideas and the violence of a regenerated Ku Klux Klan were being paraded and spread about? For during the 1920s, as during the final quarter of the last century, black musicians and black writers, like all black people who "were trying to make their voices heard, carried a heavy burden marked with all the signs of inferiority which every single black bore, no matter which tradition had lent its character to his plays or poetry or novels."

It was in this climate of derision toward anything black that the Negro Renaissance in America emerged to give some direction and significance to the black personality both in literature and in the culture as a whole.

THE EMERGENCE OF BLACK IDENTITY

The Harlem Renaissance movement which Arna Bontemps brought to life in 1921 is, in fact, the philosophical, spiritual, and artistic result of a number of movements and actions beginning at the turn of the century. Among them we should note: W.E.B. Du Bois's organization of the National Association for the Advancement of Colored People (NAACP), his editing of the *Crisis*, and his organization of several Pan-African congresses; Marcus Garvey's creation of the Black Star Steamship Line and the founding of the review the *Negro World;* and Carter G. Woodson's founding of the Association for the Study of Negro Life and History. All these projects and creations, with their fair share of generosity and radicalism (and sometimes, of utopia), directly helped the rehabilitation of black Americans.

The "Black Renaissance" was thus brought about by blacks for blacks. It was himself that the American black put forward as a subject for his own literary creations, and he went to great lengths to express for himself his own particular problems and his own aspirations and rights in a form which seemed to correspond best with his own fate.

[Critic] Jean Wagner has summed up this new perspective: "The Black Renaissance rises as a whole from a new vision of the past which the whole race shares together."

The movement was composed of many themes: there was revolt against the injustices suffered by blacks; the demand for a new personality and for a cultural identity; and finally there was nostalgia and fascination for the far-off land of Africa. The movement expressed the feelings and thoughts of blacks. And thus where literature is concerned one may speak of a realistic, engaged literature, yet it was also romantic. The nostalgia for Africa appears in fact as a wish to return to roots, coupled with a great love for the history and life of the African people. Africa also appears as a mythical continent, a lost paradise; but at the same time it is also a representation of a black past before all the denials and distortions of slavery. So by turning back and resurrecting Africa there was a possibility for self-assertion: the extent to which black Americans could feel certain about their past governed the extent to which they could place their hope in the future.

This movement for self-assertion, racial rehabilitation, and recognition of the links of solidarity with Africa was centered in Harlem and crystallized around three writers—Claude

McKay, Countee Cullen, and Langston Hughes—to which one should add the voices of Jean Toomer, James W. Johnson, Sterling Brown, Jessie Fauset, Nella Larsen, and others.

These writers produced an eminently American, but also an explicitly black, literature. The writing reflects the material conditions of existence of black writers, as well as the ideological and spiritual expression of a special group in American society. There are two principal themes: first, the rehabilitation of black history and of blacks in contact with "white" and "Anglo-Saxon" culture; and second, the reappraisal of the black race and its art in a world of cultural interaction.

This unique revolution was to be achieved through the efforts and work of the *exiles*. Although effectively exiled from their fatherlands like other blacks, the blacks in America who were to rise up were also exiles within their own culture. Many of them came from places other than Harlem: Claude McKay was Jamaican; E. Wabrond was Guyanese; Langston Hughes came from Missouri; and Arna Bontemps was from California. And several of these poets were not from the black middle class. They were academics who, through learning, had moved away from their origins: Claude McKay came from the State University of Kansas; Jean Toomer from Wisconsin and City College; Jessie Fauset from Cornell; Langston Hughes from Lincoln University; Rudolph Fisher was a professor from Howard University. So they were a minority within a minority; first, because on the level of social relations, they were black in a white-dominated country; and second, because they were the privileged among the blacks. What they began to shout out was: "I am different because I'm Black" and "I, too, am America." These shouts were to launch an important literary movement which was to have considerable influence in the United States and in other parts of the world.

PRIDE IN AFRICAN CULTURE

During the 1920s there appeared in Paris a series of publications on Africa: in 1920 there was *L'Anthologie Nègre* ("The Negro Anthology") by Blaise Cendrars, a collection of stories, legends, fables, poems, and songs from black Africa; in 1921 there was *Batouala, Véritable Roman Nègre* ("Batouala, A True Negro Novel") by Réne Maran; and finally in 1927 there was *Le Voyage au Congo* ("Journey to the Congo") by André Gide, followed by *Retour du Tchad* ("Return from Chad") in

1928. In these last two books, as Jean Wagner notes, "Black America thought it had found confirmation of its idea that France was turning back toward genuine life forces. Postwar American writers, rebels against both the system and the Victorian prudery that dominated small-town life, thought they had found in the black man a kind of noble savage whose primitive spontaneity had somehow been left untouched by the horrors of the civilization which they were surveying."

It was a period in which among the intellectuals and liberals in Europe there was a distinct interest developing in Africa and African people. The black man, in his innocence and splendor, became a kind of curiosity. This approach pervaded both the colonial administration and applied anthropology. There was a search, on the one hand, for the most efficient means of colonizing Africa and, on the other hand, to fill in the gaps in the ancient history of European man which meant describing "African savages" in terms based upon models taken from Western prehistorical accounts. Yet at the same time, the West was discovering that it was no longer the norm in history and thought, that it was not the prime incarnation of either civilization or culture, and that rational thought as an absolute value and major reference was nothing but a myth. The subjective philosophies set off by German romanticism in the eighteenth and nineteenth centuries were beginning to spread, while the notion of relativity on which specialists in the exact and natural sciences were working began to invade the social sciences and the humanities. The human and spiritual misery at the end of the 1914 to 1918 war also led to a serious questioning of the values of that Western culture which in practice could so effectively set the instruments of death in motion.

It was at this moment that white Europe discovered the American black, jazz, African art and, above all, masks. Certain ethnologists (Frobenius, Delafosse, Monod and so on) kept a wary distance from the ideology of applied anthropology and described a sympathetic, dynamic, and original African culture quite different from the mistaken images put out by colonial propaganda. At the same time there also started to be some deep questioning in the works of African scholars who had felt only satisfaction and pride up to then: what actually was African culture?

Leopold Senghor, in an excellent little book entitled *Pierre*

Teilhard de Chardin et la Politique Africaine ("Pierre Teil-hard de Chardin and African Politics") has described the as-tonishment of young black students in Paris and elsewhere in Europe who suddenly discovered good reasons for feeling pride in being Africans. And Lilyan Kesteloot has shown in her book that one of the main causes of this confidence was being in touch with black American writers.

Whenever they speak about the beginnings of their literary movement, the poets of Negritude (or, more precisely, the three apostles [Aime] Césaire, Senghor, and [Leon] Damas) give recognition to the leading role that the black American writers played in arousing their general sense of awareness and the sense of racial awareness that was worked out in the Negro Renaissance. Therefore it was with good reason that Senghor, in his paper to the Colloquium on Negritude held in Dakar in 1971, rightly called them the "fathers of Negritude."

THE IMPACT OF THE RENAISSANCE IN FRANCE

To understand the influence of the black American writers on France, it should be remembered that they brought their re-bellion to Paris. There, like other writers such as Ernest Hem-ingway and Gertrude Stein in this period, they had fled from the dehumanizing system of racial segregation and the dry-ness and conformity of American culture during the 1920s. There were three focal points to their demands—rebellion, vi-olence (both literary and political), and racial awareness.

First, they rebelled against the structure of American so-ciety (see, for instance, *Banjo* by Claude McKay), a society into which they had been thrust but yet one which disowned them ("I, too, am America," exclaimed Langston Hughes). They made claims for their rights; for the rights of American citizens; for their human dignity (as in "If we must die," for example, a poem by Claude McKay); for the right to live; and for the recognition of Africa (as in Countee Cullen's poem "Heritage"). And they denounced racial hatred by both blacks and whites.

Second, one can understand why their tentative gropings would often be toward a sort of religious mystique in which evil (sin, the devil, hell) would be symbolized by the fall of man (especially in the work of Countee Cullen, but also in that of Claude McKay). They were tempted by communism as a social system, as an ideology, and as an epistemology, insofar as communism claimed to resolve all contradictions, to end

man's alienation, and to give freedom not just to the proletariat but to blacks—crushed through exploitation, destroyed
through racial discrimination, and denied through poverty.

Third, there was the inner assertion of the exile, which is
to say the intense existential anxiety that without doubt
sprang from the rejection suffered by the black in American
society, but which was equally caused by the very fact of
Americanism. This can be seen in the rebellion and misery
and bitterness which had been sung about ever since the
first Negro spirituals, such as "Nobody Knows the Trouble
I've Seen." This torn black conscience ("the shock of Americanism on the Negro conscience," in Chester Himes's
words) would only find itself properly by going over all the
psychological conflicts, frustrations, and traumas that had
been endured by blacks since slavery.

The poets of the Negro Renaissance were the first to show
signs of a wish to discover and develop their own culture:
American jazz erupted in Europe and brought with it a new
violence in art and, more particularly, in music. The phenomenon of [black actress and singer] Josephine Baker
made a deep impression on the French ballet in 1925 with
the dazzling spectacles that she made, for example, at the
Folies Bergères. This had prompted the majority of observers to think that the black African poets involved in the
Negritude movement had only taken up the Negro Renaissance rebellion in order to assert the "African Presence."

FRENCH ATTEMPTS TO REAPPRAISE BLACK CULTURE

First of all, there was *La Revue du Monde Noir* ("The Black
World Review") published in Paris (1931–1932) which established a point of focus for all the blacks in the French capital. Previous meetings had been organized where most
black writers had worked toward one goal: the reappraisal
of black culture.

> What we want to do is offer to the intellectual elite of the
> Black race and to the friends of the Blacks an organ in which
> they may publish works of art, literature and science; to study
> and make known through newspapers, books, conferences or
> classes, everything that concerns *Negro civilization* and the
> natural riches of Africa—the fatherland that is three times sa-
> cred to the Black Race; to forge amongst Blacks throughout
> the world, drawing no distinctions between nationalities, an
> intellectual and moral link that will help them to know them-
> selves better, to love each other as brothers, to defend their

collective interests more effectively and to lend honour to their Race.

This statement was directly inspired by the manifesto of the Negro Renaissance. The contribution made by poets such as Claude McKay and Langston Hughes is by no means negligible.

Thus *La Revue,* in wishing to identify Negro values and reappraise black culture with an eye on historical truth, brought about a kind of cultural awakening through justifying its own myths. It talked about the "cultural unity of the black world" which was a unity presented as a belief in oneself and as a force acting in the face of the colonial powers. It should, however, be noted that in *La Revue,* in contrast to the Negro Renaissance, there was to be neither aggressiveness nor polemics, but rather the demand for a return to oneself—a demand made with greater serenity through writing that was sometimes not so much racist as rather conciliatory. There remained nevertheless something of the atmosphere of Alain Locke's "New Negro Movement" in the attitude of understanding and sympathy and responsibility in respect to blacks.

In 1932, when *La Revue du Monde Noir* ceased to appear, the young people from the Antilles who were studying at the universities of Paris declared themselves "suffocated" by the system of exploitation and denial which was making the black man "less than his master's object." They founded the review *Légitime Défense* ("Self Defense") which in one single issue effectively inaugurated the "New Negro" movement. Against the great alienation that the black writer experienced (because of his "borrowed personality"), protesting over the muddled poet (for whom "being a good copy of light-skinned man is meant to stand for social as well as poetic reason"), the authors of *Légitime Défense* in their own way took up the aims of the Negro Renaissance. Speaking about the militant function of the literature that they were trying to start up, E. Lero stated: "The wind that is rising from Black America will, we hope, swiftly sweep our Antilles clean of the fruits fallen from a decayed culture. Langston Hughes and Claude McKay, the two black revolutionary poets, have brought to us, steeped in red alcohol, the African love of life, the African joy in love and the African dream of death. And already the young poets from Haiti are beginning to bring us verses inspired with the dynamics of the future."

The development of the black rebellion can be traced from Negro Renaissance to "Haitian Indigenism," and from *Légitime Défense* to Negritude. But in this journey of suffering and exaltation, the writers of the Negro Renaissance were establishing the paradigm for the conscience of the race. This is why an extract of McKay's novel *Banjo* is given in *Légitime Défense* as a model for the New Negro's literary work, as the principal objective in *Banjo* was to resist European culture by turning back to African culture.

> Black American literature already contained the germs of the principle themes for Negritude, and in this respect one can claim that the real fathers of the Black cultural Renaissance in France were neither the writers in the Antillian tradition nor the surrealist poets nor the French novelists between the wars but the Black writers from the United States! They had left a deep stamp on our writers in the way they had tried to represent the whole race, and had let up a cry in which every single Black recognized himself: it was the first cry of rebellion. . . .

BLACK WRITERS QUESTION WESTERN VALUES

Recognition of their own values led black African writers to start questioning the West and its norms as well. This questioning is shown in novels such as *Un Vie de Boy* ("Boy's Life"), *Le Vieux Nègre et la Médaille* ("The Old Negro and the Medal") and *Chemins d'Europe* ("Paths of Europe") by Ferdinand Oyono; *Ville Cruelle* ("Cruel Town"), *Mission Terminee* ("Mission to Kula"), *Le Pauvre Christ de Bomba* ("The Poor Christ of Bomba"), and *Le Roi Miraculé* ("The Miraculous King") by Mongo Beti; and *Les Bouts de Bois de Dieu* ("God's Bits of Wood") by Sembene Ousmanc.

This challenge to the West, together with the situation he found himself in, finally led the African to start questioning himself. And in the end there was a meeting with the West, which is what we find in Ousmane Soce's *Les Mirages de Paris* ("Mirages of Paris"), Bernard Dadie's *Un Nègre à Paris* ("A Negro in Paris"), and Ake Loba's *Kocoumbo l'Etudiant Noir* ("Kocoumbo the Black Student"). From this inner questioning there arose an existential anxiety: the translation of frustration and the rending schism between loyalty to the race and culture of the blacks and entry into a world dominated by new and strange values. This is admirably illustrated by Cheik Hamidou Kane in *L'Aventure Ambiguë* ("Ambiguous Adventure"), and in V.Y. Mudimbe's *Entre les Eaux* ("Between the Waters"). Samba Diallo, the hero of *L'Aventure*

Ambiguë, sums up this painful quest of his own: "I am not a distinct country of Diallobes, facing a West that is distinct, and understanding with a cool head what I can take from it and what I am supposed to leave behind in exchange. I have become both of them. There is no one clear way between these two choices. There is only one strange nature—one in distress at not being two." This situation of conflict was clearly summed up by W.E.B. Du Bois, though in different terms:

> It is a peculiar sensation, this double-consciousness, this sense of always looking at one's self through the eyes of others, of measuring one's soul by the tape of a world that looks on in amused contempt and pity. One ever feels his two-ness: an American, a Negro; two souls, two thoughts, two unreconciled strivings; two warring ideals in one dark body, whose dogged strength alone keeps it from being torn asunder.

Similarly in African poetry this expression came as a liberation that can be seen in the use of free verse and breaks in rhythm similar to the jumping rhythm of the blues, which is a special expression licensed by the sensibilities and sentiments of blacks. Senghor, David Diop, and others provide eminent examples of this kind of liberty and spontaneity of form. As Senghor wrote, black poetry is a "poetry of flesh and earth; if one is to talk like Hughes, peasant poetry which has not lost contact with the telluric forces. And this explains its cosmic rhythm, its music and its imagery of running water, rustling leaves, beating wings and twinkling stars."

After *Légitime Défense,* and especially after *La Revue du Monde Noir,* the meeting together of the blacks from America, Africa, and the Antilles encouraged the dawn and rising of the great Negro poetry in French and, in a general way, the birth and development of what we today call Negro-African writing. Since then the constant exchange and circulation of ideas have been established, so that the movement can be described in three stages. First, Africa was the point of departure for black ideas that spread from Europe to America. Second, during the decade from 1920 to 1930, Harlem-America became the center of a series of new ideas which, passing first through Paris, spread into the black world in Africa and the Caribbean. Finally, today there has been established a bipolar route between Africa and the black diaspora in America and the Caribbean.

African literature, having found its examples in black American literature, takes on the same ideological character.

In fact from the ideological point of view, it becomes clear that this writing has only one single aim, namely to show how black people really are, or, to take the voluntarist terms of W.E.B. Du Bois to show: "the feeling of being in at the birth of a new criterion for happiness, a new desire to be creative, a new will to exist; as if in this dawn of life of the Black group we have been woken up from some sort of sleep." The problems, the history of black Africa, its beginnings and its mythic splendors are all brought out, but on a romantic pretext, as if to contrast all the more starkly with the misery and limitations of blacks in the modern world. Both African and American writers tend in this way to insist rather strongly upon a blockage of an ideological nature, yet they do at the same time note the essential meaning of this blockage, which is both historical and sociological in nature—the history of blacks and their status and role in the contemporary world.

This consideration can be reformulated with the help of a concept from literary realism, in order to indicate the importance and relevance of Negro Renaissance and Negritude.

Any society which has enjoyed a certain stability tends to corrupt those who are sensitive to the need to speak up for the groups least favored and for those in the greatest minority. Once corrupted, unionized bureaucracies and writers become integrated into the bourgeoisie, allying themselves with the interests of the dominant class which is glad to know them well and to see reflections of itself mirrored in them. But once these groups have performed their tasks their work should become a permanent questioning, a constant search for coherence, and, in the case of American society as in that of colonized Africa, there should be awkward questions raised about nationhood and law. . . .

CONDITIONING THE WRITER

The writer himself is, as the evidence shows, conditioned by society and by the contradictions of the group or social class that he belongs to. But at the same time this conditioning may be drastically reduced by careful use of the rules of "authentic realism." Indeed the ideological world would, thus, no longer be a simple reflection of the economic organization of society.

This call for a kind of comprehensive and radical analysis of literature is satisfactory proof that in the case of the Negro Renaissance literature, as in that of Negritude, we may find a literature that is really involved. This literature is the reflection of the material conditions of existence of black writers. It is also the ideological and spiritual expression of a group in society: the blacks.

It is fundamentally characterized by two main themes: the rehabilitation of black history; the condition of the black in contact with a white culture. On the American side there are W.E.B. Du Bois, Marcus Garvey and Carter G. Woodson; and there are Cheik Anta Diop, Th. Obenga, and J. Kizerbo on the African side.

This is a group which, because it feels itself badly integrated into another group, is clamoring for its "right to cry out and speak." It bursts out and, in declaring its differences, declares as well its right to the sun and to life. It also rises up against all received wisdom by demanding fresh judgment, by rewriting the history of the past, by interpreting in its own way the present time and its conflicts, and finally by projecting its own particular dreams into a future where it seeks to escape the dogmatism and violence of the dominant white classes in America, while in Africa it seeks to escape the white power of colonization.

The struggle of black Americans strongly attracted the first black writers from the Antilles and from Africa. The myth created around African unity which had suggested a utopian vision of Pan-Africanism... was constantly being reactivated throughout the struggle for political and cultural liberation in Africa. It had even inspired ideas of the most violent kind, like those of Cheik Anta Diop. The emergence of the New Negro in America lies in the political and cultural awakening of black Africa, and vice versa.

The first texts of Negro-African writing bore the influence of the poets of the Negro Renaissance, with *Pigments* by Damas, opening with an epigraph by Claude McKay: "Be not deceived, for every deed you do I could match, outmatch: Am I not Africa's son. Black of that black land where black deeds are done." While some poems were dedicated to Mercer Cook and Louis Armstrong, Senghor also dedicated poems to Claude McKay and Langston Hughes and translated Countee Cullen. Later these same black American writers participated in the Congresses of Black Writers and Artists in Paris in 1956 and in Rome in 1959. They published literary texts and analytical articles in the review, *Présence Africaine*, and founded the African Society for Culture. One can per-

haps now understand why so large a number of studies have
been carried out about them and why one whole issue of
Présence Africaine was published in honor of Langston
Hughes. In this fact lies recognition of the important contribution made by the American Negro Renaissance toward the
promotion and expression of blacks in Africa and throughout the world.

The Failure of the Creative Intellectual

Harold Cruse

In 1967 social philosopher Harold Cruse published his collection of essays *The Crisis of the Negro Intellectual*. These essays critiqued the role of blacks in American society throughout the twentieth century. One group he critiques is the creative intellectuals of the Harlem Renaissance. In Cruse's assessment, the creative intellectual community failed to elevate the rest of black culture to an acceptable standard. This was due to the creative intellectuals' desire to integrate with white society instead of educating the black community on the importance of maintaining a distinct cultural identity. This is significant, since it echoes W.E.B. Du Bois's argument that "all art is propaganda," an idea at which the renaissance writers scoffed. The byproduct of this is a cultural community that is capitalized upon and manipulated by white society simply for its entertainment value and lucrative draw for richer white audiences.

Racial democracy is, at the same time, cultural democracy; and the question of cultural democracy in America is posed in a way never before seen or considered in other societies. This uniqueness results historically from the manner in which American cultural developments have been influenced by the Negro presence. Since a cultural philosophy has been cultivated to deny this truth, it remains for the Negro intellectual to create his own philosophy and to bring the facts of cultural history in focus with the cultural practices of the present. In advanced societies it is not the race politicians or the "rights" leaders who create the new ideas and the new images of life and man. That role belongs to the artists and the intellectuals of each generation. Let the race politicians, if they will, create political, economic or organizational forms of leadership; but it is the artists and the creative minds who will, and must, furnish the all important content. And in this role, they must not be subordinated to the whims and desires of politicians, race leaders and civil rights entrepreneurs whether they come from the Left, Right, or Center, or whether they are peaceful, reform, violent, non-violent or laissez-faire. Which means to say, in advanced societies the cultural front is a special one that requires special techniques not perceived, understood, or appreciated by political philistines. There are those among the latter who give lip-service to the idea that Culture and Art belong to the People, but what they actually give to the people (not to speak of what is given to Negroes as people) is not worthy of examination. It is the Negro creative intellectual who must take seriously the idea that culture and art belong to the people—with all the revolutionary implications of that idea.

To bring this idea into proper focus, and into the context of our peculiar American cultural ideology, let us quote from Gilbert Seldes' book, *The Public Arts*, written in 1956:

> "This country, with its institutions, belongs to the people who inhabit it," said Abraham Lincoln, and as he was then facing the possible dissolution of the United States, he added, "Whenever they (the people) shall grow weary of the existing government, they can exercise their Constitutional right of amending it or their revolutionary right to dismember or overthrow it."

> I am suggesting that the cultural institutions of a country also belong to its inhabitants, and, not having the courage of Lincoln's radicalism, I do not insist upon the revolutionary right of the people to destroy whatever wearies them. Moderately, I propose the idea that the people have valid rights over those cultural institutions which can be properly called "the public arts."

Seldes had come a long way from 1924 when he wrote *The Seven Lively Arts*. He pointed out, in 1956, that a revolution had taken place in American cultural arts communication, which had transformed what he had called in the 1920's the "seven lively arts," into what are now the "public arts": "For convenience, the beginning of that revolution can be placed in the late summer of 1929, when millions of Americans, with more money to spend on recreation than they had ever had before, spent nothing because they were staying home to be entertained by the Amos 'n' Andy radio program."

IMPOSING WHITE SYMBOLS ON BLACK AMERICA

The fact, of course, that "Amos 'n' Andy" was a modernized version of the old-time minstrel show—in which whites blackened their faces in order to imitate the original plantation minstrels created by Negroes—probably did not strike Seldes as being highly significant in a cultural way because of "content." But the fact that the program was an imitation Negro comic show *is* significant. The Negro-white cultural symbolism involved here was expressed and given significance by Gilbert Seldes himself, during the 1920's when his critiques of American art forms damned the Negro with faint praise, condemning him forever to the back alleys of American culture. Seldes claimed then that Negro music and musicians could not hope to rise to "classic" stature. He implied also that Negro theater ought not to be looked upon as art in the sense that the devotees of Western culture think of art. "The one claim never made for the Negro shows is that they are artistic," Seldes wrote. He was then talking about such hit shows as Sissle and Blake's *Shuffle Along:*

> Set beside them [Negro shows], then, a professedly artistic revue, the *Pinwheel* [a white show], compounded of native and exotic effects. It had two or three interesting or exciting numbers; but the whole effect was one of dreariness. The pall of art was upon it; it died nightly. And *Shuffle Along, without art,* but with tremendous vitality, not only lived through the night, but dragged provincial New Yorkers to a midnight show as well.

Yet, according to Seldes, Negro shows were not art. And what, pray tell, *is* art? The peculiar and perverse tradition of cultural criticism, practiced by Gilbert Seldes and others, has severely distorted native American artistic standards by over-glorifying obsolete European standards. Seldes debased Negro creative artists by refusing to accept their native originality as truly American. He rejected what was truly American because it was not European, but Afro-American. Thus by downgrading Negro musical originality, he helped to undermine the only artistic base in the American culture in which the Negro could hold his own as an original artist. And, from this base, he could eventually, by dint of creative discipline, raise his own level of sophistication and finesse in all other American art forms. Thus, in the 1920's, Seldes' criticisms encouraged undemocratic ethnic tendencies in American culture. Yet contradictorily, in 1956 Gilbert Seldes wants the "public arts" of America democratized by returning them to the people. But which people? Seldes, of course, knows that the "seven lively arts" did not belong to the people in the 1920's. Because if they had, America would not have witnessed that un-cultural spectacle of Hemingway, Harold Stearns, Sinclair Lewis, T.S. Eliot, Ezra Pound—the lost generation refugees—hotfooting it to Paris and Madrid to escape American cultural suffocation. While all of these white intellectuals were escaping because they could not be real artists in America, the Negroes were trying to create new art in their own native American way. And, as things have turned out "culturally" in America, there is now *only one* group of American creative intellectuals who have the motivation (or at least the potential) for democratizing American culture and forcing the return of the public arts to the people. These are the new young generation of Negro intellectuals—the cultural and ethnic progeny of those very Negroes whom Seldes critically downgraded in the 1920's as being mostly primitive and non-intellectual as creative artists. These young people, however, will have to go far beyond Seldes' proposed "moderation" in techniques and will have to search for the "revolutionary rights" of confrontation that Seldes disavows.

ESTABLISHING CULTURAL LEADERSHIP

This new young generation must first clear the way to cultural revolution by a critical assault on the methods and ideology of the old-guard Negro intellectual elite. The failures and ideological shortcomings of this group have meant that no new directions, or insights have been imparted to the Negro masses. This absence of positive orientation has created a cultural void that has spawned all the present-day tendencies towards nihilism and anarchism, evident in the ideology of the young. This new generation of Negro poets, artists, writers, critics and playwrights bursts onto the scene; fed and inspired by the currents flowing out of movements at home and abroad, they are full of zeal but have no well-charted direction. They encounter the established old guard (even some lingering representatives of the 1920's) and the results are confusion and a clash of aims. The old guard attempts to absorb some of the new guard. This process has been seen at work in the Harlem Writers Guild, the Artists for Freedom group, *Freedomways* and *Liberator* magazines and in the recent proliferation of Negro Writers' Conferences. The young wave attempts to criticize *and* emulate the old guard at one and the same time, which creates more ideological confusion. The young wave cannot completely break from the old order of things cultural, because the old guard stands pat and blocks the path to new cultural frontiers. . . .

How would one define cultural leadership? How would it be differentiated qualitatively from ordinary civil rights leadership, or the overworked "civil writism" of the old guard, or the emulation of the new? This has to be clarified because American Negroes are, after all, Americans who pattern their social reasoning on white American standards of social logic. White Anglo-Saxon Protestants are fundamentally anti-theoretical, anti-aesthetic, anti-cultural, anti-intellectual. They often try hard not to be that way, but have a deep-seated suspicion of art, culture, and intellect nonetheless. They prefer the practical, by which they mean the application of practical values in the pursuit of materialistic ends. They actually look upon the enjoyment of art and culture as a materialistic end, especially if it is "entertaining." But they are not overly concerned about the cultivation of creativity. Creative values are usually subordinated to materialistic values. This outlook permeates everything in the United States, including the outlook of American Negroes. . . .

The civil rights movement cannot really give cultural leadership in any effective way—it is too suffused with the compulsion to legitimize its social aims with American standards. The leaders of the civil rights movement, along with all the "civil writers," subordinate themselves to the very cultural values of the white world that are used either to negate, or deny the Negro cultural equality, and to exploit his cultural ingredients and use them *against* him. This is one of the great traps of racial integrationism—one must accept all the values (positive or negative) of the dominant society into which one struggles to integrate. Let us examine two very prominent cultural questions out of the American twentieth-century past and see how they were handled. Both of these are issues of the 1920's that have become institutionalized in today's Americana. One is exemplified by the folk-opera *Porgy and Bess,* a cultural product, the other by [pianist and composer] Duke Ellington, a cultural personality.

LACKING KNOWLEDGE OF CULTURAL CONTENT

In May, 1959, following the successful opening of *A Raisin in the Sun*, its author Lorraine Hansberry debated Otto Preminger on a television program in Chicago, over what she labeled the deplorable "stereotypes" of *Porgy and Bess*. The film version of the folk-opera, directed by Preminger, had just been released and it starred none other than Sidney Poitier, who also headlined Miss Hansberry's play on Broadway. This was, of course, not the first time *Porgy and Bess* had been criticized by Negroes. Ever since its premiere in 1935, it has been under attack from certain Negro quarters because it reveals southern Negroes in an unfavorable light. Hence Miss Hansberry's criticisms were nothing very new or original. What *was* new, however, were the times and the circumstances. Miss Hansberry objected to *Porgy* because stereotypes "constitute bad art" when "the artist hasn't tried hard enough to understand his characters." She claimed that although Gershwin had written a great musical score, he had fallen for what she called the exotic in American culture. . . .

When Preminger asked Miss Hansberry if she suspected the motives of those who had written and produced *Porgy*, she replied: "We cannot afford the luxuries of mistakes of other peoples. So it isn't a matter of being hostile to you, but on the other hand it's also a matter of never ceasing to try to get you to understand that your mistakes can be painful, even those which come from excellent intentions. We've had great wounds from great intentions."

During this debate there was also injected a discussion of *Carmen Jones*—a white-created, Negro version of the Bizet opera, *Carmen*. Miss Hansberry did not like *Carmen Jones* either; but oddly enough (and also characteristically), she weakened her argument on the subject of artistic integrity by wanting to know why no whites had been cast in this caricature of *Carmen*, as if to imply that interracial casting would have made it more acceptable as art. Behind this query there lurked, of course, the whole muddled question of integration in the arts. Also implicit was the Negro integrationist's main peeve in the theater—the "all-Negro play" (or musical), which they deplore as a symbol of segregation, and the "all-white play," which it is their bounden duty to "integrate" even if the author never had Negroes in mind. . . .

This whole episode revealed some glaring facts to substantiate my claim that the Negro creative intellectual does not even approach possession of a positive literary and cultural critique—either of his own art, or that other art created for him by whites. In the first place, Lorraine Hansberry revealed that she knew little about the history of this folk-opera, or how or why it was written. She was only concerned with the fact that it was a stereotype. This already precluded the possibility of Miss Hansberry or anyone rendering the kind of critique *Porgy and Bess* deserves from the Negro point of view. Hence, the whole debate was worthless and a waste of time except from the point of view of making some more noisy, but superficial, integrationist propaganda.

The real cultural issues surrounding *Porgy and Bess*, as it relates to the American Negro presence, have never been confronted by the Negro intelligentsia—inside or outside the theater. The two most obvious points a Negro critic should make are: 1.) that a folk-opera of this genre *should have been written* by Negroes themselves and has not; 2.) that such a folk-opera, even if it *had been written* by Negroes, would never have been supported, glorified and acclaimed, as *Porgy* has, by the white cultural elite of America.

Lorraine Hansberry, taking to the television rostrum on art and culture *à la Negre*, was like a solitary defender, armed with a dull sword, rushing out on a charger to meet a regiment. But once having met an opposing general she immediately capitulates—"My intentions are not really hostile but you all have wounded *us.*" For Miss Hansberry to have criticized *Porgy* merely on content was, of course, her unmitigated privilege; but on this basis, her own play was wide open for some criticism on art and the image of the American Negro, which it never got. To criticize any play today involving Negroes, purely on content, is not enough. Most Negro criticism of *Porgy* has been of middle-class origin, although the Negro middle class has never been at all sympathetic to the realities of southern Negro folk characteristics in any way, shape or form. Hence, a generically class-oriented non-identification was inherent in Miss Hansberry's views. . . .

CONFRONTING CULTURAL DENIAL

To attack it, one must see it in terms of something more than mere content. It must be criticized from the Negro point of view as the most perfect symbol of the Negro creative artist's cultural denial, degradation, exclusion, exploitation and acceptance of white paternalism. *Porgy and Bess* exemplifies this peculiarly American cultural pathology, most vividly, most historically, and most completely. It combines the problems of Negro theater, music, acting, writing, and even

THE IMPACT ON OTHER CULTURES

In this excerpt, author and scholar W.E.B. Du Bois states that artistic endeavor must be used for no other purpose than to elevate the rest of a culture to a higher standard.

And so I might go on. But let me sum up with this: Suppose the only Negro who survived some centuries hence was the Negro painted by white Americans in the novels and essays they have written. What would people in a hundred years say of black Americans? Now turn it around. Suppose you were to write a story and put in it the kind of people you know and like and imagine. You might get it published and you might not. And the "might not" is still far bigger than the "might". The white publishers catering to white folk would say, "It is not interesting"—to white folk, naturally not. They want Uncle Toms, Topsies, good "darkies" and clowns. . . .

Thus it is the bounden duty of black America to begin this great work of the creation of Beauty, of the preservation of Beauty, of the realization of Beauty, and we must use in this work all the methods that men have used before. And what have been the tools of the artist in times gone by? First of all, he has used the Truth—not for the sake of truth, not as a scientist seeking truth, but as one upon whom Truth eternally thrusts itself as the highest handmaid of imagination, as the one great vehicle of universal understanding. Again artists have used Goodness—goodness in all its aspects of justice, honor and right—not for sake of an ethical sanction but as the one true method of gaining sympathy and human interest.

The apostle of Beauty thus becomes the apostle of Truth and Right not by choice but by inner and outer compulsion. Free he is but his freedom is ever bounded by Truth and Justice; and slavery only dogs him when he is denied the right to tell the Truth or recognize an ideal of Justice.

Thus all Art is propaganda and ever must be, despite the wailing of the purists. I stand in utter shamelessness and say that whatever art I have for writing has been used always for propaganda for gaining the right of black folk to love and enjoy. I do not care a damn for any art that is not used for propaganda. But I do care when propaganda is confined to one side while the other is stripped and silent.

W.E.B. Du Bois, "Criteria of Negro Art," *W.E.B. Du Bois: Writings.* New York: Library of America, 1996.

dancing, all in one artistic package, for the Negro has expressed whatever creative originality he can lay claim to, in each of these aspects of art. However, Negroes had no part in writing, directing, producing, or staging this folk-opera about Negroes (unless it was in a strictly subordinate role). In fact, the first recording of *Porgy* used the voices of Lawrence Tibbett and other white singers, because it was not at first believed that Negroes were "good" enough. As a symbol of that deeply-ingrained, American cultural paternalism practiced on Negroes ever since the first Southern white man blacked his face, the folk-opera *Porgy and Bess* should be forever banned by all Negro performers in the United States. No Negro singer, actor, or performer should ever submit to a role in this vehicle again. If white producers want to stage this folk-opera it should be performed by white performers made up in blackface, because it is distorted imitation all the way through. . . .

But the superficial Negro creative intelligentsia, who have become so removed from their meaningful traditions, cannot see things this way, so blindly obsessed are they with the modern mania for instant integration. They do not understand the cultural history of America and where they fit in that historical scheme. They understand next to nothing about the 1920's and how the rather fluid, contending cultural trends among blacks and whites were frozen in that decade, once white control of cultural and creative power patterns was established to the supreme detriment of blacks. They are not aware that the white critics of that time were saying that Negro creative artists were, for the most part, primitives; and that Gilbert Seldes, for example, asserted that Negro musicians and composers were creatively and artistically backward. They are not aware that for critics like Seldes, the Negroes were the anti-intellectual, uninhibited, unsophisticated, intuitive children of jazz music who functioned with aesthetic "emotions" rather than with the disciplined "mind" of white jazzmen. . . .

This was a personal opinion, but whether true or false, it typified the white cultural attitudes toward all forms and practices of Negro art: Compared to the Western intellectual standards of art and culture, the Negro does not measure up. Thus every Negro artist, writer, dramatist, poet, composer, musician, *et al*, comes under the guillotine of this cultural judgment. What this judgment really means is that the Negro

is artistically, creatively, and culturally inferior; and therefore, all the established social power wielded by the white
cultural elite will be used to keep the Negro creative artist in
his place. But the historical catch in all this is that the white
Protestant Anglo-Saxon in America has nothing in his native
American tradition that is aesthetically and culturally original, except that which derives from the Negro presence. . . .

The *Porgy and Bess* controversy had another important
angle. In December, 1955, the State Department sent a company to perform it in the Soviet Union. The folk-opera was
well received by the Russians and given a tumultuous ova-
tion. Truman Capote, the American novelist and playwright,
reported on this cultural exchange in his book, *The Muses
Are Heard.* One of the Leningrad critics said, in part, of *Porgy
and Bess:* "We are not used to the naturalistic details in the
dance, to the excessive jazz sound of the symphony orchestra, etc. Nevertheless the performance broadens our concept
of the art of contemporary America, and familiarizes us with
thus far unknown facets of the musical and theatrical life of
the United States."

Of course, this is an enthusiastic overstatement of the
facts of life, inasmuch as the opera was written in the 1930's,
based on a novel written in 1925. But the fact that the Russians praised the work revealed the awkward, false, and
highly irrelevant position of the American Communist left-
wing on the Negro in culture. From the leftwings's cultural
thesis on art, we get the aesthetics of Soviet socialist realism
that was imposed on leftwing Negro writers. This thesis
agrees with those non-Left Negroes who call the folk-opera
a stereotype. But, if Soviet-loving Paul Robeson, for example,
ever publicly set the Russians right on how to assess this
work of art, I am ignorant of when or how. The Russian reaction proved that it is impossible to attack *Porgy and Bess*
on content alone, for the Russians could not possibly have
grasped the real and actual "facets of the musical and theatrical life of the United States" simply by seeing this work
performed in Leningrad.

DEMONSTRATING WHITE CONTROL

In 1965, Duke Ellington, America's greatest exponent of or-
chestrated jazz music and composition, was turned down for
the Pulitzer Prize citation for "long-term achievement" in
American music. In *The New York Times* story, the Pulitzer

Prize advisory board gave no reason for refusing the citation to Ellington. For just about forty years, he has been, by general popular and professional acclaim, the foremost jazz orchestra leader and composer in America. This turn-down indicates that the same old, ethnic-group war for cultural supremacy in American music is still being waged. Ellington was quoted as saying: "Fate's being kind to me. Fate doesn't want me to be too famous too young."

Ellington could be denied this kind of recognition only because of the undemocratic way the cultural machine in America is run. Here was an affront to the entire musical and cultural heritage of every Negro in America. If the Negro creative intellectuals were really educating their people—every jazz musician, singer, and actor would have understood the meaning of this contemptuous attitude. They would have walked off their jobs and demonstrated collectively in a march down Broadway. Every movie house in Negro neighborhoods would have been boycotted, in a sympathy strike against the racist views that have for decades permeated American culture, poisoned its creative bloodstreams, corrupted its ideology, and retarded the national potential. But the incident passed with only a momentary response to its cultural implications, so blind, benumbed, amoral, crass and corrupted have we become, so aesthetically untutored are our collective sensibilities. . . .

Negro creative intellectuals, however, are neither equipped nor willing to contribute cultural leadership on a question like this. They are most adept when it comes to sentimentalizing in public about their preoccupation with the indigenous qualities of the "Folk." But somewhere deep in their consciousness is the same attitude, borrowed from whites, that jazz music does not edify but merely entertains. A jazz artist is, therefore, merely an entertainer who, in certain cases, makes a lot of money—or at least a lot more than the average Negro earns. Such artists are successful, at least in quasi-middle-class terms. Therefore, in their practical minds, jazz entertainment is rated according to what degree its Negro practitioners earn money enough to achieve middle-class status. When this earning power reaches a level that permits one to purchase a Life Membership in the NAACP [National Association for the Advancement of Colored People], an entertainer has "arrived." Sammy Davis, Jr. even went one better, for he was recently elected Chairman of the Association's Life-Membership Drive.

This is an entertainer who has *truly* arrived. . . .

Every NAACP bigwig feels exactly the same way about entertainers of color: Just as long as they do not stereotype the Negro and offend middle-class sensibilities in such vehicles as *Porgy and Bess*, they are appreciated, but not taken too seriously. Thus the real impact of the Negro entertainer on race politics in American culture does not penetrate the minds of these colored, middle-class philistines.

THE UNCHANGING ROLE OF NEGRO ARTISTS

These people do not want to comprehend the fact that the role of the Negro, as entertainer, has not changed since the 1920's. In 1967 the Negro entertainer is still being used, manipulated, and exploited by whites (predominantly Jewish whites). Negro entertainment talent is more original than that of any other ethnic group, more creative ("soulful" as they say), spontaneous, colorful, and also more plentiful. It is so plentiful, that in the marketplace of popular culture, white brokers and controllers buy Negro entertainment cheaply (sometimes for nothing) and sell it high—as in the case of Sammy Davis. But there is only *one* Sammy Davis. In the shadows, a multitude of lesser colored lights are plugging away, hoping against hope to make the Big Time, for the white culture brokers only permit a few to break through—thus creating an artificial scarcity of a cultural product. This system was established by the wily Broadway entrepreneurs in the 1920's. Negro entertainment posed such an ominous threat to the white cultural ego, the staid Western standards of art, cultural values and aesthetic integrity, that the entire source had to be stringently controlled. . . .

But the Negro creative intellectuals cannot exert themselves to deal with the *roots* of these problems, because they permit too many of the surface issues to pass without dealing with *them*. The question of Ellington and the Pulitzer Prize is a surface issue. The prize itself is not really that important, but what lies behind the denial of the prize, *is:* a whole history of organized duplicity and exploitation of the Negro jazz artist—the complicated tie-in between booking agencies, the musicians' unions, the recording companies, the music publishers, the managers, the agents, the theater owners, the nightclub owners, the crooks, shysters, and racketeers. The Negro creative intellectuals have to look into the question of how it is possible for a Negro jazz musician to walk the streets of large cities, jobless and starving, while a record that he cut with a music company is selling well, both in the United States and in Europe. They have to examine why a Negro jazz musician can be forced to pay dues to unions that get him no work, and that operate with the same discriminatory practices as clubs, halls and theaters. The impact of the cultural tradition of Afro-American folk music demands that the racially-corrupt practices of the music-publishing field be investigated.

The Negro creative intellectuals must also take action against the film-producing conspiracy in the United States, where a "one-star" system has been manufactured around Sidney Poitier. He is supposed to represent the cultural presence, the aspirations, and the social psychology of the largest minority in the United States, a minority whose population is considerably larger than many independent nations in the world. The Negro creative intellectuals cannot make peace with a cultural apparatus that will not take *Invisible Man,* or any other representative novel, and film it. Whether such works are good, bad or excellent is academic, in view of the millions of dollars wasted annually in filming trash for the movie market. . . .

But the Negro intelligentsia cannot give cultural leadership on these questions because they have sold out their own birthright for an illusion called Racial Integration. Having given up their strict claim to an ethnic identity in politics, economics and culture, they haven't a leg to stand on. They can make no legitimate claims for their group integrity in cultural affairs. They take the *illusion* of the integrated world of the creative intellectuals as the social *reality,* and do not know how to function within its cultural apparatus.

What lurks behind the disabilities and inhibitions of the Negro creative intellectuals is the handicap of the black bourgeoisie. Unless this class is brought into the cultural situation and forced to carry out its responsibilities on a community, organizational, and financial level, the cultural side of the black revolution will be retarded. The snail's pace of bourgeois civil rights reform, and white power-structure manipulation, will combine to stall it indefinitely. The problem of cultural leadership, then, is not only a problem of the faulty orientation of the Negro creative intellectuals; it is also a problem of the reeducation of the black bourgeoisie, especially its new, younger strata.

CHRONOLOGY

1917

Ridgely Torrance and Emily Hapgood present three one-act plays: *The Rider of Dreams, Simon the Cyrenean,* and *Granny Maumee;* each has an all-black cast; James Weldon Johnson's *Fifty Years and Other Poems* is published by Cornhill; Claude McKay publishes his poem "Seven Arts," becoming the first black writer to publish in a white publication.

1918

Carter G. Woodson's *A Century of Negro Migration* is published by Cornhill; Marcus Garvey begins his journal *Negro World.*

1919

Claude McKay publishes his poem "If We Must Die" in the *Liberator;* Robert T. Kerlin's *The Voice of the Negro* is published by Dutton.

1920

W.E.B. Du Bois is awarded the Spingarn award for his work as editor of the *Crisis;* Eugene O'Neill's *The Emperor Jones* is performed for the first time; Natalie Curtis's *Songs and Tales from the Dark Continent* is published by Schirmer; Claude McKay's *Spring in New Hampshire* is published by Grant Richards; Alice Dunbar Nelson's *The Dunbar Speaker and Entertainer* is published by Nichols.

1921

Shuffle Along, the first musical review written and performed by blacks, opens in New York; Charles S. Gilpin receives the Spingarn award for playing the role of Brutus Jones in *The Emperor Jones;* Countee Cullen publishes "I Have a Rendezvous with Life" in the Dewitt High School literary journal, the *Magpie;* Langston Hughes's first published poem, "The Negro Speaks of Rivers," appears in the *Crisis.*

1922

Claude McKay's *Harlem Shadows* is published by Harcourt, Brace.

1923

James Weldon Johnson's *The Book of American Negro Poetry: An Anthology* is published by Harcourt, Brace; the black musical review *Strut Miss Lizzie* opens in New York; Charles S. Johnson and Graham R. Taylor's *The Negro in Chicago: A Study of Race Relations and a Race Riot* is published by the University of Chicago Press; Clement Wood's *Nigger* is published by Dutton; the Spingarn Medal is awarded to George Washington Carver for excellence in research and agricultural chemistry; Jean Toomer's *Cane* is published by Boni and Liveright; *The Chip Woman's Fortune* by Willis Richardson is the first serious play by a black playwright to open on Broadway; Waldo Frank's *Holiday* is published by Boni and Liveright.

1924

Eugene O'Neill's *All God's Chillun Got Wings* opens in Washington, D.C.; *Opportunity* magazine hosts its dinner at the Civic Club in New York to honor Jessie Fauset's novel *There Is Confusion;* W.E.B. Du Bois's *The Gift of Black Folk* is published by Stratford; Countee Cullen wins the Witter Bynner Poetry Competition.

1925

DuBose Heyward's *Porgy* is published by Doubleday; Zora Neale Hurston becomes editor of the *Spokesman;* Countee Cullen's first book of poems, *Color,* is published by Harper and Brothers; *Survey Graphic* publishes a special March issue featuring works by African American writers; Alain Locke publishes *The New Negro,* an expanded version of the *Survey Graphic* issue.

1926

Langston Hughes's first book of poetry, *The Weary Blues,* is published by Knopf; Carl Van Vechten's *Nigger Heaven* is published by Knopf; Wallace Thurman, Langston Hughes, Zora Neale Hurston, Aaron Douglass, and Richard Bruce Nugent launch *Fire!;* The Krigwa Players, a new black theater troop, is founded by the *Crisis;* the play *Blackbirds,* starring Florence Mills, opens in New York.

1927

In Abraham's Bosom, by Paul Green, is the first play with an all-black cast to win the Pulitzer Prize; DuBose Heyward's

Porgy opens as a Broadway musical; Alain Locke edits the anthology *Plays of Negro Life;* it is published by Harper and Brothers; James Weldon Johnson's book of poetry *God's Trombones: Seven Negro Sermons in Verse* is published by Viking; Countee Cullen's *Ballad of the Brown Girl, Copper Sun,* and *Caroling Dusk* are published by Harper and Brothers; Langston Hughes's *Fine Clothes to the Jew* is published by Knopf; James Weldon Johnson's *Autobiography of an Ex-Coloured Man* (1912) is reprinted by Knopf; *Opportunity* suspends its literary contests due to the submission of weak material.

1928

W.E.B. Du Bois's *The Dark Prince* is published by Harcourt, Brace; Rudolph Fisher's novel *The Walls of Jericho* is published by Knopf; Nella Larsen's novel *Quicksand* is published by Knopf; Wallace Thurman's *Negro Life in New York's Harlem* is published by Haldemann-Julius; Charles W. Chesnutt receives the Spingarn award for excellence in literature.

1929

Wallace Thurman's novel *The Blacker the Berry* is published by Macaulay; Countee Cullen's *The Black Christ* is published by Harper and Brothers; Claude McKay's *Banjo* is published; Benjamin Brawley's *The Negro in Literature and Art in the United States* is published by Dodd, Mead; Jessie Fauset's novel *Plum Bun* is published by Stokes; Nella Larsen's novel *Passing* is published by Knopf; on Thursday, October 24, the stock market crashes.

1930

Randolph Edmonds's *Shades and Shadows* is published by Meador; Charles S. Johnson's *The Negro in Civilization: A Study of Negro Life and Race Relations* is published by Holt; Gilmore Millen's *Sweet Man* is published by Viking; Carl Whitke's *Tambourine and Bones* is published by Duke University Press.

1931

The Scottsboro Trial runs from April through July; Arna Bontemps's *God Sends Sunday* is published by Harcourt, Brace; Benjamin Brawley's *A Short History of the American Negro* is published by Macmillan; Jessie Fauset's *The Chinaberry Tree* is published by Stokes; Langston Hughes's *Dear Lovely Death* is published by Troutbeck; George S. Schuyler's novel *Black No More* is published by Macaulay; Jean Toomer's *Essentials* is published by Lakeside.

1932

Arna Bontemps and Langston Hughes's *Pop and Fifna* is published by Macmillan; Sterling Brown's *Southern Road* is published by Harcourt, Brace; Countee Cullen's novel *One Way to Heaven* is published by Harper and Brothers; Rudolph Fisher's *The Conjure Man Dies* is published by Covici Friede; Langston Hughes's *The Dream Keeper* is published by Knopf; Claude McKay's *Gingertown* is published by Harper and Brothers.

1933

Jessie Fauset's *Comedy, American Style* is published by Stokes; James Weldon Johnson's *Along This Way* is published by Viking; Claude McKay's *Banana Bottom* is published by Harper and Brothers.

1934

Nancy Cunard's *Negro* is published by Wisart; Randolph Edmonds's *Six Plays for the Negro Theater* is published by Baker; Langston Hughes's *The Ways of White Folks* is published by Knopf; Zora Neale Hurston's *Jonah's Gourd Vine* is published by Lippincott.

1935

Countee Cullen's *The Medea and Other Poems* is published by Harper and Brothers; Zora Neale Hurston's *Mules and Men* is published by Lippincott; Langston Hughes's *Mulatto* is the first full-length play by a black man to open on Broadway.

1936

Richard Wright becomes editor of *Challenge Magazine* and changes the name to *New Challenge.*

1937

Claude McKay's autobiography, *A Long Way from Home,* is published by Lee and Furman.

1940

Richard Wright's *Native Son* is published by Harper and Row; Claude McKay's *Harlem: Negro Metropolis* is published by Dutton.

FOR FURTHER RESEARCH

Arnold Adoff, *I Am the Darker Brother: An Anthology of Modern Poems by Negro Americans.* New York: Macmillan, 1968.

William Andrews, *Classic Fiction of the Harlem Renaissance.* New York: Oxford University Press, 1994.

Harold Bloom, ed., *American Fiction, 1914 to 1945.* New York: Chelsea House, 1987.

———, *American Poetry, 1915 to 1945.* New York: Chelsea House, 1987.

Countee Cullen, *Caroling Dusk: An Anthology of Verse by Negro Poets.* New York: Harper & Row, 1955.

Leo Hamalian, ed., *The Roots of African American Drama: An Anthology of Early Plays, 1858–1938.* Detroit: Wayne State University Press, 1991.

Nathan Huggins, *Harlem Renaissance.* New York: Oxford University Press, 1971.

Nathan Huggins, ed., *Voices from the Harlem Renaissance.* New York: Oxford University Press, 1976.

James Weldon Johnson, *The Book of American Negro Poetry.* San Diego: Harcourt Brace Jovanovich, 1983.

Marcy Knopf, ed., *The Sleeper Wakes: Harlem Renaissance Stories by Women.* New Brunswick, NJ: Rutgers University Press, 1993.

David Lewis, *The Portable Harlem Renaissance Reader.* New York: Viking, 1994.

CRITICISM OF THE PERIOD

Jervis Anderson, *This Was Harlem.* New York: Farrar, Straus, Giroux, 1982.

Houston A. Baker, *Modernism and the Harlem Renaissance.* Chicago: University of Chicago Press, 1987.

John Earl Basset, *Harlem in Review: Critical Reactions to Black American Writers.* Selinsgrove, PA: Susquehanna University Press, 1992.

Harold Bloom, ed., *James Baldwin.* New York: Chelsea House, 1986.

——, *Langston Hughes.* New York: Chelsea House, 1989.

Frank Marshall Davis, *Livin' the Blues: Memoirs of a Black Journalist and Poet.* Madison: University of Wisconsin Press, 1992.

Dictionary of Literary Biography, "Afro-American Writers Before the Harlem Renaissance." Detroit: Gale, 1986.

——, "Afro-American Writers from the Harlem Renaissance to 1940." Detroit: Gale, 1987.

Gerald Early, ed., *Speech and Power: The African-American Essay and Its Cultural Content from Polemics to Pulpit.* New York: Ecco, 1992.

James A. Emanuel, *Langston Hughes.* Boston: Twayne, 1967.

Langston Hughes, ed., *A Pictorial History of the Negro in America.* New York: Crown, 1983.

Gloria T. Hull, *Color, Sex, and Poetry: Three Women Writers of the Harlem Renaissance.* Bloomington: Indiana University Press, 1987.

Bruce Kellner, ed., *The Harlem Renaissance: A Historical Dictionary for the Era.* Westport, CT: Greenwood, 1984.

Reference Library of Black America. New York: Bellwether, 1971.

Robert A. Russ, *The Harlem Renaissance: A Selected Bibliography.* New York: AMS, 1987.

Cary D. Wintz, *Black Culture and the Harlem Renaissance.* Houston: Rice University Press, 1988.

WORKS BY CONTEMPORARY WRITERS

Sterling A. Brown, *The Collected Poems*. New York: Harper & Row, 1980.

Countee Cullen, *Color*. New York: Harper & Brothers, 1925.

——, *My Soul's High Song*. New York: Doubleday, 1991.

W.E.B. Du Bois, *The Souls of Black Folk*. Millwood, NY: Kraus-Thomson Organization, 1973.

Jessie Redmon Fauset, *Plum Bun: A Novel Without a Moral*. Boston: Beacon, 1990.

——, *There Is Confusion*. Boston: Northeastern University Press, 1989.

Rudolph Fisher, *Walls of Jericho*. Ann Arbor: University of Michigan Press, 1994.

Langston Hughes, *Selected Poems*. New York: Vintage Books, 1987.

——, *The Weary Blues*. New York: Knopf, 1926.

James Weldon Johnson, *The Autobiography of an Ex-Coloured Man*. New York: Vintage Books, 1989.

——, *God's Trombones: Seven Negro Sermons in Verse*. New York: Viking, 1980.

Alain Locke, *The New Negro: An Interpretation*. New York: Johnson Reprint, 1968.

Claude McKay, *Harlem Shadows*. New York: Harcourt, Brace, 1992.

——, *Home to Harlem*. Chatham, NJ: Chatham Bookseller, 1973.

——, *A Long Way from Home*. New York: Arno, 1969.

Eugene O'Neill, *Plays*. New York: Horace Liveright, 1925.

Jean Toomer, *Cane*. New York: Liveright, 1993.

Carl Van Vechten, *Nigger Heaven*. New York: A.A. Knopf, 1926.

Eric Walrond, *Tropic Death*. New York: Collier Books, 1972.

Richard Wright, *Black Boy, a Record of Childhood and Youth*. New York: Harper & Brothers, 1945.

INDEX

Africa
Barnes's art collection from, 147–49
indigenous texts from, 53
literature of, 193–94
Parisian publications about, 187–88, 190–92
perception of, 47
portrayed in theater, 59
themes in Hughes's poetry, 140
see also primitivism
African Americans, 48–49, 67, 161–62
census statistics for, 40–41
Harlem populated by, 24–25, 31
heritage of, 46–47, 49–51
housing denied to, 25–27
Hughes on self-image of, 167–70
lifestyle changes among, 33–34
Locke on changing identity of, 32–38
migration of, from the South to Harlem, 23, 27–28, 34
prejudice among, 44–45
self-image of, 51–53
slavery of, 53–54, 57, 62
West Indian population and, 39–45
see also culture; race; stereotypes; theater; West Indians
African Grove Theatre, 57–58
African Kraal, An (Freeman), 60
Aftermath (Burrill), 84
Aldridge, Ira, 58
All God's Chillun Got Wings (O'Neill), 85–86
Amenia Times (newspaper), 152
American Caste and the Negro College (Gallagher), 177
American Dilemma, An (Myrdal), 180–81

American Mercury (magazine), 121–22, 148
Amos 'n' Andy (radio show), 199–200
Autobiography of an Ex-Colored Man, The (James Weldon Johnson), 23
L'Aventure Ambiguë (Kane), 192–93
Awakening, The (Charles S. Johnson), 15
"Awakening: A Memoir, The" (Bontemps), 105–106

Baker, Josephine, 18, 49, 190
"Ballad of Margie Polite" (Hughes), 142
Banana Bottom (Claude McKay), 94, 103–105
Bandanna Land (Bert Williams and George Walker), 59
Banjo (Claude McKay), 94, 100–103, 192
Barnes, Albert C., 146–49
Barthé, Richmond, 150
Battle of Who Run, The (Hunter), 60
Bayou Relics (Brown-Guillory), 76
"Becky" (Toomer), 113–14
Bernhardt, Sarah, 60
Big Sea, The (Hughes), 10–11, 132–33
biracialism
analyzed in *Cane*, 112–14
"race-mixing," 114–15
rejection of African American identity and, 115–17
of Toomer, 108–12, 117–18
see also marriage/intermarriage
birth control, 85
Black Arts Movement, 146
black consciousness, 13–14

217